Experiencing God of the Miraculous

A Collection of Real – Life Short Stories

Greg and Bev Wootton

"Experiencing God of the Miraculous"

Copyright © 2008 by Greg and Bev Wootton.
All rights reserved. Printed in the United States of America.
Except as permitted under the Copyright Act of 1976, no part of this publication may be reproduced or distributed in any form or by any means, or stored in a database or retrieval system, without written permission of the publisher.

The authors may be contacted for personal use of any stories, photographs or materials within at:
bevandgreg2007@gmail.com

ISBN 978-1-4092-1070-2

Experiencing God of the Miraculous

Preface

We met while attending a teachers' college in Salisbury, Maryland in the fall of 1973, and within six months decided to forgoe academic life for one of following our hearts. In April of 1974 we boarded an Italian cruise ship for Naples and made our way from there to the Holy Land where we began searching for the God of Abraham, Isaac and Jacob. We lived on a kibbutz (communal farm) in the Jordan Valley for five months and afterward returned to the United States where we married on December 7th. Our firstborn, Isaac, arrived nine months later, and then on June 6, 1976 we immigrated to Israel with our young son. It was a calling of sorts to live in the land of the prophets where Jesus spent his life, and we felt from the first that it was our destiny to be a part of the unfolding history of the nation of Israel.

We have wanted to record the personal experiences of God's miraculous leadings and interventions that have transpired over the past thirty years, but could not get started without first identifying our audience. We raised our six children in an atmosphere of faith and dependence on God, and they were first-hand witnesses of His grace in our lives. Due to having married in our early twenties, we have been blessed to have the opportunity of spending time and getting to know our precious grandchildren, but it occurred to us that we might not have such ample opportunity with our future great-grandchildren, and so this book was written for them.

Neither of us have any record of the lives of our great-grandparents, although we both spent our childhood years around our loving grandparents. Thus, we have attempted in this book to briefly share an autobiographical sketch of our lives through the looking glass of "Experiencing God of the Miraculous."

A longtime dream to walk the length and breadth of the land of Israel was accomplished in eighty-six days in 2005 when we hiked the Israel National Trail. The final chapter of this book contains our trail journal with pictures chronicling our daily trek. We hope that you, the reader, will be blessed through these short stories and be encouraged in your 'walk of faith'.

Greg and Bev Wootton

Table of Contents

Chapter	Title	Page
	Dedication to Our Future Great-grandchildren	9
1	Three Promises Fulfilled	11
2	If This Is The Truth?	14
3	First Contact – Faith Comes By Hearing	18
4	The Rabbi at the Jaffa Gate	21
5	The Paycheck	25
6	Summer of Miracles	27
7	Written Off	33
8	It Has Rats	35
9	The Prophetic Dream	39
10	Dancing In The Spirit	42
11	The Holy Kiss	44
12	Call El-Al	47
13	Mother's Day Miracle	50
14	The 'Fear of the Lord' Tent Fire	53
15	Unconditional Surrender	57
16	Tongues of Fire	62
17	The I.D.F. Mosquitoes	65
18	The Blessing of the I.R.S.	68
19	The Walkabout	72
20	Return of the I.R.S. – Pack Your Bags	74
21	The Golden Triangle	79
22	A Christmas Praise – Tehila	87
23	Kiwi Station Wagon	91
24	Little Luna Gala's Big Typhoon	97

25	Crossing the Egyptian Border with $2	101
26	Start the Engine	105
27	The Word of Knowledge	107
28	Adventure in Ashkelon	111
29	Our Sealed Room	115
30	The Motorcycle License Tests	119
31	Heavenly Places	123
32	Bruce and The Almighty	127
33	30 Flights in 30 Days	131
34	Digging for 'The Voice of Hope'	135
35	Wrong Bank, Right Money!	139
36	Trouble in Paradise	142
37	The Bear Looked Me In The Eye	148
38	The Shadow of Death	151
39	As The Kinneret Wept	159
40	Walking in The Spirit	161
41	Field of Garlic	164
42	$1.85 a Brick	167
43	Best Friends	173
44	Empathizing With Bill Gates	176
45	Raise the Dead	179
46	Love Thy Neighbor	181
47	Grandpa's Yortzite	183
48	When He Speaks	189
49	"But Where Sin Abounded..."	192
50	.... The Holy Land Walk of Faith	195

Experiencing God of the Miraculous

Dedication to Our Future Great-grandchildren

To the children of our granddaughters: Lovey, Jessica, Jordie, Aliyah, Hosanna, Nephtalie, Ithiel and Nili; and to the children of our grandsons: Andrew, Israel, Ethan, Nehemiah, Ezekiel, Elijah, Luke and Roark. This book and the entirely true stories within are dedicated to you so that you might come to know the miraculous power of God's grace that has been working in our lives and is freely available to you. The curse of the law of sin and death that had overshadowed the lives of the generations that came before us was broken in our generation by the divine intervention of God who revealed Himself to us through His Son.

If in this life our days are so numbered that we do not have an opportunity to come to know you personally, then we have within recorded these short story testimonials for you. Through them, we hope that you will come to know us, and experience the God of the miraculous whom we serve. Until we meet face to face in the heavenly place that has been prepared for us, "grace unto you and peace from God our Father, and the Lord Jesus Christ."

Chapter 1
Three Promises Fulfilled

As far as oxymorons go, the fact that I was born a 'poor Jew' is quite significant in that both terms, Jew and poor, shaped my life most significantly. I do not wish for you to think that I am looking for sympathy, for quite the contrary I have become rich in faith because of my humble beginnings.

Already by the age of nine I had experienced a lifetime of misery of which I will not go into detail now, because the point I'm wanting to make is that the circumstances of my childhood shaped my future more dramatically than anything else could have, and that the God of infinite wisdom knew what was best for me even before I was conceived in the womb.

By contrast, my mother had grown up a Jewish princess in a twenty-six room mansion, accustomed to maids, servants and country-clubs, but had become utterly destitute a couple of years before I was born as a result of my grandfather losing all his riches in a failed oil venture. Two hopeless-from-the-beginning marriages later, I the eldest of now six children would again be fatherless after the desertion of my stepfather, and was beginning to feel the strain of the many bad decisions made by my parents and grandparents.

Going back to the story of the 'three promises fulfilled'… an unexpected turn of events was to take place before my tenth birthday that would alter the course of my life. In the summer of 1963, my mother and her mother suddenly decided to take an unheard of vacation to Cedar Point, Ohio. I believe that my grandmother had come into some bonus commissions in her telephone-soliciting job. I was invited along to baby-sit for my two youngest siblings who were both under four years old. I imagine that the rest of my half brothers were sent off to their father for the summer. As far as vacations go this was the best that I could expect and was a great relief from the stifling heat and boredom of the city of Chicago in the summer.

The island of Cedar Point, off the coast from the city of Sandusky, was a peculiar world in itself. I had already from a tender age explored all the neighborhoods around the north-eastern part of the city that I grew up in, so I had no trouble mapping out this entire vacation oasis within a couple of days. It seemed that the singular one-story hotel took up at least half of the place, with rooms that continued down long corridors without end. The long sandy beach in front of the hotel was my outdoor job-site, as I was employed full-time without pay to watch over my younger brother and sister. This rather boring stretch of coast took up maybe another third of the tiny landmass. Then there was the unreachable heavenly place just down the way, in plain sight of my longing eyes day in and day out.

The Cedar Point Amusement Park was not huge, as far as amusement parks go, but it was compact and filled with roller coasters and every imaginable exciting ride possible. Yet it might as well have been on another planet for all intents and purposes, as it stood like a giant at the end of the beach, beconing and mocking me continuously.

One day, toward the end of our stay at Cedar Point, I was playing with a bat and ball by myself outside while my brother and sister were napping, and I suddenly felt that I couldn't take it any more. I had never spontaneously prayed from my heart before and had not felt that the God of Abraham, Isaac and Jacob was anywhere close-by the few times that I had been taken to synagogue services by my grandfather on the Jewish high holidays. Nonetheless, not having a nickel to my name and knowing full well that my mother probably didn't have much more than that to her name to spare, I decided in sheer desperation to give prayer a shot. So I prayed a simplistic and childish prayer, "God, if you will let me go to the amusement park, I will believe in you all my life."

I guess the Creator of heaven and earth was quite amused that day as he hadn't heard from me before, and I was asking a pretty small favor for such a large commitment, so He surprised me and granted my request. Out of nowhere, my mother up and invited me to come to the amusement park for the day with her and her new boyfriend. I was in such a euphoric mood that I don't remember much except that as the new boyfriend was footing the bill and the younger children were with my grandmother, I had the time of my life and rode every ride as often as I wanted. It was truly a miracle.

The next day I began to ponder the events of the previous day and it occurred to me that it might have all been a coincidence and that maybe God really hadn't answered my prayers after all. So I did the only thing that an almost ten-year-old kid could do, and struck up another bargain with God. I prayed the same prayer and made the same promise but this time with twice the earnest.

Now I'm sure that the LORD was more amused by the second prayer than the first because He answered it almost immediately. Another boyfriend mysteriously invited my mother and I to a day at the amusement park, just shortly after I finished praying. Well it turned out even better that the previous day, because I knew exactly where I wanted to go and what I wanted to do so I didn't waste any time, but got a double-portion of fun out of what I figured would be the last time in this life that I would ever visit this place.

By now you probably can see where this is going, so I'll cut to the chase. Although I knew it couldn't have been a coincidence that I had been struck by lightning twice, so to speak, each time immediately after praying, I felt that there would be no harm in asking for a third trip to the park with the exact same promise appended to the request... *"God, if you will let me go one more time to the amusement park, I will <u>really</u> believe in you all my life."*

It is now almost a half-century later, and by His grace and to the best of my ability I have been trying to keep my promise, for God looked into my heart that day and granted my third petition, knowing that it was a small price to pay for such a thing as a boy's heart.

"Truly I say to you, unless you are converted and become as little children, you shall not enter into the kingdom of Heaven."
Matthew 18:3

Chapter 2

If This Is the Truth?

From the little that I knew with any certainty, I thought that Jesus was a good man and possibly a misunderstood Jewish prophet, but nothing more. For me, the Hebrew 'Tanach' or Bible began with Genesis and ended in Chronicles, and the 'New Testament' was just an interesting Christian book written by, and for, the Gentiles. I was born a Jew, raised in a Jewish home, and was certain that at the end of my allotted time on earth, would die a Jew – for we had survived as a separate and unique people for over fifty-seven centuries. Christians were born Christians. Moslems were born Moslems. Hindus were born Hindus, etc. and never once did I conceive of the idea that one could change whatever religion, race or species that he or she was born into.

But the question of Jesus' resurrection posed a serious problem for me intellectually. If it were true, then it was a very serious thing indeed. If not, then millions of Christians all over the world who believed in his resurrection were royally deceived. What concerned me was this, short of dying – how could anyone know for sure one way or the other, if Jesus really had risen from the dead?

Putting philosophical issues aside, at the age of twenty-two, I heeded the command given to me in my bar-mitzvah scripture reading nine years earlier, 'Lech Lecha' (Go Out). This was originally God's call to Abram (Genesis 12) to leave his homeland and go to the Promised Land. With ten dollars and two suitcases to our name, my wife and I immigrated to Israel with our young son, Isaac, on June 6, 1976. We returned to the kibbutz (communal farm) in the Jordan Valley that two years earlier we had spent five months on, and became candidates for membership – a process that was scheduled to take a year.

My wife, Beverly, reluctantly put our son in the babies' home where he had to remain for eighteen to twenty hours a day with four other children his age, and be raised by a 'metapelet' or house mother. He could be with us each afternoon and evening until bedtime and then would have to be returned. Bev was assigned to work in the communal laundromat and I was sent to the olive orchards. Although communal life on the kibbutz was stress-free, with no bills to worry about, meals to prepare, taxes or rent to pay, etc., it was extremely stifling for those of us who had grown up in the USA, a nation that encouraged freedom of thought and action from early childhood.

Quite frankly, I hated picking olives eight hours a day. Ten minutes after beginning work each morning I was already bored out of my mind. Therefore, I found every excuse to avoid work, which was the worst thing a candidate for membership on a communal farm could do. I came late and left early, took two-hour lunch breaks and averaged one sick day per week! The temperatures were in the 100-105 degree range, and with the extreme humidity along the Jordan River, we had to begin our workday well before dawn at around 4:30 AM, six days a week, to avoid the sweltering heat.

After a month or so of this, I had reached my lowest ebb spiritually. We were stuck in the Promised Land without any promise of a better life. The kibbutzniks (members of the kibbutz) wore the same clothes, did the same jobs, ate the same food, carried on the same meaningless conversations about nothing, day in and day out and what was worse, didn't even seem to mind it. Watching television a few hours a week (one station only) in one of the kibbutz bomb shelters was about the only mental stimulation we had, and so depression deepened daily in the depths of my soul.

I must admit that I wasn't even considering how by precious wife felt about all this, since she was five months pregnant, struggling with our firstborn being in the children's house, working in a pressure cooker (literally) laundromat, and barely able to communicate in Hebrew. I was just plain self-centered and only focused on my own misery, and regretting my decision to come to Israel in the first place.

I knew that it would be impossible to call our parents and ask for help to return to the States since they had been adamantly opposed to our leaving in the first place. No, we had to stick it out just to prove them wrong even if they had been right. When we had left for Israel, no one in either one of our families would even drive us to the airport in New York. My ex-roommate, Mike, from my college days had driven us up to New York's international airport from Maryland with absolutely no money to even buy gas to get back home again. The story is that Mike had become a Christian since he had left school and was now a full-fledged Jesus freak. Even so, it was very touching that he took the time and totally illogical leap of faith to take us to New York. on the first leg of our journey to Israel. He had also given us both New Testaments before he left us, but I had given my copy away at the airport even before we boarded the El-Al flight to Tel-Aviv.

In the book of Ecclesiastes it says, "There is a time and a season for everything under the sun." Little did I know what God had prepared for me from the beginning of time. One day, I was just so miserable that I didn't go to work and sat down in our tiny kibbutz apartment in a state of despair. On the table was my wife's New Testament, one of the first editions of the New International Version translation that had recently come out. On its cover were the faces of over a dozen happy people from all walks of life who seemed to be beconing me to join them. I was sick of everything and especially my rock-n-roll albums so I began looking through them more carefully to try and find something to play to cheer me up. There, in the middle of the stack of records, was a Christian album called 'Hope' that obviously Mike had slipped in. I thought that I might as well put in on just to have something new to listen to, and then I opened the New Testament to the middle and began to read.

I usually begin reading in the middle of a book because it seems that it takes so long to get to any of the real good parts if you start at the beginning. And, if you're the impatient type like I was, it could also be a waste of time starting at the beginning of a book if it turned out that it was no good. I figured that if the middle of a book were interesting then it would be worth it to go back and read it through from the first page again. Anyway, here I was in the middle of the New Testament, reading about some guy named Saul on the road to Damascus in the ninth chapter of the book of Acts. The music playing on our stereo was very soothing and the words to one song in particular kept penetrating my thoughts... "Everybody needs. Everybody hopes. Everybody dreams, but time doesn't seem to answer it all... Everybody needs. Everybody hopes. Everybody dreams, but time doesn't seem to answer it all..."

I read all day until I finished the last chapter in the book of Acts and then realizing that I hadn't read the first eight chapters, began to read it over from the beginning. I got back to the story of Paul's conversion on the road to Damascus about 11:00 PM and gently closed the book. I was feeling deeply moved and yet confused by what I had read. I just couldn't understand how Jesus' followers had all that joy, enthusiasm, faith and power after He was dead. I hadn't prayed once since I was a kid so the words didn't come out too easily. I just quietly said out loud, "Lord, if this is the truth, change my life" and then I went to bed.

I woke up five hours later to go to work in the olive grove and I experienced something that I had never experienced before. It felt like I was a very small child without a care in the world. I was happy, and I mean deep down unbelievably happy. I was at peace for maybe the first time in my life... and I was absolutely sure that Jesus was the Messiah, the Son of God and that He truly had risen from the dead!

I took the New Testament with me to work, in my back pocket, reading a few paragraphs every so often, and then I would go back to picking olives while I meditated on what I had just read. Over the next few days almost everyone I worked with came up and asked what had happened to me (probably concerned that I had been out in the sun too much or something). As a result, with only the little bit of the Word that I knew, I had a chance to witness to my co-workers and friends of the miracle of the resurrection of Jesus – and proclaim to them that He was the Messiah of the Jews.

After a few days, my wife asked me out of curiosity, "Why are you so happy?" and I gave her the same testimony. She immediately took the New Testament and began to read it with all her heart. From that moment on we had to share the book between us. We began to pray the 'Our Father' prayer that Jesus taught his disciples together because we didn't even know how else to pray.

From that point on I became one the best kibbutz olive pickers. I never missed another minute of work because I was so grateful to have such a great job. I could read the Word of God, and then meditate on it while I picked olives in autopilot for hours at a time. I would look over at the Jordan Valley and the natural beauty all around me, and tears would come into my eyes. For the first time in my life I truly cared about the happiness of others, especially my precious wife and helpmate. Most importantly the joy and peace I experienced that day I first believed never left me, not even for one moment during those next months. Truly I had been born again, the greatest miracle of all.

"Therefore, if anyone is in Christ, he is a new creation; old things have passed away; behold, all things have become new."
1 Corinthians 5:17

Chapter 3

First Contact – Faith Comes by Hearing

It truly had been a wonderful worship and praise service that snowy December night in Jerusalem, and I had felt moved on by the Holy Spirit to give all the money I had by faith in the offering. To be honest, I had no trouble doing so because my wife, Beverly, was holding half of our money in her purse, so I was sure that we would be all right financially until I found a job.

It came as quite a shock to both of us later that night that my precious wife had also felt moved on by the Holy Spirit to give all she had in the offering, knowing that I had half of our money in my possession. We obviously had been of one mind and one heart that night, and now we were in one word, BROKE. Looking back at the situation, I guess it would not have been so bad except for the fact that we had two small children to care for, were living with our pastor's family in the basement of their home, and as I already mentioned, I was unemployed.

As far as prospects went, the future didn't look all that bright either, for the fact is that I hardly spoke Hebrew and hadn't quite gotten around to finishing the requirements for my college degree before we had immigrated to Israel six months earlier. It did not help a bit that we had no savings, owned little materially except for a few personal belongings and possessed nothing whatsoever that we could sell. But as I said, it had been a wonderful worship and praise service that night, so we prayed together before going to bed and committed ourselves into our heavenly Father's hands before falling asleep in perfect peace.

The next day, I felt that as the head of our small but growing household, I had better get serious about praying and hearing from God before things got much worse. So when all was quiet, the children napping, and our pastor's family out shopping, I went down to the basement to seek the LORD. Looking back, I guess I should have told my wife what I was up to before I began, but it seemed that everything was under control and I wouldn't be needed for a while. You see, I told the LORD that I would not get off my knees until He answered me. I was so desperate at that moment that I had determined that I would not get up off my knees before hearing from God.

Well the devil saw what was going on and decided that it was time to test my commitment. I don't believe that I had been praying very long when I heard a tremendous uproar going on upstairs. I didn't know much about spiritual warfare at that time, as I had only been a believer for a few months, but it did seem like there was a battle being fought around me. So, as all the commotion continued upstairs, I blocked everything out of my mind and 'kept praying through'.

Now I only have my dear wife's word for what occurred while I was detained in the heavenly realms, so I will here be giving a second hand account of the events that transpired in my absence. It seems that the children woke up on the wrong side of the bed, both at the same time, while at that very moment the washing machine broke down completely and began pouring water out in great quantities, flooding the upstairs and threatening to fill the basement as well. About that time, the family's dog, a rather large and frisky German shepherd, sensed that it was time to join in the action and was yelping and slipsliding all over the place with his muddy feet. I can honestly say that I quite understand what provoked my wife's outburst when she called down to me in a rather loud voice, " Don't you care what's going on up here? Get up off your knees and come up here and help me!"

I believe that when I didn't respond that she may have thought I didn't hear her, for I do remember hearing her say it again after she came downstairs and stood right above me. I know your thinking that it was kind of callous of me not to at least let her know why I wouldn't get up to help her out, but I had made this vow and hadn't heard from the LORD yet, and well I was sure that if I got up or spoke to her or anything else but pray I would never hear from God... so I continued to pray even as my wife left the room having given up hope on me completely.

I'm not exactly sure of what I was expecting to hear because I can't really say I had ever heard the voice of God up until that day. I only know that some time later while I was praying, I was completely overwhelmed with the idea, as if I was being commanded by an audible voice, to get up off my knees and go upstairs and call the Ministry of Education immediately. There was no denying it because the impression was so strong, and the idea seemed so ridiculous, that I was sure that the LORD had spoken.

Thankfully the children had been quieted, the dog put outside, the washing machine turned off and the water mopped up by the time I got off my knees or I might not have made the call right away. Not having been given any other instructions except "call the Ministry of Education", I dialed the number for information and got the phone number. Amazingly I got right through. At this point, I'm not sure what I said, but the secretary I spoke with made an appointment for me for the next afternoon.

I arrived by bus the next day right on time and without having to wait for even a minute was ushered into a room where three distinguished looking people sat. They spoke with me briefly in Hebrew about my background, family and purpose for arranging this meeting, which I don't think I was all too clear about. Anyway, after a few minutes one of the men said, "Tell us why you want to be a teacher since you have no teaching experience, don't speak Hebrew very well, and don't have a college degree."

At that moment I understood what Jesus had meant when He had said to his disciples, "Do not worry about how or what you should speak. For it will be given to you in that hour what you should speak." Out of my mouth came words that were not my own. I answered and said something like, "I know that you have many teachers with advanced degrees that cannot teach, but I was born a teacher and I love children." There was such a silence afterwards that you could have heard a pin drop, and then I was asked to step outside the room and wait while they conferred together.

After five minutes or so, I was called back in and told that I was to be given an opportunity to get my teaching degree, if I agreed to take an intensive five month training course for new immigrant teachers. Furthermore, since I had a family with two small children, I would be furnished a two-bedroom apartment, nearly rent-free, and a small monthly stipend until I completed the program. I was then given all the information about how to get the apartment through the Ministry of Absorption, as well as instructions on how to get to the Greenberg College in the German neighborhood by bus, since classes were to begin the following week.

I cannot really describe the feelings that welled up in me when I walked out of that office in a spiritual daze. Although the home we were staying in was a good many miles away, I could not sit and ride the bus, but instead I ran all the way, singing and praising God, so grateful that that the Creator of heaven and earth cared so much for me that He had taken time to speak to me personally.

"So then faith comes by hearing, and hearing by the word of God."
Romans 10:17

Chapter 4

The Rabbi at the Jaffa Gate

I was walking along one afternoon in Jerusalem on my way home to my apartment at the absorption center for new immigrants, when, out of nowhere I had the distinct impression that the Holy Spirit was speaking to me saying, "Go to the Jaffa Gate tomorrow and wait for the person I will send to meet you."

The Jaffa Gate, or Gate Beautiful, is the most western of the eight gates that leads into the Old City of Jerusalem – the ancient three thousand year old walled city that lies within the modern metropolis of Jerusalem. The Jaffa Gate opens to a market square just to the north of King David's Citadel, between the Christian and Armenian Quarters of the Old City. From there it is only a fifteen minute walk due east to the Western Wall and the Temple Mount.

If it hadn't been for the miraculous answer that God had given me in prayer a few weeks earlier when He clearly spoke to me to call the Ministry of Education, I probably would have ignored the voice thinking it was only my imagination, and continued on my way. That evening, I couldn't get the impression out of my mind that I had to go and wait for someone at the Jaffa Gate. Not wanting anyone else to think I was 'hearing things' I kept this to myself.

The next morning I got up and plastered several Messianic tracks entitled 'Never Again' onto a large cardboard box. This powerful track had haunting images of the Holocaust on its cover, and had been published by the 'World of Yah' ministries in New York. I then strapped the box on the back of my bicycle with a stack of these same tracks within and headed off to the Jaffa Gate to keep my divine appointment.

I had no clue as to whom I was to meet or what the person would look like. It was all as big a mystery to me, as it is to you, but I decided that if whoever it was didn't show up I wouldn't be any the worse off for trying. I sat outside the Jaffa Gate on a concrete bench with the box beside me for a couple of hours without anything of particular importance occurring. I was reading my Bible and praying and just waiting in anticipation of the person the LORD wished for me to meet. A young religious man wearing a yarmulke on his head (a small round cap) walked up to me and after ascertaining that I was a messianic Jew told me that if I didn't leave by the time he came back that he would physically remove me.

Well, that more or less put a time-table on events as far as I was concerned, so I prayerfully told God, "LORD, if whoever it is that you want me to meet isn't here within fifteen minutes, I'm leaving." I just didn't see the point in provoking a violent confrontation for no good reason.

Ten minutes later an ultra-orthodox Hassidic rabbi dressed in full black robe came up to where I was seated and began looking at the tracks. He wore one of the Orthodox big round wide-brimmed black felt hats, had a long beard and the traditional side curls, and looked rather menacing. The Hassidic Jews are a type of the Pharisees of Jesus' day, living today in modern Israel and in other ultra-orthodox Jewish communities scattered throughout the world. They love the Holy Scriptures and truly are zealous to keep all of God's commandments that they believe were given to them by both the written and 'oral' law. Although they have many different sects within their community, they have a common thread of hatred for anything to do with Jesus, the New Testament and especially Jewish 'believers'. As a matter of fact they refuse to even say the name of Jesus, but derogatorily call him 'Yeshu' meaning "let his name be forgotten", rather than pronounce 'Yeshua', which means 'salvation'. Though, they may be as the Apostle Paul said in his epistle to the Romans, 'enemies of the gospel', truly they are also 'beloved for the sake of the fathers'.

After a few minutes this rabbi spoke to me in perfect English and said, "Ah, you're a Messianic Jew that believes in Jesus, hah?" He went on to say that he was familiar with the 'World of Yah' as he was from the same area where they are located in the United States and that he too had read the New Testament but that it was clearly not the truth. It seems that this rabbi had studied the New Testament scriptures in order to lead ignorant wayward Jews (like myself) back to Judaism. He took my Bible and showed me where one of the kings of Israel listed in the genealogy of Jesus had been cut off by God. He then spoke of what he termed as other inconsistencies and falsehoods in the New Testament. Lastly, he explained that the messiah, who was to be cut off according to the prophesy in Daniel chapter nine, was merely 'an anointed one' as King Cyrus had been called in the scriptures, and was not referring to 'The Messiah' or to Jesus.

Under my breath, I prayed, "God, is this really the person I'm supposed to meet?... If so, please help me." I finally admitted to the rabbi that I was a new believer in Jesus and didn't really know the answers to the supposed scriptural paradoxes and inconsistencies that he was pointing out. I told him that he obviously knew the Bible better than I did, but then I gave him my testimony of how I had been saved on the kibbutz. I told him how I had read the book of Acts and felt the touch of the Holy Spirit when I read it, and how I had prayed a simple prayer, "LORD if this is the Truth, change my life." I then witnessed to him about the changes that had taken place after I had received the baptism of the Holy Spirit. I told him that I now loved the Word of God more than anything else and that my only desire was to do God's will in my life. Furthermore, I let him know that it was in obedience to the Holy Spirit that I had come to the Jaffa Gate that day to wait for the person that God had told me He was going to send for me to meet.

What happened next is hard for me to believe even after all these years. I saw tears rolling down the rabbi's cheeks. His whole countenance and tone changed from one of antagonism to humility as he simply said, "The Holy Spirit is a promise for our people." He told me that he never passed by this way from the yeshiva (orthodox Hebrew school) where he taught, and as a matter of fact, he was supposed to have been there for another hour but for some unexplainable reason had suddenly felt a strong urge to leave the yeshiva early and come this direction on his way to the post office on Jaffa Road. I could tell that he was now visibly touched by the Holy Spirit and the events of the last hour.

After asking where I lived, he agreed to come over to my apartment later. When he arrived that evening he further agreed to stay for a Bible study which was being taught by a visiting pastor from Elizabethtown, Kentucky, Leo Jordan, who was speaking about a new book that he had just completed on the subject of "Angels, the Messengers of God".

Over the next few weeks, like Nicodemus in the Gospel of John, my rabbi friend would indiscreetly come to my apartment only after dark and talk about the Word of God until the early hours of the morning. He was generally argumentive, as if he was trying to convince himself that this was not the truth.

One night, I said to him, "Why is it that you only want to talk about Jesus? You never want to talk about sports or politics or anything else? Why do you love Him so much that He's all you want to talk about?" After a few moments of silence, he answered me with tears in his eyes, "Jesus is everything that the Torah (the five books of Moses) ever taught that a Jew should be."

With that statement, uttered by his own lips, he was converted and I never detected any more doubt from him nor heard any more arguments on subsequent visits. A short time later, he was filled with the Spirit of Holiness and became a vessel of God's grace.

It has now been over thirty years since we met at the Jaffa Gate, and though we live in completely different worlds, the two of us have remained the closest of friends and brothers in the LORD.

Nicodemus said to Him, "How can a man be born when he is old? Can he enter a second time into his mother's womb and be born?" Jesus answered, "Most assuredly, I say to you, unless one is born of water and the Spirit, he cannot enter the kingdom of God."
(John 3:4-5)

Chapter 5
The Paycheck

For five weeks all the teachers in Israel had been on strike. With no end of the impasse between the Teacher's Union and the Ministry of Education in sight, we were caught in the middle of something much larger than ourselves. At the onset of the strike, rather than waiting around for it to end, Bev and I had travelled up north with our three small children for several weeks to participate in an evangelistic outreach to the Arabic people living in the town Nazareth.

This was in the fall of '78 and Israel did not have the social services for the poor that were common place in the U.S. and in Europe. On top of that, with over a hundred-thousand teachers abruptly unemployed, there just weren't any temporary jobs available. Credit cards were unheard of at the time so there just wasn't a 'safety net' to fall back upon in such situations. We knew the LORD was our Provider, and not my job as an English teacher at the local highschool in Eilat, so we had not been overly concerned during this time of the strikes.

A couple a weeks after we arrived back in Eilat, the last of our provisions and money ran out on the morning of the thirty-fifth day of the strike. I walked down to the bank to see if anything had come into our account from the Ministry of Education or from one of the various funds that the government had set up for new immigrants. I can honestly say that I was a bit disappointed when the account balance showed the same amount as the day before... zero.

When I arrived home, Bev and the children were sitting on top of a short stone wall near the the walkway that led up to our apartment. I said, "Well, we are officially broke now, so let's praise the LORD". And we did just that. Right there on the street, we all began praising the LORD!

After a few minutes we headed up the walkway to go into our apartment on the third floor, and as we reached the stairway I noticed that we had a letter in our mailbox. When I opened it, my wife and I began to cry, for inside was a check for $400. It had been sent a couple weeks before by a man I had only met once in Shreveport, Louisiana six month's earlier. In the note accompanying the check, he explained that due to a back injury, he had been out of work for over a year and had promised the LORD to send us his first paycheck when he was able to work again. He could not have known how perfectly timed that first paycheck of his was for us on that day.

> *"I have been young, and am old; yet I have not seen the righteous forsaken, or his seed begging bread."*
> *Psalm 37: 25*

Chapter 6
The Summer of Miracles

We were managing to live meagerly on Greg's salary as a teacher in the remote desert city of Eilat, located at the very head of the Red Sea in Israel. Preparing a good pot of soup had become my forte, and I thank God for Lucille Farmer's visits; she came once a week with a sack of vegetables, usually with just the right stuff to make an interesting soup if seasoned up properly.

Lucille had faithfully served the Lord as a missionary in Ecuador for over twenty years and had recently been led by the Holy Spirit to dwell in Israel where now her encouraging tutelage was spiritually profiting for our young family of four. Her presence temporarily eased the homesickness for my own mother, whom I missed terribly. She moved from Jerusalem shortly after we did, conjecturing that she wanted to be in a warmer climate, but I ascertained it was to be with us in Eilat. Although she was in her sixties and I was in my twenties, she was my best friend whom the Lord had miraculously led us to on Prophet Street in Jerusalem when we had first stepped out in faith and asked the Lord to lead us to someone with whom we could share our newfound belief in Jesus. Lucille had come with us that glorious day when Greg and I were baptized for our faith in Jesus in the Jordan River and had all of our sins washed away by faith when Tom Marshall immersed us in the Jordan's murky waters. We had begun having bible studies regularly with Lucille after that time and continued doing so as often as possible.

That summer of '78 when I was very pregnant with my third child, people wondered how I managed to get around walking all over town in the desert heat holding onto two small boys and pushing bags of groceries up and down the steep hills in a flimsy stroller. I happened to be a very happy mother because of my relationship with the Lord and I was excited about the new addition. I read my bible fervently in those days and believed that the last three months had the greatest spiritual influence on the child in the womb, so I was determined to stay close to the Lord.

While on a seven-day water only fast I had learned of this pregnancy and continued to remain on a spiritual 'high' throughout the duration. During the fast, while reading in the book of Ezra in the Old Testament, God spoke so clearly to my heart from chapter

8:21, "Then I proclaimed a fast there at the river of Ahava, that we might humble ourselves before our God, to seek from Him the right way for us and our little ones and all our possessions." Ezra cared about the spiritual condition of God's people and he encouraged them to obey the word of God.

After dinner that evening, I shared with Greg the word I had received from Ezra Chapter 8 and told him God had shown me we were going to have a little girl and her name was to be Ahava, in Hebrew Ahava means love. His reply was that he too had been reading the book of Ezra that morning and God had spoken to him from Chapter 6, (the word Ahava is mentioned only twice in the bible, in Chapter 6 and 8) and that God had also shown him that Ahava should be our next child's name. What a miracle that the Lord revealed to both of us on the same day from different verses but the same book of the bible that we would have a daughter and her name would be Ahava. I never sought medical knowledge of the sex of the baby in the womb and more importantly, I never doubted that the baby would be a girl.

Eight months into this third pregnancy, we received a surprise gift from Lucille's home church in America and to our delight a brand new Maytag washing machine arrived. For several years I had been hand washing everything; in the late seventies in Israel, disposable diapers like 'Pampers' were not available so we had acquired a heap of cloth diapers with our two boys still requiring them at night. Now life would change with the brand new Maytag that was too big to fit though the front door and had to be hoisted up to the third floor and permanently placed on the tiny balcony off the kitchen. It had been packed tight with the most adorable clothes. Can you believe every thing was for a little girl? We were so excited over the machine's arrival that the whole family stood and watched it do the first load. Over the next three years we would spend many hours sitting out on the balcony waiting for laundry to finish and just enjoying the awesome view of the bustling new desert town of Eilat set before the deep blue Red Sea and distant pink mountains of Jordan and Saudi Arabia.

Now that I had more time on my hands not having to hand wash everything, I could be more involved in the summer outreach planned with our first and only official pastor in Israel, Tom Marshall and his family, who had rented a house in Eilat for several months just for the evangelical outreach. There were others from the

States who would be joining us, and there was even mention of a youth group that might make it for a few days as well. It was going to be our first intense time in Israel since we were saved, openly witnessing every day in courtyards and malls, busy business areas, on the beach and in the marketplace. Each evening after outreach in town, we planned to have a fellowship dinner at the Marshall's house and invite all the new contacts, which meant I would be making many pots of soup.

Greg was busy reading 'The Mystery at Bear Hollow' to the kids who loved hearing the Sugar Creek Gang mysteries before bedtime, and Lucille was over visiting so she and I had a chance to read the Word together. We had just gotten started when there was a knock on the door from a young fellow we had meet only once before in Jerusalem, Jim, who had just arrived back in the country of Israel now with this youth team. However, the team had arrived earlier than expected so they came as planned to Eilat to be with us for one week to participate in the outreach, and here they were all standing at our doorstep at 8 P.M. They began to quietly and slowly pile into our small third floor apartment, and after greeting this gentle, kind and exhausted looking group, the room was wall-to-wall young people, twenty-seven in all. Tom Marshall had given Jim our address so that when they arrived at the bus station in Eilat after riding the bus for many hours through the desert they walked an exhausting several miles from downtown uphill to our apartment, so we felt obliged to help them. Since we did not have a phone and there were no cell phones in those days either (only in the James Bond movies) they had been unable to contact us and they apologized for the late intrusion many times.

Our hearts were touched with their peaceful and appreciative attitudes, so the most logical thing to do was feed these weary travelers knowing that is what Jesus would do. It was not the normal lifestyle in Israel to hurry down to a carryout restaurant for a crowd like this, in fact there were no fast food restaurants in all of Eilat, and visitors were mostly fed in homes in the Middle East. Lucille and I gathered in the kitchen racking our brains over how we would feed them, as we were aware that no stores were open at this late hour, not even a loaf of bread could be bought after 7 P.M.

When Lucille said in her smooth sweet voice, "Now, just get the pot of soup out of the refrigerator and warm it up." I hesitated but did not inform her that there was only a third of a pot of soup left. I lit the two-burner gas stove, put the pot on and removed two frozen loaves of hala bread from the freezer, all while I kept wondering what she was going to miraculously come up with to add to this more than half empty pot of soup. I filled a container of water and before I was able to add a drop to the pot of soup Lucille grasped my arm and said, "No, that will not be necessary."

At that moment, an awesome presence of the Holy Spirit permeated the kitchen with faith and peace, and not another word was spoken between us. The word of faith hit my ears and I knew not to question anything, but to just stir the pot of soup while Lucille cut up the bread and began warming it in our little toaster oven while I set out the many plastic soup bowls I had borrowed from my neighbors. The group was cozy sitting on the floor on their duffle bags and on the few chairs we had around the living room, and now the sweet sound of the group softly singing a praise song filled the house.

Lucille held the soup bowls for me while I ladled them full to the brim, I intentionally never gazed down into the pot, I just continued faithfully ladling. These young people had been called by God to come to Israel to be a blessing. God knew their needs and I was aware that He wanted to use us as instruments to meet their needs. Not one of our guests would have requested food or have complained if there had been none, but they all showed appreciation and many thanks for such delicious soup and bread. That night I witnessed the miracle of a third of a pot of soup feeding twenty-seven young adults. It is surely a fact that God has a sense of humor because after we had finished serving and the group left to walk with Greg to the Marshall's house where they would sleep the night, there was still some soup left in the pot.

Now that the summer outreach was in full swing, I rose up very early to avoid the heat of the day to start cooking whatever would be my contribution to the evening meal. I would get involved in the day's activities with my children until they were worn-out and then take off for street evangelism as soon as it was their naptime. I love any opportunity to witness for the Lord, although in Israel there is a very hostile environment for speaking about Jesus Christ. My first afternoon out with the group witnessing in the open market I distributed a number of tracts but stumbled pitifully with my Hebrew. I lacked confidence and felt very ill equipped to share the gospel, and if I had listened to the devil lying in my ear, I would have missed the opportunity to talk with Edwar.

Edwar, a young man in his early twenties, approached me after having taken a tract from one of our boxes and told me he was a Christian, an Arab Christian. He humbly admitted that he did not go to church and he had fallen away from God. Sadly, he also confided in me that most people hated him because he was an Arab and because he was a Christian. I asked him if he had been born again and he lowered his head and said no. As I began to share with him what it means to be born again, tears came into his eyes, and he responded that he really wanted to know more. We spoke there, oblivious to the noisy hubbub of the market, about what it means to be born again for about an hour before I had to return home, but I made sure that I invited him to the fellowship dinner that night and I gave him a New Testament.

Edwar was saved that night before we ate dinner and he was baptized the next week. A month later, we visited his home in Nazareth where we were treated like royalty. He became a very close friend of our family as he grew spiritually and in less than a year, he flew with our family to the U.S. and traveled with us for two weeks.

The outreach continued successfully and crowds were now gathering at announced locations where our group would be gathering to play our instruments and worship the Lord publicly. One afternoon, while in a large courtyard in town singing with guitar music and boxes of New Testaments, a Rabbi came up to one of our brothers and began to intimidate him. The Rabbi had four scruffy looking henchmen surrounding him wherever he went and after getting very riled up, he started yelling and causing a crowd to gather saying, "Missionaryem', Hootza", meaning missionaries, get out! This Rabbi grabbed our box of New Testaments, took out his huge cigarette lighter, and was trying to set the books on fire with a flame that was several inches tall. Even though it was in the high 90's Fahrenheit that day, not one book caught fire. The furious Rabbi became very enraged and he and his henchmen began slinging our New Testament books around on the ground in the town's center in a rage. Now a crowd had begun gathering and pressing in and we supposed there might be a riot so our group signaled to one another to split up quickly and get out of sight! It was then, while I was making my way out of the crowds that I saw the young crippled man who had been hanging around us for days, stand up on top of a wooden box and start swinging his crutches over his head yelling out in Hebrew, "What is this, Russia? I don't believe like these people do, but they have a right to believe whatever they want. Is Israel a democracy or not? Do we have any real freedom?"

Once back at the house our excited group began to pray for protection for we knew that the Rabbi had power to cause much more trouble if he wished to pursue it. After a few days, Greg was called up to the office of the Ministry of Education to meet with the director who was a lady who spoke nicely to him and warned him that if he were caught teaching or preaching in the name of Jesus again, anywhere in Eilat, he would be fired from his job. Otherwise, she said, "This country is a democracy and you do have the freedom to do whatever you want but make sure it is in the privacy of your own home."

August 18th was the last day of the outreach that summer, and that night I gave birth to the most precious little girl, Ahava, born at home in our bedroom on the third floor of our apartment in Eilat.

During my birthing labor, I was blessed to have been surrounded by a spiritual group of ladies who sought the Lord in song and praise throughout the night at my bedside. The next day all the outreach team came to pray over us before departing as well as rejoice over the spiritual birth of Arab and Jewish souls that had come to Christ that summer; it **was** a summer of miracles!

"Ahava", our daughter of "Love"

"And whatever things you ask in prayer, believing, you will receive."
Matthew 21:22

Chapter 7

Written Off

"That's it! I'm never witnessing to Mike again," I said in frustration to my wife as he left our apartment late that night.

We had met Mike a couple of months earlier in a local pizza parlor. He was a young Englishman that was backpacking through Israel, and we had felt to invite him to stay the night in our apartment. It was still cold outside in the early spring, and Eilat didn't have any youth hostels at that time. A few weeks later, Mike decided to become a volunteer worker on Kibbutz Eilot, which was only a mile north of Eilat. He enjoyed coming over and visiting with us after he finished work during the week. Mike was a deeply spiritual young man who was looking for a purpose in existence, and he had studied several far-eastern religions and philosophies in his quest.

Quite often the subject of our faith in Jesus would come up and then lengthy discussions would ensue. I knew that Mike was a sincere 'seeker', so it usually didn't bother me that he was often on the offensive and attacking our beliefs. However, as the weeks wore on, I became increasingly impatient with him and sensed he was becoming even more entrenched in trancendental meditiation than before we had first met... and so after a particularly long 'intellectual' discussion about Jesus that I was sure was not getting through to him ... I wrote Mike off for good. I figured that he was beyond hope, and so I spiritually shook the dust off my feet.

Suprisingly, at five o'clock the next morning we heard a loud knock at our door, and there was Mike standing in the hallway with tears in his eyes. He said that after leaving our home that he hadn't been able to sleep all night, and could only think about what we had shared with him...that Jesus was different from all other prophets and 'holy men' since He alone had risen from the dead. It was clear to me that when the LORD saw I had given up and would not be interferring any longer, He had begun a lasting work of grace in Mike's life.

Mike went on to tell us that as soon as he acknowledged Jesus as Lord, that he had been overwhelmed by a peace that he had never experienced in his life up until that moment... and that he now wanted to be baptized, this very morning!

Walking down to the beach on the Gulf of Eilat together for a sunrise baptism, we rejoiced in the miracle that God had wrought with this precious man who just a few hours ago I had written off as lost forever. After his baptism, Mike continued to grow in the grace and knowledge of our Lord Jesus Christ. A few weeks later, he returned to England, a much different person than had come to Israel... for now he was 'born again of water and the Spirit'. To God be all the glory!

> *Jesus said, "I am the Resurrection and the Life!*
> *He who believes in Me, though he die, yet he shall live."*
> John 11:25

Chapter 8

It Has Rats!

Riding a bus across the U.S.A. can be a bit tedious unless you are one of those world travelers from another country armed with a thirty-day bus pass and have chosen this method as a relaxing way to see the sights in America. If you are not a tourist but just too broke to drive yourself or fly, it is another matter altogether. If you are traveling with small children, then my heart really goes out to you and I hope you had the common sense to bring along a few of their favorite toys and coloring books to pass the time. However, if your are traveling across America on a Greyhound Bus with three young children who are sick with the whooping cough, and are vomiting every hour or so, then I would have to say that you have lost your mind completely and should have stayed home. That advice that 'we should have stayed home' was given to us by our dear friend, Pastor Pogue.

We desperately wanted to get to that conference in Salt Lake City with our three children, and we had no other choice. Pastor Pogue had even hinted that we might be burying those kids on the way, which really did not smack of having much faith for a man of God, but we boarded the bus in Cleveland anyway, believing that God would provide and take care of us. We only had about a hundred dollars to our names after we bought those one-way bus tickets, so we were as poker players say, 'all in' when we headed out west with our three small whooping and coughing children that day.

We had been 'walking by faith' for several years by now but had not ridden a bus by faith yet, so this was altogether a new experience for us. By the time we had to change buses in Chicago, we were exhausted and at wits end as to how to stop the coughing and throwing up that the children seemed to be taking turns doing every few minutes. Prayer always worked in the past, and we did trust that 'all things were working together for the good', we just could not see why the answer was taking so long this time. I believe that it was while we were in the bus terminal in Chicago, waiting to board the 'express' to Salt Lake City that I had an idea and suggested to my wife we give the kids Alka Seltzer to settle their stomachs. I do not really know why but the idea sparked faith and hope in us so we bought some just before we boarded the bus. Between the fizzy tablets and God's intervention, the vomiting slowed down to an acceptable pace as we hit Nebraska.

By the time the bus crossed the Utah state line, the children were doing much better, and I for one fell asleep, worn out from exhaustion. We had not made any plans in advance as to where we were going to stay in Salt Lake City, but it was just as well since we could not have afforded any of the hotel or motel rates anyway. Sometimes when you hear from God you just have to go and hope the Red Sea parts before you drown or get run over by an Egyptian chariot. As the bus pulled into downtown Salt Lake City, I was sleeping as soundly as I ever had in my life. Suddenly, I woke up in a daze, glanced out the window totally disoriented, and heard the voice of the Holy Spirit speak to me clearly, "That place is where you will stay." I immediately began to make a mental note as the bus made another turn or two as to where 'that place' was located in relationship to the downtown bus station where we were heading.

Five minutes later, we pulled into the terminal and unloaded our children and luggage. I immediately said to my wife, "Honey, I know where we're going to stay. Wait here with the kids, I'll be right back." I didn't give her much of a chance to respond and I'm sure she was wondering how I knew where we were going to stay because neither of us had ever been to Salt Lake City before. She was well aware that I was as clueless as she was concerning accommodations in this city especially during a large convention or conference. Seizing her moment of astonishment, I ran off in the direction that I had pictured in my mental map.

On my way back to 'that place' I had seen from the bus which had no name or sign for that matter, I dropped into one of the local downtown hotels and was informed they were all booked up for the week. The desk clerk offered that we could stay one night only, for sixty dollars, but I graciously declined. By this time, I was sure that either a miracle was about to take place or we were in very deep trouble here. The children were still sick with the whooping cough but appeared to be on the mend after having slept a few hours during the past day's bus ride.

I got to 'that place' that the Lord had showed me in about ten or fifteen minutes, and walked up to what looked like an office of sorts. I asked the man that was standing around in there if he had a room to rent. He said that he was just now in the process of fixing up some apartments that he intended to rent out by the week but only had a couple ready and was not open for business yet. I told him that I had a wife and three kids down at the bus station waiting for me and that we were in Salt Lake City to attend a conference for the week. Suddenly his face lit up and he said, "Oh, then you'll need two connecting apartments, because they're only one bedroom each." Well, that sounded all right with me, so I hesitantly asked him, "How much would that cost me?" When he replied, "sixty dollars," the same price that the local hotels were charging, my heart sank and I figured that one night was going to be it. Since, we were exhausted from the trip, I pulled out three of our last twenty-dollar bills and handed it to him. He took the money, and began to write me out a receipt as said, "Okay, that is sixty dollars for the week. Will that be all?" I could not believe what I had just heard and asked him if he was really saying that it would only be sixty dollars for the week. When he confirmed it, I began to get a little suspicious so I said, "Can I take a look at the rooms?"

This was beginning to seem too good to be true even for a person like myself who had traveled several thousand miles by faith with less than a hundred dollars. I have to admit that I was skeptical to say the least. As this kind man grabbed his keys, he said that he had recently bought the place and was refurbishing it, one apartment at a time, but that it was not really finished yet. I figured that he was letting me know in advance not to get my hopes up too high.

I was speechless when I saw the two nicely decorated connecting apartments, and could hardly believe that they both had a kitchenette, bedroom with double beds, bathroom with tub and shower, refrigerator and color television – all which worked perfectly. After a two or three minute tour, I shook his hand, grabbed my receipt and ran back to the central bus station. When I got there out of breath, I said, "Honey, I just rented two beautifully furnished apartments for the week for sixty dollars!"

We laugh about it now, but it was not quite as comical at the time. She looked at me with an expression of unbelief, like she was about to cry, and said, "It has rats!" I tried to reassure her that it did not, though in all honesty I was not a hundred percent certain that it didn't. I quickly told her the whole story of how I found the exact place that the Holy Spirit had said, "That is the place where you will stay." I then mentioned that whatever the situation was I had already given the owner the last of our money anyway, so we might as well go check it out together.

We were a quite a sight for sore eyes after we had walked the mile or so back to the apartments with the children and luggage. After a thorough inspection, my wife lifted her hands and praised the LORD with all her heart... there were no rats (or even roaches) anywhere! The next day when Pastor Pogue arrived after his flight, with his wife, brother and sister-in-law to spend the week together in a hotel room about the size of one of our kitchenettes, he looked at our two apartments with unbelief. Without hesitation, he pulled out sixty dollars from his wallet and apologized for his lack of faith, stating that he would be blessed if we would allow him to pay for the rooms.

That was only the first of several more wonderful things that God did for us that week, and miraculous does not seem to be a strong enough word to describe them all. Oh, by the way, the kids were never sick another minute after we checked into 'that place', the one that the Lord had provided for us long before we had boarded the bus in Cleveland.

"And Abraham called the name of the place, The-LORD-Will-Provide; as it is said to this day..."
Genesis 22:14

Chapter 9
The Prophetic Dream

I sat straight up in the bed, bewildered and confused. Wow, it was only a dream! Why had I dreamt of Francis? Was she pregnant as I had just seen in my dream, and who was that man with the two suitcases who said, "The Lord has sent me"?

After breakfast I shared the strange dream with my husband, Greg, and we prayed for Francis. She had been our neighbor when we lived in the absorption center in Jerusalem. She was a sweet fifteen year old, not a pretty girl, but she had a very endearing smile. She had immigrated with her mom, Kay Miller, from the Bahamas who was a podiatrist. Kay had opened a business in downtown Jerusalem on King George Street and was always busy working. Francis hung around me most of the time and became interested in knowing about Jesus.

I began reading the New Testament with Francis and eventually she asked for one. Knowing that there is a law against proselytizing in Israel, and she was under the age of eighteen, I could only assure her that I would be here for her and if her mother agreed, then she could get herself a Bible. It had now been over three years since we had had any contact with Francis.

After breakfast, we enjoyed our mile long walk across town to Eilat Christian Academy. The morning air was still crisp here in the desert, but it would soon become unbearably hot outside. Our school enrollment was up to twentynindm students. We had experienced many miracles in the establishing of this school. Our two eldest boys, Isaac and Isaiah, were in the ABC'S of A.C.E. (Accelerated Christian Education), which I taught. I was so thankful that our own boys were able to get a Christian education in this remote desert city in Israel. A.C.E. is an independent learning curriculum that we purchased in Texas. That is a whole other story about our school that I will tell elsewhere. So, being maxed out in our enrollment, Greg was overloaded teaching more than twenty students in twelve different grades in just one classroom. We had begun to seek the Lord for a new teacher.

For over a week I had been having racing heart palpitations. It left me feeling weak and nauseous and did not go away. I mentioned it to Greg and we decided after praying that I would walk up to the hospital clinic on the weekend if I were not any better.

To our surprise, that afternoon we had a very unexpected visitor. She had spotted Isaac and Isaiah in the playground and the boys came bubbling through the door all excited with Francis. We were happy to see her again. I had just dreamt about her.

She and I had a good talk before I started preparing dinner. She explained how she had gone to great lengths to find out where we lived. She had gotten herself in trouble and wanted to move out of her mother's house. Her mother was angry that her only daughter was unmarried and pregnant. But, when Francis told her she was coming to see us, her mom surprised her by saying, "That's a very good idea. Maybe they can help you." This was a big change in attitude from her mom who had at one time, three years before, started cruelly beating Francis for coming to our apartment after forbidding her to have a bible or have anything to do with "those Jesus freaks".

After dinner, Francis sat on the couch reading bible stories to the kids. Greg was in the kitchen helping do the dishes. I had gone to my room to lie down. The dizziness and palpitations had worsened. There was a knock on the door and I dragged myself to get up and answer it.

When I opened the door, I saw two suitcases standing by the door and in the shadows, a tall man. It was getting dark out so I could not make out his face. He introduced himself saying, "Hello. My name is Howard Axtell. The Lord has sent me." With that, I invited him in and showed him into the kitchen where he began to speak with Greg. Though weak and faint, I leaned on the doorway just listening.

The man pulled out a long grocery receipt and began reading a list of scriptures he had written on the back that he claimed the Lord had given him. He said he was a physician, and had gone through a number of tragedies in his life, including a divorce, and now he had told the Lord he would obey. Therefore, he closed his practice in Texas and bought a one-way ticket to Israel. Upon arriving in Tel Aviv, he caught a sharuut (Israeli multi-passenger taxi) to Jerusalem, where wandering around on King George Street he saw a sign in English that read 'Kay Miller - Podiatrist.' He knocked on her door and introduced himself, "Hello. My name is Howard Axtell. The Lord has sent me." With that Kay replied, "Well, I'm not the one to help you but my daughter is visiting with a family who lives in Eilat. I'm sure they will help you." She gave him our address.

Having caught the next bus to Eilat, he was now on our doorstep. It was then, while Greg and Howard were still talking and Francis was on the couch reading to the children, that I remembered the dream. There sat Francis, pregnant, on the couch; there were the two suitcases I had seen in the dream and here was the man I had not recognized who had said, "The Lord has sent me." Greg excused himself and came to speak to me privately about the situation. I reminded him of the dream I had shared with him just a few weeks ago. We decided to let Francis sleep in the kids room on a mattress and we would let "the man the Lord had sent" sleep on the couch.

From the moment that Howard walked into our house, I never experienced another irregular heart palpitation. All the heaviness on my heart lifted and I have never had that problem again. Howard also turned out to be the answer to our prayer for a new teacher. He stayed with us for six months teaching in Eilat Christian Academy before returning to the U.S., but we would be seeing him again in the future.

Francis met a nice young man and got her own apartment in Jerusalem where they have been raising her boy together. She is always in our prayers and she has grown spiritually and shared her faith with her husband. On separate occasions, we went down to the Rea Sea with Howard and Francis where Greg baptized them on the profession of their faith in Jesus' name.

I cannot help but think that if I had not had that dream we may not have taken Howard seriously and would have said goodbye to a stranger on our doorstep claiming "The Lord has sent me." I would have missed my healing and so much more.

> *"For 'who has known the mind of the Lord*
> *that he may instruct Him?'*
> *But we have the mind of Christ."*
> 1 Corinthians 2:16

Chapter 10

Dancing in the Spirit

As far as we were concerned this place was a complete nut-house, but we were just too polite to get up and walk out. With high hopes of hearing the Word of God that evening, my friend Howard and I had gone to the 'Church of the Cock Crow' to attend a service where the Mt. Zion believers met. The church is built on top of one of the most authentic religious sites in Jerusalem, and the actual remains of the High Priest Caipha's house have been excavated there providing irrefutable proof. Thus, the courtyard is where Peter denied the Lord, and the political prison in the basement is where Jesus was scourged. All of this of course has nothing to do with the craziness that was taking place above this hallowed site.

Howard and I were there to worship the Lord, but everyone in the place was singing and dancing around like they were intoxicated. A couple of times we looked at each other in disbelief and smiled. Every few minutes, one of the sisters would come up to us as we were the only ones sitting, and say something like, "We're really free in the Spirit here brothers. Won't you join us?". I would politely answer each time, "Are we also 'free' to sit?" which seemed to un-nerve whoever was inviting us to 'dance in the spirit' and they would waltz away with a little bit less of a bounce in their step.

We wondered with increasing curiosity what was next on the agenda for this service. Anyway, neither of us moved; we just sat there very dignified like two bumps on a log. About the time that I was fairly certain that things couldn't get any weirder, one of the few brothers in the meeting sauntered up to me and said, "I would like to give you my testimony." Well, I'm always in for a good testimony so I replied, "Sure, go ahead", whereupon I was treated to the absolute strangest story I had ever heard. Now, I want to assure you that I'm not making stuff up or trying to paint the picture more colorful than it was, because every word of this is true.

He began his testimony by saying, "Brother, I was once like you - bound in the Spirit." I had never considered myself 'bound in the Spirit' before, so I just decided to grin and bear with him. He continued on with his testimony and said, "Then one day the LORD set me free, and I began to 'dance in the Spirit', and the LORD showed me that in every country and in every place that I danced before Him, He would send revival. For many years now I've been traveling all over the world, going from country to country, dancing in the Spirit before the LORD."

I don't want to make fun of anyone because I know that it takes all kinds to make a world, or even the body of Christ, and since we really are a body, we must have a funny-bone included in us somewhere. I just shook my head in disbelief while this brother danced off into glory.

About a half hour later, I gathered that the dancing was the main attraction in this fellowship, and I was literally getting bored stiff from sitting on the hard wooden pews in this cathedral. I had already examined every fresco on all the walls and ceiling several times and felt that it was probably about time to get out of here. I got up to stretch my legs, and in the corner of my eye caught that brother's eye. I imagine that he thought that his testimony had touched my heart because I was now standing, so he danced over in my direction.

To this day I can't really tell you what came over me. I think I was feeling a bit mischievous and figured that I was certainly never going to see any of these folks again. Whatever the case, I just spontaneously grabbed this brothers two hands and started hopping about and acting like a fellow nut. Now, the strangest thing happened that was altogether unexpected. Instantly, I was absolutely overcome by the power of the Holy Spirit. I glanced around and to my amazement so was Howard. There he was, one of the most conservative brothers I knew, dancing like a pro.

I can't really say how long I was 'dancing in the spirit' that night, but it was long enough that all the inhibitions and fears of embarrassment that were hidden in my soul were released, and I was genuinely set free. Howard and I stayed up late that night at the hostel trying to rationally and logically analyze what had happened. In the end we came to the conclusion that God had definitely done something very different in our lives that night.

Although I have continued over the years to dance in the Spirit, when God moves on me in that way, I've never heard Him once say that He would send revival in every place that I danced... but then again He may well chose to do so, for truly He is a sovereign God.

"Let no one deceive himself. If anyone among you seems to be wise in this age, let him become a fool that he may become wise."
1 Corinthians 3:18

Chapter 11
The Holy Kiss

Israel naturally attracts all kinds of folks, and over the years, we have seen our share of the spectrum. A million or more tourists may pass through our borders in any given year and for the most part these are just normal Jewish, Moslem and Christian tourists making a once-in-a-lifetime pilgrimage to the Holy Land. Now, I'm not saying that there are not any abnormal Jewish tourists who believe that their favorite 'rebbe' is the Messiah, or Moslems who believe that Tel-Aviv ought to be returned to their Palestinian brothers, but by and large, it is the Christians in particular that make the sport of 'tourist watching' a national phenomenon. Once again, the majority of these evangelical and non-evangelical pilgrims are just normal people being herded about like sheep on a whirlwind tour of mostly inauthentic holy sites. It is the 'peculiar people' that the book of Peter refers to that are the most interesting.

The 'messiah complex' runs deep in some who are borderline mental patients and who are reading their bibles with a different twist on it than the rest of us. Usually, by the time they get to the Book of Revelation, they are fairly sure that they are one of the two prophets or witnesses who are to die and resurrect in the city of Jerusalem. Instructions are included in eleventh chapter of Revelation for those reading this that may think they qualify as a candidate. They never come over together with the other prophet as they probably figure that they will meet up with him after their arrival. Now, the first thing that they do is give themselves a very 'biblical name' and not one like Ahab or Judas, but something with a bit of a flare to it, like 'Koresh Jerubbaal'. Next, they have to dress the part, so they rent the movie Ben Hur, and after watching it a time or two go about acquiring the appropriate dress. A staff like the one Moses carried is also required, which takes some imagination on their part to carve out since the original was cut up into pieces by King Hezekiah a few thousand years ago.

Okay, so you got the idea that every year we have a few prophets and would-be messiahs running around the streets of Jerusalem, preaching their version of some gospel, and in general entertaining the Jewish people and embarrassing the poor Christian believers who are forced to disassociate and denounce them when push comes to shove. These messengers generally do not gather much support, become discouraged and leave on their own volition once their three month visa is up; unless they do something like incite a riot down at the Wailing Wall on the Day of Atonement, in which case Israeli security arranges for their early departure from the Promised Land.

The next colorful category of folks is the long-term missionaries, usually not sent out by any denomination or church but what you would call 'independent'. These zealous ones do not usually bother with trying to renew their visas every three months, knowing full well that they will not have any chance of slipping by the watchful eyes of the Ministry of Interior more than once or twice. They have some ministry or other to some group or other, and in general because they are not technically in the country legally will behave themselves and remain as invisible as possible. The exception being, the Black Hebrews who now number several thousand and are centrally located in the Negev desert town of Dimona. Originally, from Chicago, they have their own messiah, Benyamin Carter, and have multiplied rapidly through their wide-scale practice of polygamy. They live communally with as many as twenty in a two bedroom apartment, are strict vegans, dress very colorfully and have had the political clout to finally establish themselves in the land after being persecuted for over twenty years. Originally, the founders went to Liberia in the late seventies but decided Africa was not really the land of promise that they had thought it was and so slipped into Israel as tourists. Renouncing their American citizenship and screaming 'racial prejudice' to whatever black U.S. congressman or congresswoman would listen when Israel tried to round them up and deport them in mass, they ended up defying the odds and making it, becoming full fledged Israeli citizens only two years ago.

After the fall of Saigon, an Israeli patrol boat picked up six-hundred Vietnamese in a sinking ship out in the Indian Ocean somewhere, and brought them to Israel. How these Buddhist refugees arranged political asylum in Israel is still somewhat of a mystery, but at the time no one else wanted them and the movie Exodus still conjured up images of Jews being turned back at the shores of Palestine by the British. Anyway, we got about six-hundred Chinese restaurants out of the deal and these people have become a perfect model for any non-Jewish immigrant group wanting to make Aliyah, the Hebrew term for immigration – blend in and find your niche in society.

Well, I have wandered away from the Christians who have made such a colorful impact, and I want to tell you about the 'Holy Kiss' before time runs out or you get tired of reading this. We have had all kinds of evangelists and self-proclaimed teachers wander amongst our fellowships while visiting Israel and these have had the most far-reaching effect. Their doctrines, prophesies and teachings have added spice to what would normally be rather boring 'believers meetings'. It is better if each meeting is limited to just one such guest and self-invited speaker, but you can not always spot these dear ones in the crowd before its too late.

Now, Dougie was such a character. His carrying around an autoharp at all times could have given him away, if he just hadn't had the countenance of an angel and such a sweet spirit. He loved Jesus with all his heart and spoke of nothing else but praise for the Lord and the 'Holy Kiss'.

Your guess is as good as mine as to what the Apostle Paul meant when he on three different occasions exhorted the Romans, Corinthians and Thessalonians to greet one another with a holy kiss. Customs in Eastern Europe and the Middle East differ greatly in the way people greet one another, but in general, hugs and some sort of cheek kissing are the norm. Now, Dougie and his fellowship back in England had gotten sort of a revelation about what the real 'Holy Kiss' was to entail... smack on the lips and nothing less. Brothers kissing brothers, sisters kissing sisters, and brothers and sisters kissing one another on the lips. Dougie himself mentioned that on occasion a brother and sister had 'fallen' by lingering on the holy kiss, but that did not deter his commitment to the doctrinal revelation he had received.

Now the 'Holy Kiss' never really caught on in any of the fellowships on a large scale, and was only popular for a time with a few folks who didn't seem to get embarrassed very easily. But I for one thought it to be strange enough to at least qualify to be put on the list of things to avoid that had the appearance of evil. If anyone out there is reading this and has a 'true' understanding of Paul's exhortation, I for one would really like to hear it.

> *"Greet all the brethren with an holy kiss."*
> 1 Thessalonians 5:26

Chapter 12
Call El-Al

In 1980 the United States began building two massive air-bases in the southern Negev desert of Israel in compliance with the Camp David Accords. Hundreds of men came to Israel to be a part of this massive building project and most had brought their families with them. However, just prior to the start of the school year, it was announced that only those who had been authorized by the company to bring their children with them would be allowed to attend the newly built Oovda airbase school. Many families were left out in the cold by this decision and had to look for an English speaking educational alternative in a Hebrew speaking nation for their children.

For us this was nothing short of the miraculous as we had completed the administrative training to begin an Accelerated Christian Education (A.C.E.) school the year before and had just rented a vacant apartment with the intent to begin a private English speaking Christian school by faith. At the time we did not have any idea where we would find students for our proposed school, which we had already named 'Eilat Christian Academy'.

Now, within days of that decision we registered twenty-nine students in grades K-12. We required only a one-hundred dollar deposit for each student which we intended to use to purchase the A.C.E. curriculum from Lewisville, Texas. However, a month later we were still waiting for the arrival of the curriculum. Finally, we were informed that the Israeli authorites had confiscated the entire $2000 worth of books at the port in Haifa due to the fact that unauthorized Christian literature was not generally welcomed within the Jewish nation.

The next day I received a Western Union telegram from my mother in Chicago letting me know that my beloved grandfather had passed away the day before. I knew that religious law forbids Jews from being embalmed; therefore I would not be able to attend his funeral, which would almost certainly take place very soon.

That same night I humbled myself before the LORD and sought Him with all my heart. I cried out for direction, for help and for His miraculous intervention. The loss of my grandfather deepened my sorrow greatly. I had been prepared to go to jail for circumventing

Israeli law for beginning an illegal Christian school, but wasn't expecting such a setback before we had even gotten off the ground.

Summer Students of Eilat Christian Academy

While on my knees, the Holy Spirit clearly spoke to me and said, "Get up immediately and call El-Al... Make reservations to fly to the United States tomorrow." Within minutes, I was on the phone making reservations to fly to Chicago without a cent to pay for the ticket!

The next morning I packed just a few things and prepared to go on a journey of faith. Before lunch a man knocked on our door, and after introducing himself, informed us that he had a nine year old daughter named Diane who was an excellent student but was not being allowed to attend the Oovda Air-base school. We briefly gave him some details about our 'proposed' Eilat Christian Academy and the cost of our monthly tuition. When I told him that a $100 deposit was required to reserve a place for his daughter, he quickly handed me $900 instead and insisted on paying for the whole year in advance!

That evening I arrived at Ben Gurion airport in Tel-Aviv and payed for my ticket at the El-Al counter. Thinking that I could now relax, I was shocked back into reality a few minutes later. As I went through passport control, I was informed that my Israeli passport had expired three weeks earlier and as an Israeli citizen, I would not be permitted to leave. Without thinking, I told the security guard that my grandfather had recently passed away. He asked me if I had proof, and when I reached into my pocket I was amazed to find that I had with me the Western Union telegram that my mother had sent the day before. Within minutes I was given a temporary exit permit and allowed to board my flight.

I returned the following week with enough of the curriculum in two large suitcases to get the school started. A pastor in Milwaukee who deeply loved Israel donated the curriculum from his own school when he heard of our dilemna. He then arranged for a set of the entire curriculum to be air-freighted to Israel. He also arranged for it to be personally cleared through customs by one of the men in his church who was co-owners of Burlington-Northern Airlines.

This was just the first of many miracles that we would witness in the life of Eilat Christian Academy over the years…

"Call to Me, and I will answer you, and show you great and mighty things, which you do not know."
Jeremiah 33:3

Chapter 13

Mother's Day Miracle

I prayed like a child: "Lord, bless mom and dad. Make a way for them to come to Israel. They have never flown on a plane or ever dreamed of such a trip. They are getting older now, so please do not take long to answer. Lord, you know my heart, so I am going to release this idea to you and trust you to bless them. Amen."

For years my parents had dreamed of retiring in Florida. Daddy had worked hard all his life as a farmer. The Korean War called most young men away but my dad, a mere twenty-one was the most responsible son chosen to remain and manage all of the area farms. Though it seems he always felt like he had been left out of the excitement, God was probably sparing his life. Thus, he set his heart to be the best farmer in the land. He was blessed with a perfect helpmate, my mom, and the most loving wife and mother any child could ever have.

My husband, Greg, and I with our five children had been in Israel now two years without seeing our family and I was very homesick. I was packed and ready for this upcoming five-month trip. Sadly, we would have just two weeks with mom and dad before we would have to hit the deputation trail. When we finished deputation, we would spend another week with them before flying back to Israel. Deputation meant that we would be driving from coast to coast, over 6,000 miles, visiting hundreds of churches. We would be sharing our vision and experiences about the work of the Lord in Israel and according to the Pentecostal Church program, raising monthly support that would enable us to live and minister in Israel.

Mom was brokenhearted over having been separated from her grandkids. "Why can't you work with the poor in the Appalachian Mountains? Why do you have to go over there to Israel anyway?" She had a point, but then how could I get her to understand the leading of the Holy Spirit. We had a call of God on our hearts that meant I would just have to die to self, and family, and go – go wherever the Holy Spirit was leading.

The thought of this adventure sent excitement through my veins, though the reality of such a task with five small children really scared me. How would our children manage sitting still in a car for hours and days as we drove across America? How would they sit quietly through hundreds of church services? How would we afford the gas? What vehicle would we travel in? So many questions, so many unknowns! We needed to start trusting the Lord now more than ever before.

There was a bright side for the kids because visiting America meant eating at McDonald's, new tennis shoes, watching TV cartoons, going to the movies, playing video games, miniature golf, swimming pools, maybe even Disney World or Six Flags. It also meant visiting grandparents and Uncle Ricky and Uncle Ronnie. The children felt so at home away from home around my family.

After five months of traveling, our deputation was a success. We had only one church left to visit before we would drive to Maryland from Illinois. We had been blessed and raised our support in record time. There were so many wonderful experiences to remember and now very shortly we would be leaving and going back to Israel. The time had just flown by. We were excited now about our two weeks at home in Maryland before leaving. Tears welled up in my eyes just thinking about it.

It was high time for me to let go of that secret hope of being able to buy my parents tickets to come to Israel. I repented before the Lord for placing such importance in my heart for something that now seemed obviously was not His will. We had a few hundred dollars in cash that we would use in Maryland to buy some clothes and extra stuff we wanted to take to Israel with us. I was content.

The church was large and packed out. We took our place down on the front row as we always did. The children's behavior had been outstanding on this trip. Another hour or so of just sitting still on a church pew and we would be finished. Greg preached his brief message and the pastor announced a special request. He asked me to come up to the platform with the children. So, we lined up and stood facing this very large congregation. He explained that it was Mother's Day and he wanted to do something different. He asked that only the women in the church get out their checkbooks, and for Mother's Day he wanted them to bless Sister Wootton. I had been so busy getting the family ready for church I hadn't realized that it was Mother's Day.

While the choir sang and the offering was being collected, I stood there with the children around me and hung my head down fighting tears. The ladies started coming up, one by one, with hugs and more tears. I was bathed in love. What a rich experience.

After the service, the pastor presented Greg with an envelope and told him this offering was to be given to his wife, all of it. He said it was the largest single offering the church had ever collected - $2,600.

This money was all mine. Temptation hit me hard on our drive to Maryland. Satan kept whispering in my ear how desperately we needed this money and how we would not have any other opportunities to buy the things we need, on and on…. Greg assured me that this was the miraculous provision from the Lord to bless my parents. God had answered my prayer and I was not to question it. On the way to Maryland, we stopped at a travel agency and had the exact amount to purchase round trip tickets for my parents and my youngest brother, Ricky, to fly to Israel.

We entered the driveway of my parent's home and there was Daddy up on a ladder mending the roof. Mama ran out of the house to greet us. I anxiously waited for Daddy to climb down off the ladder before giving him the envelope with three tickets to Israel. A spring of joyful tears and kisses followed. It would be much easier saying goodbye this time. We knew they would be embarking soon on a trip of a lifetime to visit us in Israel. Praise the Lord. He hears our prayers, boosts our faith and gives mothers' miracles.

> *"Hear my prayer, O Lord,*
> *And let my cry come to You.*
> *In the day that I call, answer me speedily."*
> Psalm 102: 1,2

Chapter 14

The Tent Fire

You were introduced to Dr. Howard Axtell in my story "The Prophetic Dream." Howard kept in contact with us after he left Eilat and returned to Israel some three years later. Only now, circumstances were very different. We again needed his help but this time in our new business "Computer World."

We were in the process of renting the vacant house across the street for him to live in. The Lord had blessed him and he would now be coming to Israel with his son and new wife and her three children. Together, with the adopted old man, Mootz, who lived with us, we were fourteen at the dinner table. Their two oldest teenage girls loved being in Israel and were very enthusiastic about helping out with our small brood of five. Their younger brother fit in like a pea in a pod with our gang.

There was big excitement over the tent sleep-over being planned in the back yard because the Reed family was visiting from Jordan. They were missionaries there and they crossed into Israel regularly. We loved their visits. Gary and Linda Reed had three great kids also around the same age as our kids.

We had not yet rented the house across the street for the Axtell's so it seemed like a good idea to let all twelve kids have their sleepover. Though we had a big house, it was still nice to get all the kids 'out for the night'.

Beyond a row of big old pine trees behind our house were peanut fields, as far as you could see. Our back field and yard had over twenty avocado trees that had been hand planted by our adopted grandpa, Mootz, who had moved in with us. His son had higher aspirations, he wanted to sell the whole property, and would have if Mootz, now an obstinate eighty-four years old, had not violently opposed. We were renting the son's house while he was off in the United States studying for his PhD. Mootz had become a cherished addition to our family.

In preparation for setting up the tent, the men decided to clear the overgrown, dried-out backfield beyond the grassy yard so that it would be safe for a campfire. Gary Reed suggested a controlled burn as a quick way to clear the field. Therefore, within a few hours the site was ready.

We had a big army-navy tent that claimed to sleep eight. It would sleep twelve tonight. The kids assembled it early on the lawn and then set about making an ideal campfire a safe distance in the unplanted area of the garden. All the sleeping bags were dragged out and who knows how many stuffed animals and toys were included. It was a grand ordeal and nothing could suit the evening better than hotdogs and marshmallows. The kids did not mind that the Israeli marshmallows sorta' turned to glue on the stick in the fire and the hotdog buns were not buns at all but pita bread. Even though the adults were not included in the sleepover, we were welcome to join in with the food preparation and fun.

After dark, we sat up late enjoying the campfire. The flashlights in the tents blinked like lighting bugs as twelve kids rustled around giggling and whispering way after we had called "lights out". They would surely sleep late in the morning.

Once inside the cramped tent, I began to pray with the kids and left Amy, the second eldest girl with every instruction I could think necessary. She was very responsible and there would surely be at least one potty trip inside. She assured me she could wake up very quickly if need be. That girl will become a good mom.

After ten years of rearing babies, I had learned to awaken at the drop of a pin, often gazing down on my little ones as they opened their eyes. I could keenly hear their movements stretching under the covers from another room. I inherited a great sense of hearing from my mother, which is not such a blessing when you are a teenager.

In the middle of the night, I sat straight up in bed thinking that I heard the crackling of a fire. Now already awake, I got up and went downstairs to make sure everything was all right. It was then that I heard Amy crying out, "Help!"

At the first sight of what seemed to be the world on fire, I hollered to the adults asleep inside, "Get up! Help! There's a fire outside!" I ran to the tent, which seemed to be transparent from the glow of blazes all around. The huge row of pine trees set off vociferous crackling noise and towering blazes.

Amy was struggling to unzip the tent while carrying sleepy little Israel in her arms. She handed him to me and went back inside the tent to grab another sleeping child. I put him down on the patio and raced back. Thus, we continued struggling to extract the kids from what was now a very hot environment. The kids just would not wake up and we struggled to drag them to safety.

Greg was quickly on the scene in quite a panic. I ran past him several times seeing him hold onto the end of the hose that was not long enough to reach the fire yelling for someone to turn the water on. Praise God, eventually he went inside and phoned the fire department.

Howard's wife, Diane, and Gary's wife, Linda, were now on the scene getting the startled but dopey kids, who wanting their stuffed animals and whatnot's from the tent, settled down. Howard and Gary hastily carried buckets of water trying to put out the flames closest to the tent. I watched Howard as he walked barefooted over hot coals trying to throw buckets of water on the flames closest to the tent.

It was a horrendous struggle for all of us. When the fire department finally arrived, Mootz also arrived on the scene shaking his cane at us for making such a racket in the middle of the night. It took the fire department over an hour to get the flames under control. We got a whopping water bill from them a few weeks later.

The men sat up the rest of the night guarding the remaining glowing embers. The exhausted, smoky group of kids all piled into bed and fell right off to sleep again. All except Amy, she had a good cry and we all thanked the Lord together that not one was hurt. Howard never complained about his burnt feet.

Upon inspection in the morning, we became fully aware of what an amazing miracle had taken place in the middle of the night. Despite such tremendous heat and close proximity to the flames, only small melted areas, not even revealing holes, could be found on the tent. It was also assumed that a spark from the controlled burn earlier the previous day had fallen into an old woodpile undetected in the overgrowth by the pine trees. It had been much later in the night that it caught fire and caused our drama.

Gary was thankful that not once had anyone pointed the finger in blame for his suggestion to do a controlled burn. Experiences like these bonded our families even closer together. We later built on the tent fire site a lovely children's park with a flying fox, sand pile, tree house with an escape pole, a hanging rope bridge, a chicken coop

and rabbit cages, plus a newly planted garden.

We have laughed about one another's reactions during the crisis over the years but the "fear of the Lord" remains the primary lesson.

"Nor shall any plague come near your tent;
For He shall give His angels charge over you,
To keep you in all your ways."
Psalm 91:10,11

Chapter 15
Unconditional Surrender

Sometimes truth and reality can be so much stranger than fiction that one is tempted to under-exaggerate, or play down the facts, to make them more palatable to the reader, or to the listener. Stories that make us laugh or even cry are more preferable than those that make us think about the closeness of eternal judgment, which is merely a heartbeat away from any of us at any given moment.

I was extremely alert as I sat there that day in the middle of the convoy of Israeli soldiers headed to the front lines of battle for 'The Peace of Galilee'. It has always amazed me at how hard the military tries to make war seem justified by naming it with lofty titles. This war in Lebanon would neither bring peace for the Galilee nor to anyone else for that matter. It would only prove to us the limitations of our military strength and become a Vietnam type debacle for the Israeli Defense Forces.

The Israeli army has always risen to great heights when called to defend our tiny little country from another holocaust at the hands of those who curse our existence. However, this was not the case in this situation. Our offensive attack on the sovereign territory of Lebanon in the summer of 1981 was the brainchild of then Defense Minister, Ariel Sharon, who had assured Prime Minister Menachem Begin that it would all be over within seventy-two hours. Ten years later, the last of our soldiers would cross back over our border, officially ending the conflict that had no military solution to begin with.

Here I was, caught up in the middle of this mess, only a year after it had all begun with such fanfare and high hopes of swift victory. I had completed basic training and had been discharged from the Israeli army a couple of years earlier, and now I was being called up for a thirty-five day reserve tour of duty, which everyone who received such a notice was fully aware of what it would entail. Instead of the normal eight to twelve hours of guard duty on some then quiet remote Jordanian or Egyptian border, we were going to be thrust into the thick of it in Lebanon. My unit was assigned to Sidon, which is close to the Mediterranean Sea, just an hour or so from the northern Israeli city of Nahariya. That one-hour's drive each way to

Sidon and back was one of the most dangerous trips that I have ever made.

This was ten years before 'Desert Storm', the war that United States' fought with Iraq to liberate Kuwait from Sadaam Hussein's armies. Suicide bombing as a terror tactic was only in its infancy at the time, but was rapidly growing to maturity as it created its intended effect on civilians and soldiers alike. Roadside bombs were regularly detonated by remote-control devices as convoys passed by, which in the end succeeded in killing more soldiers than hand-to-hand combat ever had.

Every soldier had a bulletproof flack jacket on, which worked extremely well as long as the enemy aimed for the small area of your body that it covered. Although we all wore metal combat helmets to protect our skulls, they also baked our brains in the intense July heat that characterizes the Middle East. Each of us had been issued six empty magazine clips, which we had filled with bullets, along with several hand-grenades that we now had secured in pouches on our belts. Our M-16 weapons were cleaned like brand new, fully loaded, and pointed outward with the safety mechanisms off, ready in less than a fraction of a second to obliterate anything that threatened our lives.

I firmly believe that 'those who live by the sword will die by the sword' and so this whole thing had me spiritually and physically concerned. My wife and our five young children were at home in Raananna praying for me. I was heading north through Lebanon praying for them, because Bev was nine months pregnant with our sixth child and was expecting to give birth any day. God was listening, and He had already sent the answer and His deliverance to us in a most unconventional way.

Being caught up in war is one of those times that makes everyone aware of his or her own mortality as the Angel of death awaits the next victim on his list. It is when we are facing the annihilation of our existence that we know for sure that as we were born naked into this world, we also will take nothing of this material life with us. It is both a dreadful as well as an exhilarating experience, because with the unconditional surrender of our will comes a sense of rebirth, and with it the freedom and the courage to test the limits of our faith in God. Such were the thoughts that crossed my mind as I prayed that day for my family, my fellow soldiers, and myself.

It seems only logical that given my family circumstances, the I.D.F. would have released me before sending me to Sidon that day. The army bureaucracy was just unable to deal with so many requests by reservists needing special consideration for various civilian 'emergencies'. Therefore, they simply ignored them all and sent everyone north. No one was being released for any reason, so I didn't bother asking to go home when I gathered with my unit to pick up our equipment from our assigned army base. After getting dressed in uniform and signing for all my military gear, weapons, ammunition and such, I found a quiet place to read my Bible and seek the Lord before we headed out.

We reached Sidon by midday, and were soon assembled together on the roof of one of the tallest buildings still standing in the center of the city, which the I.D.F. was using as a headquarters at the time. Our commander informed us that there were at least a half a dozen militias and armies fighting each other in the area. The Moslems, Druze, Southern Lebanese Army (made up of Mariannite Christian soldiers), as well as various splinter groups were ruthlessly and savagely slaughtering one another. The only thing that most of them had in common was their hatred of us, the Israelis. We were assigned to man all the checkpoints around the city, examine the trunk of every vehicle, and confiscate every weapon that anyone was carrying.

After a very quick orientation from the rooftop of the sections of the city that the various armies were trying to control, we ducked back into the building for cover and got ready to head out on patrol. We were broken up into various shifts so that we could cover the city twenty-four hours a day, seven days a week. I was to go out first thing in the morning, and was told to try to get some sleep on one of the army cots that had been placed along an interior wall of one of the rooms that still had walls to protect us.

After a very uneasy night's sleep, I woke up in the morning soaked in sweat and suffering from a very high fever. Our unit's medic pronounced me unfit for duty that morning and I was told to get some more rest as I would be re-assigned to the evening patrol. When the men headed out, I realized that I had a small window of opportunity to make a quick phone call home to my wife, and was given permission by my commander after I alerted him of my wife's situation. Amazingly, I got straight through and Bev was as shocked to hear my voice, as I was to hear hers. I told her more or less where

I was because the army is a bit paranoid of soldiers giving out any information that might be used by the enemy against us. I assured her that although I was running a fever that it was the least of my concerns at the moment. Her words to me where something like, "Well you'd better get home right away, because I'm beginning to go into labor."

We were very short-handed here in Sidon and I did not think I had any chance whatsoever of 'getting home right away' but conveyed my wife's urgency to my unit commander. To my surprise, he immediately wrote me out a two day pass and said, "If your wife doesn't give birth in the next forty-eight hours, you are to get right back here or you will be A.W.O.L. If she does give birth then report to your assigned military base commander back home and he'll issue you another pass if it's a boy." In Israel, circumcisions are only performed on the eighth day after the birth of a boy, in accordance with Jewish law. In one of the rare gender biased military rules in an army that has almost as many women as men, husbands are given eight days leave if their wives give birth to a son, but are required to report immediately back to their units the next day if it's a girl.

Now the effects of being in the middle of a war zone, having little sleep, running a high-fever, and having been unexpectedly given a free pass to go home to my family were making this whole experience seem surrealistic. For a brief while I thought I was dreaming, and would wake up any minute. In the meantime, I got my gear together, put it all into my duffle bag and headed out into the streets of Sidon hoping to catch a military convoy back to Israel. We were strictly ordered not to travel alone or in a single military vehicle anywhere in Lebanon, so I took in the sights and smells of the urban battlefield while I waited by the headquarters' entrance.

Gunfire or explosives had damaged every building everywhere, and there wasn't one structure standing that didn't have at least a dozen bullet holes in one of its walls. People nervously walked, ran or drove quickly to wherever they had to risk their lives to get to, or come back from. Absolutely no one was allowed to park his or her vehicle on the side of the road or sidewalk where one of our military convoy's would be passing by. The fine for such a parking violation was very expensive indeed; in that such a vehicle would be blown up on the spot by the lead tank assigned the task of protecting our troops. There were no warnings issued or other advance notices given. I was amazed at how quickly people ran in and out of the shops and back to their cars after purchasing whatever they felt was so necessary that it warranted risking their lives.

Within the hour I was going back the same way that I had arrived less than twenty-four hours earlier, in the middle of an armed convoy with my weapon locked and loaded, as alert as possible, and ready to literally 'get out of there'. I arrived back in the Tel-Aviv area that evening, and was miraculously by my wife's side that night in the private hospital room we had arranged for the birth. Instead of sowing death, I was being given an opportunity to help in the bringing of a new life into the world. God arranged that our doctor was busy and not in the room when the baby was ready to emerge from the womb, so I had the honor of deliverying our son, Israel, myself.

The next day, when I went to the army headquarters in Tel-Aviv to extend my leave for the eight days that I knew I had coming, I was informed that I was being taken out of the war altogether. The birth of a sixth child is considered by law to be an undo hardship on a family, and therefore the husbands in such circumstances are released from combat. I was freed to go home and continue to serve the LORD as an unconditionally surrendered soldier of Christ.

> *"No one has power over the spirit to retain the spirit,*
> *and no one has power in the day of death.*
> *There is no release from that war ..."*
>
> Ecclesiastes 8:8

Chapter 16

Tongues of Fire

Twenty first century life in Israel was becoming a travesty that was emerging from the constant danger imposed upon every household by indiscriminant acts of terrorism. It was stressful managing six small children, ages one to eight, while my husband, Greg, was away on extended business trips. This time he would be attending a Pastors' Conference in Belgium for two weeks, which was not near as bad as his annual Israeli military reserve call-up for a month at a time.

We owned and operated two computer learning centers that needed supervision, not to mention all of the 'spiritual babes' that came to our house twice a week, once for bible study and again for Shabbat, our worship day. You could say my hands were full.

Following our goodbyes at the airport, I became aware of an angelic presence surrounding me just as I had experienced at other times when Greg had been away. The divine omnipresence of the Lord caused me to feel especially peaceful and secure.

Greg had been away for almost a week; I missed him and was expecting him to phone tomorrow. Persistently staying organized was a key to keeping up with my busy schedule. After dinner all the kids were bathed and we had our prayer and bible reading time together. Even Israel, the baby, loved huddling together over a story. We usually read a chapter or two in a Sugar Creek Gang mystery. When Greg was away the kids always talked me into reading 'just one more chapter'. They also took turns sleeping in our bed (to keep me company) when Greg was away. Tonight I had left the two eldest boys, Isaac and Isaiah, in my bed reading while I did a few last chores. It was their turn to sleep in my room

We lived in a big rented 3-story house in Ra'ananna, Israel. I had gone around and locked up the house just before dark, leaving our big collie, Samson, inside. He usually stayed on the bottom floor at night, in the warm laundry room. I was just too tired to carry the ironing board down a flight of stairs so I left it standing in the hallway before turning out the lights and heading up to bed.

I climbed under the covers between the two sleepyheads, put their book up, and gave them a kiss each. They immediately fell fast asleep. I too was so drowsy but felt an urgent need to pray.

Thinking I could just lay there and get the job done proved unsatisfactory. The more I prayed the more urgent I sensed the need to seek the Lord and get up and get on my knees. This had to be the Holy Spirit because I knew I was too tired, and my flesh wasn't so happy about this.

As I knelt at the end of the bed talking to Jesus, I was not sure what it was that seemed so urgent. I began worshipping the Lord in my spiritual language. After a few minutes kneeling in the darkness, I realized that I had been praying very loudly. I didn't want to wake the boys so I got up to go into the closet. It was then I heard the ironing board screech across the floor downstairs. I assumed the dog knocked it. I went back to my worship prayer in tongues while on my knees in the closet. Then I heard the ironing board screech again. This time the sound sent a distracting wave of fear over me. I knew it wasn't the dog and I was sure someone was in the house. But why wasn't the dog barking?

The baseball bat was conveniently behind the closet door, so I grabbed it and held it perched up over my shoulder and started creeping down the dark hallway leading to the stairs. I was making a great effort to overcome my fear in order to check things out and ensure that no harm come upstairs where the children were sleeping. Once at the edge of the stairs, I reached for the light switch and when I flipped it on, I gasped at the sight of a dark-skinned young man, wearing only boxer shorts, jut across the living room headed for the front door.

In a quivery voice I cried, "What do you want?" He replied in broken English, "I'm sooorry, I'm sooorry," while covering his face with his arm. He dashed toward the front door and could be heard struggling with the lock. I ran back to my bedroom and went to the window and shouted across to my neighbor, "Neelie, bring your dog, bring your dog." This woke up all the neighbors, and in just minutes they were knocking on the door, and dogs were barking everywhere, including Samson.

This commotion had awakened the boys who were up and following me down the stairs, so I composed myself, sensing we were no longer in danger. I went downstairs carefully and unlocked the front door. The intruder, unable to get out of the locked front door, had gone into the kitchen, knocked the plants from the windowsill, and opened the kitchen window which he climbed out of, ripping down the curtains and the screen as he escaped.

The panicky neighbors helped me thoroughly check the house and Neelie offered to spend the night. Curiously, we discovered the doors and windows were still locked. It seemed that this intruder must have entered the house before I had locked up earlier. Also, he must have befriended our collie, Samson, who had not barked when we had needed him to bark. Greg always claimed that he was a dumb dog, not a bit like Lassie whom we had grown up watching on television.

Once again I became very aware of that angelic presence. I expressed my appreciation to my neighbors and said goodnight. My heart beat sharply when I saw my two little boys looking so pale and afraid. I assured them we were safe and then took them by the hand and walked with them in the dark around the entire yard of the house several times that night, praying and asking the Lord to give us peace and protection. Dealing this way I hoped to conquer our fears. I do not recall my boys praying more intensely than they did that night.

I turned the lights out once again and climbed back into bed snuggling with my boys. Thankfully, my other four children had slept through it all.

What had just happened? Could the loud prayer language I had been worshipping the Lord in have been a message for the intruder? Had the intruder understood the heavenly tongues that I had spoken and had it frightened him away? This would remain a mystery. He was obviously endeavoring to get out of the house and he did say, "I'm sorry" twice.

Praise the Lord! I forgave him.

I was tempted to inform Greg over the phone the next day of our 'little excitement' in the night but did not want to have him distracted and concerned about us. I would prudently wait until he returned next week. He did tell me that the entire conference group had prayed specifically for our family subsequent to his preaching on 'spiritual warfare' that very night.

"For he who speaks in a tongue does not speak to men but to God, for no one understands him: however, in the spirit he speaks mysteries."
1 Corinthians 14:2

Chapter 17

The I.D.F. Mosquitoes

Mosquitoes have been responsible for the deaths of more people on earth by unintentionally spreading malaria than any other creature alive, including man. But if it weren't for these insidious little vampires, I would never have become an officer in the Israeli Defense Forces (I.D.F.). However, I am getting way ahead of myself here, so I will back up a bit and explain what lead up to such a twist of fate.

After being drafted into the Israeli army in the winter of '79, and enduring three months of 'hell on earth' in boot camp, I was only beginning to understand what sacrifice 'in service to God and country' really entailed. You see, everyone including women serve in the I.D.F. because the enemies of Israel surround her and there just isn't any other choice in the matter. All young people begin military training at age eighteen, with men serving three years and women two years respectively. That's actually only the beginning of the military's interference in one's life because then there is an additional thirty to forty-five days of mandatory annual reserve duty that each individual must serve, up until that point in time, the age of fifty-five. Women of course only serve in the reserves until they have a child, which seems to have worked the desired effect of them getting married and pregnant shortly after their discharge from regular army service.

Now the I.D.F. isn't really all that bad considering the circumstances that warrant such sacrifices by the struggling nation and its resilient people, but I for one am just not cut out for guard duty, which is what ninety-percent or more of reserve duty actually involves. I can honestly say that I wasn't a very good soldier. Although I can endure the tasteless food and the company of smelly men for five to six weeks each year without any great difficulty, it's staying awake and 'watching' hour after hour, day after day, that is just cruel and unusual punishment for me personally... which brings me to the point of this story.

God, sensing my dilemma and the vexation of my spirit, intervened in a most unusual way. It so happened that in the winter of '83, after nearly thirty days of unbelievably boring guard duty near the West Bank, I took it upon myself to repair the automatic electronic gate that was our first line of defense on the military base that I had been assigned to guard. The gate hadn't been working for a while and we had to get up and manually open the thing every couple of minutes after checking out whoever and whatever was trying to enter the base at all ungodly hours of the night. Well, boredom had its way of inspiring me and one particularly quiet night, at around 3:00 AM, I fixed the thing so I could just push the button and it would magically open like it was designed to do. That daring act of bravery (I could have made that gate worse off and not work at all) got me my first recognition by my superiors and I was duly recommended to take a squad commander's course the following year.

There was nothing much to becoming a squad commander but taking part in an intensive thirty-five day training course that after the first day reminded me a lot of boot camp. The only real hardship was that I would be away from my wife and six children for that time, but that was a part of military service that everyone had to endure. The real snag in the whole process as far as I was concerned was the problem of the mosquitoes. I thought that possibly the army had bred a special strain of mosquito that was more aggressive and blood-thirsty than the normal type that civilians endured, but that may have just been a figment of my imagination brought about by lack of sleep due to the horrible whining in my ears during those few hours that I was allowed to lay down each night.

Finally, when I could take it no longer, I declared war on my enemies and got up one Friday night determined to fight fire-with-fire, so to speak. Since I couldn't sleep anyway and the base was nearly deserted for the weekend, I set about to make my barracks mosquito proof. To this day it still amazes me to think that the Israeli Defense Forces hadn't considered putting up screen doors or screens on the windows to keep the mosquitoes out of the barracks. It seems even more amazing that for nearly forty years, thousands of recruits had endured these irritating little pests by hiding under their blankets, which I found to be most intolerable that dreadfully hot summer.

Quite miraculously, I found all the things I needed: screen, hammer, nails, screws, hinges and a long spring to keep the door from staying open when the men came in and out. Within two hours of the battle, the door was on and built strong enough that it may still be functioning to this day, even after all these years. When my other roommates saw the marvel of technology that I had built, they decided to pitch in and we had the windows completely screened off in no time at all.

The following Friday, the camp commander came around inspecting each of the barracks as well as the men before releasing us to go home to our families for the weekend. His face lit up upon entering through the screen door and he inspected the workmanship thoroughly. Finding no defects and seeing that it seemed to be built according to regulation, he inquired as to who had initiated the project. He mentioned that this was the first time in the history of the base that anyone had thought to do such a thing and promptly ordered the camp carpentry shop to build exactly the same type of door on all the barracks and to cover the windows with screens as well.

The following month I was sent to an officer's training course, which I graduated from as a second lieutenant after an additional six very intense weeks. Although going through such a course was strictly on a 'volunteer basis', I was easily talked into it by the mere fact that Israeli military officers never have to do guard duty.

"You therefore must endure hardship as a good soldier of Jesus Christ. No one engaged in warfare entangles himself with the affairs of this life, that he may please him who enlisted him as a soldier."
2 Timothy 2:3-4

Chapter 18
A Blessing from the I.R.S.

As far as I can tell the Internal Revenue Service fell in love with the personal computer age that began in the early 80's and initiated a campaign of tax collection not seen since the days of Caesar Augustus at the time of Christ's birth. Unfortunately I had been blissfully ignorant that I owed taxes to the United States government for many years since we were busy ministering the gospel in Israel and trying to raise our six children by faith. I am sure that you are aware that its nearly impossible to answer a computer generated letter especially if you are living oversees, so I made the only decision reasonable at the time and ignored the letters and put the whole matter out of my mind.

Both the elephant and the computer never forget, and the letters from the I.R.S. kept coming regularly, which was a shame because it was about the only mail we got in those days. Surprisingly, the letters were programmed to become more threatening as time went by, and at the same time these computers were able to calculate the amount that we owed in back social security taxes including penalties and interest to the nth percent each day that our debt accumulated.

I was not overly concerned for the first year or two and did not see how the few thousand dollars I owed Uncle Sam would make any difference to the United States' overall budget deficit. However, the tone of the computer generated correspondences eventually led me to the conclusion that it might be wise to talk with a professional before throwing any more letters away.

Now, it's ironic that our accountant in America also happened to have been the president of the Certified Public Accountants Association for over twenty years and had met and advised every president from Truman and Eisenhower on. This brother, and his wife who was also an accountant were very spiritual people who did volunteer work for oversees missionaries, so they freely advised me to pay up or else. In a most serious and frightening manner, I was told that the I.R.S. had signed a reciprocal agreement with Israel and had the authority to come to our home and seize everything we owned including our vehicles, furniture, appliances, as well as personal and business bank accounts if we did not immediately render to Caesar that which was due to Caesar.

Well, that put an entirely different light on the matter and I realized I was in really big trouble because we didn't have but a few hundred dollars to our names. I confess that I had not been diligent in many areas of my life up until this point, but now this matter was something that was threatening to not only ruin my family but wipe out years of ministry in Israel as well. It seemed like all of a sudden the Beast of the book of Revelations had surfaced to destroy me and that I unwittingly had been feeding him all along with my ignorance.

Fear and panic set in almost immediately and I began to become more and more anxious every time I went to the mailbox. As I said, there was absolutely nothing I could do to answer these computer generated letters and I began to think that these 'impersonal' computers really were the way in which the Anti-Christ was going to overcome the saints in the last days. Over the next year or so I repented before the LORD for my laziness and lack of diligence and for a host of other sins that were brought about by those first two. Still, the dread and fear continued to grow in my heart and paralyze my spirit to the point that I was unable to do anything but worry.

I thank God for His wonderful Word because it is all that sustained me through this dreadful trial as I walked alone through the valley of the shadow of death. I did the best I could to hide my fears from my wife and children but I am sure everyone around me sensed the anguish in my spirit during those dark months... and still the letters kept coming at increasingly closer intervals.

When the fullness of time had come, the LORD looked down from heaven and I imagine, figured that I had been through enough already, having confessed and repented with tears till none were left. Faith suddenly stirred in my heart and like the prodigal son, I decided that I would go back to the United States and throw myself at the mercy of the government. It wasn't much of a plan but it gave me a measure of peace, which I hadn't had in a long time, and I made the arrangements to fly out to Los Angeles, California. I was scheduled to attend a conference for a week in Holland anyway, and the additional flights to and from L.A. only cost a few hundred dollars more.

In Los Angeles, I spent a few days with my grandmother who was dying of cancer. I was extremely glad for the opportunity to be with my grandma who had been so close to me when I was growing up, even if the circumstances of my coming to America were pretty dismal. Somehow, we both sensed that this would probably be the last time I would see her alive. We made the most of the time by taking a trip to San Diego, spending a day at Sea World, and by going to some other places she hadn't been in all the years she lived in southern California.

The day before I had to leave, when I could put it off no longer, I drove downtown to the I.R.S. building and went in as a sheep prepared for the slaughter. It didn't matter anymore, as one way or another, the whole mess was hopefully going to be over soon. Walking into the gigantic government building, I felt so insignificant by the world's standards but significantly loved by God because of my faith in His Son, Jesus.

As soon as I entered the office where I had been directed to go, which dealt with American taxpayers living overseas, I broke down and began to spill my entire life's story to a rather large African-American lady who was the only person in the office. I told her I was a Jew who had come to know Jesus as the Messiah in Israel where I had been living for the past ten years, and that I had six small children (five born in Israel) and was trying to work for the Kingdom of God and was having Bible studies and worship services in our home... and on top of that (oblivious now to where I was or who I was speaking to) I told her that my wife and I were living by faith, had no houses or savings anywhere with which we could use to pay this enormous eleven thousand dollar debt, and that we were paying taxes in two countries as we were dual citizens of the United States and Israel...

I lost track of time, but probably poured out my whole story in about fifteen minutes or so and amazingly wasn't interrupted once. It felt good to get everything out into the open and I was glad to get it all off my chest. When I finished speaking there was silence for what seemed like a half-a-minute, and then I heard the strangest words I had ever expected to hear from the I.R.S., as this lady said in a loud, almost angelic voice, **"Praise the LORD! Honey, what the government has been doing to you is wrong --- and I'm going to fix it!"**

Needless to say I was speechless, dumbfounded and not sure that I had come into the right building or office after all. This precious sister in the LORD (I never learned her name) went on to tell me that she attended Andrea Crouch's father's Pentecostal church and that she knew it was God's will for her to be in that office that day to help me. She immediately made a phone call and then got on her computer terminal. As I was leaving she said that I could expect to receive more letters for a while but to ignore them, and to go back to Israel and not worry any more about it. Her last words were that she was definitely going to take care of the whole matter.

Around eighteen months later I received my final letter from the I.R.S., which said …. Well that's another story and another answer by our 'God of the Miraculous'.

> *"When a man's ways please the LORD,*
> *he makes even his enemies to be at peace with him."*
> *Proverbs 16:7*

Chapter 19

The Walkabout

A 'walkabout' is an Australian Aboriginal term meaning a spiritually cleansing journey into the outback or 'the bush' for an indeterminate amount of time. More than two decades ago I began a walkabout that had its starting point in the southern city of Melbourne, Australia and continued along thousands of kilometers of dirt tracks before finally ending in the northernmost town of Darwin.

I am not sure what prompted my spiritual quest, but I guess that I just needed to know that God still loved me in spite of myself. Having begun in the Spirit several years earlier I had for the past few years been trying to become perfect in the flesh, and had failed miserably.

Having hitched a ride from Melbourne, I was still seven hundred kilometers or so from Darwin when I began to get extremely hungry as all my supplies and money had by now run out... so I went fishing. Now, you may be questioning the validity of this story, or wondering how a person goes fishing in the middle of the desert, but its all true I tell you. The outback of Australia is amazingly beautiful with vast expanses that remind a person of eternity at every step. There is an abundance of wildlife also, such as kanagroos, brombies (wild horses), dromedary camels, cockatoos, iguanas (huge lizards), and at least a dozen types of poisonous snakes slithering about. I was there after the winter and spring rains, so the rivers were all flowing at maximum capacity. The famous Australian barramundi is a fish that sportsman from all over the world come to the outback rivers to catch, and I was sure that I was going to catch one, and that it would be sufficient to feed me for several days.

I do not believe I have ever had a more disappointing day of fishing in my life. Everyone around me was reeling them in left and right. I had asked every question imaginable from these eager and extremely helpful anglers concerning the bait, line, tackle, technique, etc., so I knew I was doing everything the way you were supposed to do it, but I did not get one nibble all day.

As it was now getting dark out, I was even hungrier after all that wasted effort and was on the verge of total discouragement and disillussionment in myself and God. I just stood there wondering what life was really all about anyway. In such a state of mind, it seemed like I was in a trance of sorts when this man dressed in a full blown diving suit, including snorkel, face mask and flippers walked up to me and simply said, "What kind of fish do you want?" I was in shock, probably brought about by lack of nourishment, I answered, "It doesn't matter." After that I watched him walk into the dark river and disappear out of sight. In a few minutes, I rubbed my eyes in disbelief as this same aberration came walking back out of the river holding a huge fish on the end of his fishing spear. Without a word he handed it to me and walked off. All I could do was weakly mumble, "thanks".

It wasn't until I had finished grilling that delicious fish and gorging myself to the point where I couldn't eat another bite that I realized I probably had had a visitation from God, or at the very least had probably seen one of his angels. Anyway, over the next couple of weeks I experienced many more such miraculous provisions which I won't recount in detail. What is important is that I found out that God really did love me, and that 'His grace is made perfect in weakness'.

Shortly thereafter, I completed my walkabout in Darwin, changed my ticket at a two hundred dollar savings and flew back to Israel by way of Singapore and Bangkok. The process of spiritual healing and restoration had already begun in my heart and soul.

> *"After these things Jesus showed Himself again to the disciples at the Sea of Tiberias, and in this way He showed Himself...*
> *Simon Peter said, "I am going fishing"... and that night they caught nothing.*
> *But when the morning had now come, Jesus stood on the shore;*
> *yet the disciples did not know that it was Jesus.*
> *Then Jesus said to them, "Children, have you any food?"*
> *They answered Him, "No."*
> *And He said to them,*
> *"Cast the net on the right side of the boat, and you will find some."*
> *So they cast, and now they were not able to draw it in because of the multitude of fish."*
> John 21:1-6

Chapter 20

Return of the I.R.S – Pack Your Bags

It is extremely rare for me to see visions or have prophetic dreams for that matter. In over thirty years, I can only count on one hand those instances where I knew that God was giving me a vision of an event that would come about in the future. Although, the Word of the LORD specifically states in the book of Joel that all of Israel's young men would see visions in the last days, in my case it just does not happen that often. However, when it does...

Standing in a busy travel agency in downtown Bangkok, Thailand was hardly the place I would have expected to see a vision or hear God's voice, but that is exactly where the Holy Spirit revealed to me that my wife and I and our six young children would 'go around the world by faith.' Now to be clear, it was revealed to me in a vision that we would all be standing here in Bangkok with Mr. Visidhi, the travel agent who was confirming my reservation to fly back to Israel the next day. The 'faith' part I added because at the time we did not have the finances to take a bus to Tel-Aviv, which was only twenty miles from our home in Raananna, Israel.

I have never been one to dilly-dally when I hear from the LORD, so a minute or so later when Mr. Visidhi got off the phone, I asked him, "How much would it cost for two adults and six children to fly roundtrip from Tel-Aviv to Bangkok?" Now, I am not sure he took me seriously, but the Tai people are so courteous that you cannot tell whether they believe you or not from their facial expressions or demeanor. Mr. Visidhi had been making several calls over the past half-hour to confirm my reservations and was not expecting to receive any payment whatsoever for his efforts since I already had my ticket.

Anyway, my faith must have sparked his curiosity, because he then asked me something like "Wouldn't you like to visit some other countries while you're in Asia? It would practically cost the same." I said that that would be great, and he told me that he could get some excellent deals on Egypt-Air out of Cairo. After about fifteen minutes he gave me a price of $10,400.^{00}, which would include ten tickets for the eight of us, open for a year at any of the destinations I would choose. The key to the great deal was that we had to use the first of the series of tickets last, so that Egypt-Air would assume that all the flights had originated in Bangkok instead of from Cairo. At that time, it was costing us around $6,000 every few years for all of us to fly back and forth from Tel-Aviv to the United States to visit our family in America. I could hardly believe the price, but quickly told him to make the arrangements for the following month and that I would wire him the money when I got back to Israel. He had explained that he would have to have the exact amount in dollars in a certified bank check or electronic wire transfer before he could send the tickets to me in Israel by courier. I instinctively trusted this man I had only met the day before and shook hands with him confirming 'the deal'.

At the time, I didn't bother him with the details that I did not have any money and wasn't sure my wife and children would even want to travel to Thailand or all around the world for a year. When I got back to Israel, I simply said to my wife, "Honey, pack the bags, we're going around the world!" Well, she looked at me as if I was joking or mentally deranged because we both knew that our computer business was on the verge of bankruptcy, we were in an overdraft situation of several thousand dollars at our bank, the I.R.S. in the States was still trying to collect eleven thousand dollars they claimed we owed in back social security taxes, and like I said we didn't have the bus fare to Tel-Aviv. I wish I could tell you that she had such great faith in my 'hearing from the Lord' that she began packing right away, but I had been wrong on more than one occasion so she was not packing anyone's bags until she saw the money.

Over the years, I have gotten used to people looking at me funny when I tell them that I have heard from God, so I do not usually blurt stuff out like that except when I am sure that the person I am talking with won't try and have me committed. Nevertheless, it was a surprise to find my dear wife so greatly opposed to such a great vision. If I have learned anything, it is that God does not require my help to work out His plans, so I just let go of it for the time being.

A few days later, another computer generated I.R.S. letter arrived in the mail. We had been harassed beyond measure for years by this government office, and even though I had been promised by a clerk in the I.R.S. office in Los Angeles, California over a year earlier that I should ignore these letters because she would take care of the problem, it was hard to do so. I might have ripped the letter up and thrown it in the trash without even opening it, if I hadn't been awaiting a notice letting us know that it really was 'all taken care of' as that African-American lady had promised me. When I opened the letter, I nearly wept because of the goodness of God. It formally stated that our entire debt to the U.S. Government had been canceled ... and furthermore upon review it had been determined that all of the social security taxes that we had paid over the past six years would be refunded in full.

The refund was to come in separate checks, one for each year in the various amounts that had been paid, which altogether totalled over $14,000. My wife, Beverly, started packing and this was only the first of several miraculous events that would take place over the next few weeks that God used to send us to the ends of the world and back.

We immediately decided to sell our computer business, but knew that because the Apple Computers in our school were five years old we would not receive much for them. Besides this, we really did not own the store, but only leased this prime location next to the bank on the main street in Raananna. The owner, Mr. Golan had clearly informed me that he wanted the store back after our lease was up. It seems that one of his children wanted to start a flower business and had been eyeing the location for a while. We also knew that we had to finish paying off the leases on our computers before we could sell them, and the overdraft at the bank had to be paid before we could leave. Selling the business was our only option but a bleak one to be sure.

Receiving the letter from the I.R.S. ignited faith in me that the 'vision' was going to somehow work out, so we mentioned to a few people who we knew might be interested that we were selling the computer business. One person who expressed keen interest never actually made an offer but I was able to use his enthusiasm for an advantage. Within a day or so of our announcing our intentions to sell, two rather sharp looking Israeli businessmen showed up at our store. They were beginning to put together a new chain of computer stores and instantly recognized that our location was the best in the area. We had been there for five years, and had taught over four-thousand kids and adults computer programming in our courses. Besides this, we had hundreds of loyal customers who bought books, software and peripheral equipment from us regularly.

Now, in the Middle East you cannot even buy a toothbrush without having to haggle over the price. Usually, the asking price is simply whatever you are willing to pay, which makes things a bit fuzzy when you are trying to do business. We had learned to never ever quote someone the actual price you wanted to sell something for, because they automatically assumed that was the initial bargaining point and would offer you no more than half to start off the negotiations. Therefore, I doubled the price in my head and told these gentlemen that I was going to sell the store and everything in it before the end of the day (by faith) to someone for that price. They offered me half, which I refused, and again told them in Hebrew that I was sure that the business was worth what I was asking for it. They came up a few thousand more but I did not budge. I simply said that I had another buyer in mind and by the end of the day I was selling this business to someone for the full price and was not willing to take one cent less.

They genuinely seemed puzzled, for as far as negotiations go this was definitely not going according to the unwritten rules of bargaining, since there was absolutely no give and take. Finally, they sensed my seriousness and said okay, but only on the condition that the owner would give them at least a three year extension on the lease. We shook hands on it and arranged to finalize the sale the next day.

The LORD was very gracious to me that day when I went up to Mr. Golan's office to speak with him about the extension. I knew he liked our family, but he was also a very shrewd businessman, and business is business. It just didn't make any sense for him to do what I was asking him to do because there was not anything in it for him, and he would be hurting his own self-interest by going against his children's wishes. After we spoke for a few minutes and I told him about the conditions of the proposed sale of the computer business, he said, "Greg, I can't do anything to hurt you or your family. Although this is going to cause me problems at home, I'll give you the extension on your lease."

After selling the business for double what it was probably really worth, Bev and I paid off all our debts and had our bank wire the $10,400 to Mr. Visidhi. In turn, he faithfully sent the tickets directly to our home by courier within forty-eight hours. We had arranged by phone to include tickets for all eight of us to fly to New York, return to Cairo, continue on to Bangkok and then Hong Kong, Auckland, Sydney, and Manila, before returning to Bangkok and ending up back at our starting point of Cairo, 364 days after our departure on June 25th. All tickets were open for a year from the date of arrival, but the trip had to be over in 364 days in order for the last flight to Cairo on Egypt Air to remain valid.

We then went about selling all our personal electronic goods at full price, as the luxury taxes on such things are very high in Israel. We cleared another $4000 or so on the television, personal computer and stereo system alone. As we finished packing, and were getting ready to leave for Cairo and then Bangkok, we received notice that we were entitled to draw out approximately $6000 from a pension fund set up in our names that had been accumulating for years, one which neither of us knew anything about.

A few months later, it was just as I had envisioned: a truly beautiful day in Bangkok and Mr. Visidhi meeting my wife and children as we prepared to take a train up north to Chang Mai for a weeklong jungle trek into the Golden Triangle, but that's completely another story…

"Now to Him who is able to do exceeding abundantly above all that we ask or think, according to the power that works in us,
to Him be glory in the church by Christ Jesus throughout all ages, forever.
Amen.
Ephesians 3:20-21

Chapter 21
The Golden Triangle

The children had repeatedly been informed that a person under the age of sixteen was not permitted on organized treks into the jungles of Thailand. Despite the warning, our youngest son added to the end of his bedtime prayer ... "Oh, and Lord, please let us ride elephants on the jungle trail tomorrow" which received a unanimous "Amen" from his five older siblings. They enthusiastically waited for the guide to arrive who would determine our fate.

It had been a pleasant first night in the charming guesthouse on the river, just a short walk out of town, where the travel agent had suggested we stay. We had hounded the kindly manager to register us for the trek only to repeatedly hear him say in his finest enunciation, "I sorry, no good, no good. Only adult go to jungle trek," until he finally agreed to send his top guide out to meet us in the morning and if his top guide agreed, then maybe he would plan an "easy" local trek for our family.

Our six excited and enthusiastic children were up at dawn, dressed in their hiking clothes and downstairs in the lobby before we could even catch an unoccupied restroom down the hall. We found them studying brochures on the jungle adventure treks available in the lush tropical rain forests north of Chang Mai. The lobby was already busy at 5 A.M., due to the schedule of the local trekking companies. Customers who, from what we observed there in our lodge were exclusively young adults, would be picked up by four-wheel drive vehicles and driven to the edge of the jungle where they would begin an early start on a week-long hiking trail.

The travel agency sent two young Thai brothers with broad grinning faces and the readiest smiles I have ever witnessed. Instead of advising us against making a trip into the northern hills as we expected, these young men immediately sat down in the lobby with our children crowded around, watching as they spread a map of the Golden Triangle out on the teak wood coffee table. By the time my husband and I joined them, the trip was a sure deal and we knew the Lord had intervened and made a way for us to experience a trip of a lifetime visiting various native tribal villages in the Golden Triangle.

Ahava, our inquisitive ten-year old daughter, asked our guide if we would discover any elephants hauling teak logs out of the forest. The guide grinned as he launched into a vivid narrative about teak wood harvesting; it was obvious that he enjoyed children and he laughed hilariously listening to them try to correctly pronounce his name, so they nicknamed him Mr. James. He had agreed to contract us for a weeklong trek on the conditions that we hire his brother, David, as well, (also a nickname). David could assist in carrying the extra food and supplies required for a group our size for seven days and nights. Once our plans were settled, they furnished us special backpacks designed for the correct weight for each hiker, a list of what to bring along, namely a poncho for sudden cloud bursts, and said "Sawadee-cop" goodbye in Thai. We rejoiced that a jeepney would be waiting for us at 4 A.M. to take us on a trip we knew that only the Lord could have made possible.

After a hot breakfast of glutinous rice and hard-boiled eggs, we piled into the open jeepney, which drove us several hours up a rugged gravel road pass lush countryside, where only a few folks have cleared enough land for their farms from the dense forest, to the tiny village of Tha Nom on the Mae Kok River. There, to the children's wild delight, we walked over a rushing muddy river clenching a swinging rope bridge. We were startled at the monkeys screaming upon our arrival on the opposite banks of the river. Countless numbers of them in unison can frighten the bravest newcomer, and they awaited us like a band of robbers in the adjacent park. After a brief stay trying to defend ourselves from the aggressive monkey thieves, three large elephants arrived with three small Thai's, who were no bigger than our children, and each one carrying a threatening club. One loud call from the lead bull elephant had us aware of the need for the clubs, and I was thankful that our safety had been placed by faith into the hands of the Lord. This was the jungle, and we were about to ride elephants for several hours through an area that only upon the backs of such mammoth beasts could we traverse safely.

Boarding an elephant was accomplished by climbing high upon a bamboo structure resembling an environmentally friendly jungle gym, and once at the highest rung the small Thai's grabbed you and swung you up upon the elephant's royal bench built for two. There were eight of us, so I sat with Tehila on one elephant, Greg with Israel and Kezia upon another, and Isaac, Isaiah and Ahava rode the largest bull elephant. Mr. James and his brother David rode with the elephant guides, straddle-legged across the neck of the elephants. Our gear was packed under our bench seats.

We were certainly not comfortable at all crossing the mountain riding on elephants! You had to hang on or else slide from side to side on your bench with each shifting elephant step, and the moist dense tropical forest demanded most of our attention or else you would get a good drenching smack in the face from a bushy tree limb. A musical opus greeted us with the first warm rays of sunlight from an array of rare colorful birds dedicated to their task. Then the jungle began to perspire a misty cloud of fog that made the whole trip uniquely mysterious. At this point, it was hard to conceive that a more exciting journey could lie ahead for us over the next six-and-a-half days than what we had already experienced over the first few hours of our jungle trek.

Mr. James announced it was time for a lunchtime break, to the delight our eager hikers, but they were puzzled by his request for each of us to locate a sturdy reed from the bush until he took out his whittling knife and began demonstrating how to carve chopsticks, which we would use to eat our lunch. James knew the jungle well enough to find edible roots, berries, and wild vegetables, which we curiously added to our banana leaf holding our serving of rice. Now, using chopsticks when you are as hungry as a jungle jaguar does not work out welll; it would take time and practice to gain the dexterity we needed to eat rice in this fashion.

The area we were entering lies isolated from civilization and we were about to have an enlightening step back in time. With our packs upon our backs and lunch under our belts, we waved goodbye to our elephants and began following Mr. James on a footpath through the jungle, while David stayed at the rear. Mr. James and his brother, both of Burmese birth, told us stories to enlighten us about the history of their people and the indigenous tribes in the area. Just a few minutes into the hike, before we could extract our poncho's from of our packs, we experienced a lukewarm cloud burst that halted as quickly as it had begun, and it appeared like we had been doused with a fire hose, only we were amazingly refreshed and had a good laugh.

The Shan, Lao, and Thai people, all members of the Thai race, originally lived in southern China, but about sixty-years ago, fierce fighting in the Shan State caused many of the hill tribe people to migrate south across the Burmese border to find some peace in the isolated hill country of northern Thailand. The Shans remained in the dense mountain areas of northeast Burma and are but one of a score of distinct and autonomous tribes who occupy the Golden Triangle. Each tribe has its own separate culture and distinct language. Mr. James modestly admitted that he spoke only eleven of the over twenty-five different tribal languages spoken in the region, which would come in handy over the next few days.

After an afternoon of sloshing through rice paddies, we came to another stream to cross, and we once again sat down on the ground to take off our hiking shoes and socks and wade barefoot across the sometimes waist deep water. Except, at this crossing, we watched as our adorable youngest son, Israel, just marched into the water with his boots on. When we asked him why he had not taken his boots off, he replied, "I am fine, my boots are waterproof!" We all had an enjoyable laugh at his comical reasoning and were very surprised that he never complained about wet feet for the remainder of the day.

In the early evening we could hear thumping that vibrated the ground that we were walking on as we approached a village occupied by some fifty Lahu peoples, and understood from Mr. James that the noise came from their crude grain mills, run by foot power, which were no more than log seesaws with a weighted pestle on one end.

The Lahu women were grinding grain for a dinner we would soon be eating with them. As we drew near, we could see down the river in front of us, girls fishing from the bank with their minnow nets, and we could discern small thatched huts stilted high above the marshes, backed by a densely sloped forest.

This village was extremely poor and the majority of the children ran naked. The adults wore mostly old and tattered Thai shirts and sarongs and everyone went barefoot. Like other remote tribes, the Lahu women wear their distinctive colorful clothing involving yards of material, which usually hangs loose, leaving the breasts exposed and accessible to the babies, which most of them are seldom without. We were an unusual attraction to a tribal people who had never before seen western children. They hurried around to get a glimpse of us as we walked through the village to our thatched stilted hut just hovering above the mosquito-infested river where we would spend the night.

Once into the rhythm of hiking, one of our family members would usually initiate a song and all of us would join in singing, whistling or humming as we walked. Mr. James, after hearing us singing praise songs to the Lord, became very excited about telling us of his conversion from being a Spiritist to a born-again Christian. He had been an English teacher in his hometown in Burma when government unrest demanded that he flee for his life, so he crossed very dangerous military security into Thailand. Once in Thailand, he found work as a laborer carrying bricks. Eventually, due to his English skills, a missionary hired him as a translator to travel with him as he brought the gospel to the tribal natives. After translating for the missionary for several months, James learned about Jesus Christ and he gave his life to the Lord. He shared with us how he had continuously snuck across the border into Burma until he successfully smuggled his entire family, one by one, to safety into Thailand.

The next day we would be visiting a Lisu village comprised of only ninety people but we would find it to be much more prosperous and progressive than the Lahu village we had already visited, and Mr. James said it was because many of the Lisu had become Christians. He asked if we would divert from the trail for a few hours to visit friends of his that needed prayer. Indeed, James was right; these people needed help, and all we could offer them was prayer, which is why the Lord had arranged for us to walk hours off our course just to be a blessing to these humble believers. Several of the children showed bloated stomachs of malnutrition, and after Mr. James examined a few of the frailest, he dispensed some medicine to the tribal chief with precise instructions for use.

This night our thatched hut was not up on stilts, so early, before daybreak, I awakened to the sound of the pestle pounding on the ground as a few women had already begun grinding grain. I awoke extremely thirsty so I arose from my sleeping bag and quietly felt my way in the dawn light to the bamboo windowsill near the doorway where I knew we had stored our water canteens. I grabbed one, opened the top and held it above my head in order not to put the rim to my mouth, a technique I had almost gotten down pat so I didn't choke on my drink, but this time after a few big gulps I realized something terrible was wrong. The water from the canteen had a horrid foul taste and a smell that spread through my mouth and some slimy foreign objects slid down my throat causing me to gag, cough, and spit as I ran out of the hut awakening the whole village. I then recalled that Isaac, Isaiah and Israel had been catching prawns in the streams earlier the prior afternoon and were hoping to keep them alive. I had given them permission to safely place them in their water canteens. The entire day I would be bringing to mind the smell and taste from experiencing that big gulp of day-old, half-cooked, slimy, rotten prawns I had for my early morning refreshment. Our family always enjoys a sidesplitting laugh when the episode of Mommy gulping the rotten prawns arises.

On our third day of the trek we would spend most of the day traveling down the river on three half-submerged bamboo rafts guided by twenty foot poles which one person on each raft used to prod us along with from the bottom of the river. We had a heart breaking wait at the edge of a leper colony while a third raft was being constructed for our use to travel down the river where we observed half-a-dozen destitute souls covered in sores peering at us from a distance while we sat in one designated place near the shore. The jungle can be uncomfortably hot and humid, and although we deeply felt for the condition of these poor souls, moving on was a priority. All day we had looked forward to playing in the river on the rafts, and now that they were built, we would enjoy the treat despite the many dangers lurking around - primarily snakes.

Today would be our longest day of trekking into the mountainous enclaves to arrive at the village of the Akha peoples before dark. Greg was encouraging Israel to keep up the hiking pace but it had be a long day of hiking for this youthful four and a half year old and he was lagging behind, dragging his feet, kicking stones, all sweetly with a few audible requests for his abba (father in Hebrew) to carry him piggyback. We were all growing weary from the oppressive heat of mid-afternoon and a snack break for cookies was in order, so we relaxed prone in the grass munching on our power cookies when two Thai hunter's, acquainted with Mr. James, rambled up together where we were resting in the bush. They held a flock of tiny birds each flying from strings attached to their feet. This brought an excited squeal from Israel whose face lit up as he jumped up to greet these men, and one of them immediately handed him a foot long string, which he tied around Israel's forefinger that had a tiny little bird tied by the foot that flew round and round in circles on the end of the string. For the remainder of our hike that day, Israel had a dance in his step and skipped along with his little birdie that he had named Ricky-n-Ronnie, after my brothers, his favorite two uncles.

The Akha peoples are intensely proud of their tribal identity and, like each tribal group, clings tenaciously to its own style of dress, jewelry, agriculture, family structure, and social customs. Most of them live by the age-old 'slash and burn' method of farming – felling trees, clearing stones, and then burning off the undergrowth before planting in the ashen soil. It is a monumental task when you consider their simple tools, the steepness of the hillsides, and the rapid soil depletion that forces them to abandon their fields within four years to clear new land elsewhere. This shifting cultivation eventually spurns the migration and rebuilding of entire villages.

The "Golden Triangle" did not win its fame because of these primitive people living off the land. Here, in their mountain seclusion, inaccessible and perilous to outsiders, they also produce the bulk of the world's crop of raw opium. Most of the tribes we visited had been "discouraged" from cultivating opium commercially, but those who live farther back in the mountains, like the Akha tribes, beyond the realm of authority, still cultivate vast fields of opium poppies as their main crop. Our first Akha acquaintance was with a grinning toothless lady who appeared humorously as if she had been sucking on purple popsicles all day. Her mouth and lips were heavily stained, and from her inebriated look, her glazed eyes and her filthy dress, it was obvious she was a heavy user of opium. Mr. James explained to us that the opium users were harmless and they would be separate from the village area where we would be lodging for the night in a bamboo hut. That night, about forty of our Akha neighbors, dressed in tribal costumes, invited us to join them around a campfire to listen to them play their homemade instruments and watch them sing and dance. In turn, we were expected to entertain them, so Greg played an old guitar they produced, and our family worshipped the Lord in song as they joined in clapping, waving, laughing, beating on gourds, and playing stringed instruments.

The Akha erect a "spirit gate" each year to guard the entrance to their villages, which appeared as a simple wooden gateway with small ornaments of woven straw and silver work and crude figures of men and women as symbols of fertility. It was a blessing to know we could lie down that night in our hut and sleep peacefully protected by the Lord from the spiritual darkness that inhabited the hearts of the Akha peoples. Our journey would end soon, but our memories would keep this Golden Triangle hike alive in our hearts at least until we could return again to visit Mr. James. The next time, we would travel with him to his village on a private tour for two weeks, but that is another adventure story that will have to be written some other time.

> *"The Lord shall preserve your going out and your coming in,*
> *From this time forth, and even forevermore."*
> Psalm 121:8

Chapter 22
A Christmas Miracle of Praise - Tehila

It was Christmas Eve, 1987, and I had no idea I was about to lose my six-year old daughter in one of the busiest cities in the world. We were staying at Mr. Anthony's Guest House up on the tenth floor of a two star hotel in the middle of the busy Kowloon district of Hong Kong. We had met Mr. Anthony at the airport in November on the first evening of our prior arrival when we had flown in from Bangkok, Thailand on the second month of our twelve-month trip around the world.

It was good to be back in civilization after traveling around the length and breadth of Mainland China. We had been away from the major cities since our weeklong trip down the Yangtze River from Shanghai to Chunking. Hong Kong was so modern in comparison, and the Hong Kong Chinese, although non-Christians celebrated Christmas with a passion like nowhere else in the world. Every thing was excessively decorated with Christmas lights. The tallest skyscrapers had Santa and his reindeer lighting the night sky. We were all tired of eating rice and exhausted from the primitive conditions we had been enduring since we had left Hong Kong a month earlier.

I was grateful to have returned at our own little guesthouse. We wedged through the rather small door into a narrow hallway that lead to a metal caged elevator. I never noticed any sign that would indicate there was a Guest House through this doorway. It was a hold-your-breath ride to the tenth floor. Mr. Anthony and his family operated this very cramped Guest House, though it was somehow sweet, friendly and very modest. He had turned out to be most helpful arranging to change money for us, get the visa's we needed to enter into mainland China, and even doing our laundry.

We carried with us only the most necessary items in our eight backpacks. Our youngest son, Israel, now four-and-a-half years old, was delegated the job of carrying the toilet paper and cookie container in his backpack. He enjoyed his important responsibility to pass out treats at snack time.

We had planned a big spending spree here in the 'shopping Mecca of the world', knowing there would be bargains for purchasing a much wanted video camera and other needed items. Each of the children had already picked out their own hand-held electronic video game. With the most important items already taken care of, we could now enjoy the children. First, I would take the girls to the mall shopping (I was familiar with how to get there without getting lost) and when we would return, Greg would take the boys. We would shop for a few small gifts for one another and then meet back at the Guest House before going out to dinner. Reviewing our drill was important – If anyone is separated, do not move. Just stay put and blow your whistle loudly every ten seconds. Do not give your name to anyone unless it is a policeman. Most importantly, pray.

According to plan, I set out with Ahava, Kezia, and Tehila down the rickety elevator onto the crowded street. I had never walked on such crowded streets before. It would be impossible for us to walk side by side, so we held hands tightly with me in the lead and Ahava, the oldest (nine-years old) and tallest, in the back. The street crowd could rather push you along and, since we were "sardined" in the crowds on the sidewalk, it was important that I pay close attention to our location. I was able to look over the heads of most of the short Chinese crowd, but the girls couldn't see anything but the close encounter they were having with the public. For a moment, I wondered if this was a safe thing to be doing and quickly remembered that I had committed all of our ways unto the Lord this morning and I knew to overcome fear immediately with praise.

After walking for what seemed like forever and ever, I spotted our street crossing. We wedged our way through the oncoming pedestrians to a small fenced-in waiting station where, when the traffic light turned green, we would cross the noisy and traffic jammed dual highway. On the other side we would be just minutes away from the gigantic mall. I took the first side entrance to avoid any further push from the hoards of people heading to the main entrance.

Once inside the mall we relaxed and started window-shopping. The girls were delighted. We would hunt for a toy store first. It was not until we had meandered up to the eighth floor of this very extravagant and overly decorated mall that we found the perfect shop. I located the card racks and adjacent from the cards were rows of small toys and souvenirs. The girls were engrossed in discovering the appropriate gifts.

A moment later, Ahava approached me and inquired, "Mommy, where is Tehila? Kezia and I don't see her." I quickly spanned the area and began searching the adjacent aisles. With no sign of her, I called Ahava and Kezia and positioned them to stand on either side of the only entrance to the shop. I then went to the cashier and asked her if she could use the public address system to call for Tehila. There was no PA system. That is when I make use of my God-given PA. Immediately everyone in the store began to look for her. Realizing that she could have left the store put me into panic mode. I looked out into the crowd on the eighth floor and knew that I needed to stay focused. "Lord, what do I do?" I considered how Mary and Joseph must have felt when they discovered that Jesus was not with them on their journey to Nazareth from Jerusalem.

After instructed Ahava and Kezia to remain together at the entrance of the store and just wait for me to return, I ran to the security guards near the escalators and asked if they'd seen a little blond girl about four feet high. Due to their broken English, they could not comprehend my anxious appeal. I dashed down to the next floor racing to each security guard asking the same question, "Have you seen a little blond girl…?" With no sign of her, I finally came to the side entrance where we had entered the mall from the main street below.

I stopped and cried out to God, "Lord, please put your angel with Tehila. I trust you." With that, I approached the last guard standing at the entrance. "Excuse me, have you seen a little blond girl about…. " Yes," he said, "she went that way." He pointed out into the crowd. At this point, I was pressing my way through the crowds headed back to the Guest House. I knew that I must get Greg. It seemed like the longest walk in my life. I continually had to overcome my negative thoughts and just believe that the Lord had His angel with Tehila. She was too small to see over the crowds to find her way back, and how would she know where to go even if she could see. Even if she were blowing her whistle, with all the noise from the cars honking, Christmas music, and street hubbub, how could I possibly hear her? It was even challenging for me to find the small entrance to our Guest House and once there I felt my heart pounding and I was faint as I made my way up to the 10th floor. While I knocked on our door, I was fighting back hot tears in my eyes. How could I tell Greg that Tehila was lost?

My second eldest son, Isaiah, answered the door saying, "Mommy, where have you been? Tehila came to get Abba (daddy in Hebrew) to go find you. She said you got lost." I grabbed the boys and flung them around with joy. What had just happened? How did she arrive back here to get Greg? Oh, what a happy moment to know that she was safe. I immediately returned to collect Ahava and Kezia.

Now my step was lighter. God had actually placed an angel with her. I seemed to be flying over the crowds where moments ago I had almost fainted. The girls were rejoicing with me as we all returned safely back to Mr. Anthony's. Nevertheless, where were Tehila and Greg? We waited for over two hours before we heard them noisily returning down the hallway.

Tehila's incredible story was that she had returned to get Abba to help her locate us.... for we where lost! When she directed him out onto the streets it was obvious to Greg that she had no idea where she was going. They wandered around together, never even finding the mall. When I asked Tehila what had happened she said, "Well, Mommy, you were lost so I knew to go get help." "How did you find your way back to the room?" I asked. "Oh, it was easy! I have an angel with me."

That night we ate the most wonderful Christmas dinner together

at the largest McDonald's we had ever seen anywhere in the world. Although I normally do not care for this kind of food, I did enjoy eating everyone's McDonald's coleslaw. This would be one Christmas Eve together we would forever cherish.

"Tehila", our daughter of "Praise"

*"For He shall give His angels charge over you,
To keep you in all your ways."*
Psalm 91:11

Chapter 23
Kiwi Station Wagon Miracle

We where exhausted and disappointed after spending our first day in the city of Auckland searching for the right used vehicle to purchase for travel around North and South Islands. All expensive imports, due to the obvious, we were on an island where there was not a public transport system designed to take us sightseeing and our options seemed, well... nil. We had hoped to come across something we could buy or rent for a few thousand dollars. Now I knew we needed to hear from God. He surely had a plan for us; it had not been precisely revealed yet.

New Zealand is such a pristine island. In our research before our trip we learned about the world famous hiking trails where trekkers may possibly spend months exploring rain forests, fjords, snowy mountains, deep jungles, gorgeous coastal beaches, and getting acquainted with warm friendly locals called Kiwi's. We would be hiking three fabulous world famous trails; five days on the Abel Tasmin Trail, seven days on the Kepler Trail and four days on the Corimandel Trail.

We arrived on the North Island of New Zealand the day before New Years' Eve, 1987. Auckland is such a lovely city with rolling hills and awesome vista's of the countryside, even from downtown. It was like stepping back in time fifty years. The natives, called Maoris, lived as headhunters just a couple hundred years ago. Our travel book guided us to the ideal place to stay; the Georgia Guest House. It was an imposing antiquated farmhouse that had been restored to the "in" place for the largely young-adult backpackers touring or on summer break from all around the world. We felt like young back-backers ourselves, only we were the only visitors with six kids. To our

delight, everyone swarmed around us. The kids enjoyed getting so much attention. Here we learned all the in's and out's of what-to-do and what not-to-do from fellow travelers.

The next day we would take a trip to the Auckland Museum and Greg and I would continue to search the papers for a vehicle. While meandering through the different departments of the museum, the boys inquired about the displays of flesh eating instruments and other very strange utensils. As there are not any native mammals in New Zealand, the kids concluded these native Maoris had been headhunters and cannibals. Now we would have great stories develop throughout our trip on this subject.

That evening, after fixing dinner in the spacious kitchen at the Georgia Guest House, Greg came across a few numbers in the telephone book of local car dealers and decided to try them. The first number dialed responded to Greg's request about a vehicle to take us around North and South Island for maybe two months. The man enthusiastically replied, "I think I've got the perfect vehicle for you. A woman drove in last night and I bought her vehicle. I have not even given it a test drive yet but it sounds perfect for you. I'll even buy it back off a' ya' when ya' finish if ya'd like." Immediately after eating, we called a taxi to drive us to the auto dealers a few miles away. We left the kids at the guest house to prepare for bed. They had many young people around to read them stories while we were gone.

By the way, it was New Years Eve and a Friday evening, so we knew it was a miracle that this place was still open. We entered a simple little office. The man behind the desk never got up. He was very friendly and quickly told us that for $2000 we could have the station wagon out front. We could have the title and, either register it in our name, or leave it in the car dealers name and have their insurance cover us. Greg told him that we did not have but half the money on us. He responded, "It's an Island. Where are you going to go? Just bring the rest of the payment in when you pass through next time." Could this be true? Handing over the keys and the title, he said if we found another buyer and wanted to sell it for more when we finished our trip to go ahead, but he would be happy to buy the car back from us for $1800 if not.

Therefore, within fifteen minutes we were "out of there." We had purchased ourselves a Kiwi Station wagon on New Years Eve for just $1000 down. We were praising the Lord while climbing into our new "rust bucket" to drive back to the guesthouse. It was a genuine rust bucket! The salt had been eating away at the exterior since the 1979 model Ford Valiant had been built. The bottom was completely corroded. There were a few holes where you could put your feet right through to the ground from inside if you wished. It had a monster roof rack and it seemed built out of tank steel. So despite the rust, we felt we had been really blessed and God had provided the perfect vehicle for us. What a New Years Eve miracle!

All the kids and guests back at the guest house were ready to celebrate the New Year with us when they saw is drive up in our muddy brown colored, rusty Kiwi Station wagon that would take us over 10,000 kilometers over in the next two months.

The next morning we were all comfortably packed in and ready to go. There was room for three in the spacious front seat. Four kids sat comfortably in the middle seat and we laid the back seat down and placed our sleeping bags down to make a sweet comfy bed. The three youngest argued over who would get to ride there, until one of the very nice fellows who had been staying with us at the guest house kindly requested to ride with us around north island. Well, that settled it. Ahava, Kezia, and Tehila would have the back bed and Isaac and Isaiah would sit with John in the middle and Israel would ride up front with us. All the packs were tied onto the monster roof rack.

We settled in quickly and enjoyed the scenery immensely. Most of the highways in the countryside are only one lane. It was important to stay very alert and drive slowly, thus we really enjoyed the millions of sheep grazing on idyllic hillsides, there are far more sheep than people in New Zealand. As a family, we usually sang together while hiking or traveling. Thus, to the Beatles tune of "We all live in a Yellow Submarine," we began singing, "We all live in a Kiwi Station wagon, a Kiwi Station wagon, a Kiwi Station wagon....", over and over again.

On our journeys around New Zealand, we experienced such friendliness found from the locals that we have never found anywhere else in the world. While camping at the northernmost point of North Island at North Cape, a friendly NewZealander named John with his two boys approached us and insisted we visit his home when we went through Napier. While hiking the Abel Tasman Trail for five days, Isaac befriended a boy playing on a beautiful beach at Tasman Bay. His parents, Ian and Lorraine Rider, insisted that we come have dinner with them in their cabin. We later stayed in their home near the bay. While on the west coast watching seals, Jim Peach, on his first vacation from the other side of the island, ran up to us in Greymouth, and begged us to come stay with his family on his farm while in Timaru. The list goes on and on. However, there was one character I will embellish upon, simply because he became a part of our family while traveling with us for four weeks around the South Island.

Everyone was sound asleep. According to the map, we calculated it would take two hours to get to the next town. We needed to get some money out of the bank for the weekend, fill up the tank with gas and buy some salt to go with our bag of potatoes for a campfire dinner. The paved road we started on turned into a gravel-bar road, which turned into a very dusty dirt one-lane road across a serious mountain range. None of this was on the map!

We were now five hours into our journey with no end in site, seeing only more mountain ranges ahead. It was stifling hot, so all the windows were down. I was fighting drowsiness while driving but the dust kept choking me. One glance inside the vehicle alerted me as I burst into laughter at the sight of all the sleepy heads plopped over on one another, all with a thick layer of brown reddish dust, accentuating even their eyelashes. Just ahead, on the side of the road, stood what looked like a statue all covered with the same stuff. I could not make out if it was human until I pulled along side of him. Yes, there stood someone, backpack on, with little to no enthusiasm at our appearance. I woke Greg in the passenger seat when I called out, "Do you need a ride?" His reply, "Sure." He threw his pack on top and pushed some sleeping bodies over and off we went.

Now, with someone to talk to I was not tired at all. Steve was from Maryland. Imagine that, my home state. We began to get acquainted. He informed us that we were several hours from the nearest town. Suddenly, after going several kilometers, up a rather steep incline, we came to a halt. No gas. Steve said he knew a place to get gas at a lake marina just where we had picked him up.

It is nice to give a guy hitch-hikin' a ride but now we needed to ask him for money to buy the gas to get to the town we thought we'd already be in. Furthermore, he was the only one who knew where to buy the gas. Therefore, our new friend set off walking in the extreme heat with Greg back to get gas. Within an hour, they returned with the gas and Greg had a small box of cookies, which we would all share. Steve had his own box of cookies, which I discretely told the kids to stop starring at after devouring ours.

Filled up, we were off again only to sight in the rear view mirror Steve's pack and our sack of potatoes rolling around the road behind us. Steve's camp cooker was ruined from the fall and so were the potatoes for our campfire. At this point, we felt rather indebted to the guy. As it turned out, Steve grew fond of us and sorta' found himself a family. He traveled with us for four glorious weeks before parting ways. He was headed for another seven-day trek that would be in very high altitudes and maybe bad weather (he would get some painful frostbite). We missed him a lot but enjoyed his first postcard when we got back to the Guest House in Auckland. He wrote, " I miss you guys. I feel really guilty now when I buy a box of cookies and have no one to share them with."

And so, the memories in the infamous rust bucket and all our precious new friends have been preserved forever in our hearts. As we said goodbye to our Kiwi Station wagon at the car dealership, the owner kept his word and gave us $1800 cash back. We prayed that another family would continue to enjoy our New Years Eve Miracle Kiwi Station wagon. It never broke down, no, not once (and had only one flat tire)! We were once again "out of there" (the dealership) in fifteen minutes and on our way to the airport to fly to Australia. We all discussed and wondered how the Lord would provide for us once we got to Sydney.

"No good thing will He withhold
From those who walk uprightly."
Psalm 84:11

Chapter 24

Little Luna Gala's Big Typhoon

Today the white caps on the sea gave the impression like she was angry and frothing at the mouth. Not a soul knew of our whereabouts. If we capsized into the deep blue sea, who could possibly locate us? The world had not yet embarked on the technological revolution; consequently, the days of cell phones and cyber space had not yet arrived.

We were all set to sail to islands subject to typhoons, whose torrential rains can cause devastating floods. Over the next few years, the Philippines would be pummeled with three major natural disasters: an earthquake, a devastating super-typhoon, and a volcano violently erupting. With strong resolve, we encouraged ourselves in the Lord, knowing that He would place His angels to guard over us on our two-week journey.

We chuckled at the shoddy attempt to secure long cumbersome bamboo poles crosswise these coarsely hulled skiffs for balance. The awkward poles tangled with the volatile sea and created an exceptionally risky adventure for us in our attempt to reach Mindoro Island. Could these Filipino's safely transport six children and two adults to Puerto Galera in the two skiffs we were about to board?

Now roughly a half a mile out to sea fright came knocking on our hearts when the undersized outboard motor on our skiff sputtered to a halt. Our three young daughters, who were in the boat with me, now drenched from the sea spray, anxiously gripped their wooden seats. Our backpacks that had been stowed under the front bow were soaked in seawater. The two Filipinos onboard labored intensely to get the engine restarted and let out a sigh of relief when they heard Greg bellow from the adjacent skiff, "Let's return to shore, now!" The engine restarted and we were shortly scrambling out of the skiffs and onto dry-ground. We had been aware of a large Ferry sailing sometime after lunch and wondered if we could still obtain tickets.

Our family had worked up a ferocious appetite thus we responded to the call of an itinerant street vendor shouting "baluuuuut!" We were persuaded to order "balut" with our lunch, as it is considered a Philippine national street food icon, like falafel is for Israeli's. Balut is a nineteen-day-old fertilized hardboiled duck egg. The locals demonstrated how to take a big bite, shell and all. The street vendor drew a crowd trying to entertain our children who themselves were an amusement to the neighborhood kids. Tasting this delicacy became a comedy act as one by one the kids had a go. One by one their noses wrinkled up and they gritted their teeth at the texture of premature feathers on the roof of their mouths. The children's reactions were hilarious. It was no laughing matter when Ahava almost cried after taking a bite. Crunching baby beaks, limbs, eyes and all made even Greg gag. It was difficult to maintain an appetite for the oversized bowls of rice and chicken eggs being served in this uninviting setting. Greg soothed the situation over by treating us to vanilla flavored rice-sicles on a stick. Yuck again, but as for the kids, these frozen popsicles made from rice were a hit.

This ramshackle neighborhood did not appear to be the safest place. It was imperative that we keep a close eye on the children and our packs. They were reminded to use their whistles if anyone perturbed them. Throughout the duration of this trip I was accountable for sixteen passports (two each, American and Israeli), eight Israeli identity cards, all visa's required for travel, bank cards, health records and our traveler's checks and half the cash, which I secured around my waist in a fanny pack and wore as unobtrusively as possible under my shirt.

The majority of dwellings in this area were shacks erected on stilts. In certain seasons, this coastal region could be completely submerged for weeks on end. Albeit, this was the dry season but hygienic conditions remained appalling in this densely occupied area on the coast. We were only passing through hoping the islands would be a much better place as we had been told. So far, after experiencing life in Manila for a few days too many, our plans were to return with just enough time to reach to the airport for our departure flight.

We arrived in Porta Gallera after a pleasant Ferry ride and from there we rented a Jeepney, a small open jeep, for the incredibly bumpy drive on dirt roads across the mountainous island to Little Luna Gala. We had also been advised that there were affordable bungalows on the beaches and great places to hike, fish, snorkel and swim. Our journey was spectacular through mountainous tropical rain forest filled with coconut, papaya, and bananas trees everywhere. The islands have one of the world's greatest stands of commercial timber.

The island populace lives in simple thatched huts and the majority has never left the island since birth. They appeared exceptionally friendly and not out to pursue us for money, as had occurred on the mainland.

We arrived just before sunset to what would become our paradise island for two weeks. Our bungalow cost us $6 a day. Stairs on the front veranda lead right onto the white sandy beach. Each cot had mosquito netting draped roundabout and we found it roomy and extremely cozy. Just before dark we all bounded into the sea to cool off in the lucid waters of the Verde Island Pass. The shoreline was graced with coconut trees and thatched roof huts all along the coast. We were too exhausted for dinner and fell asleep promptly. In the morning we looked forward to exploring our newfound island.

We were amazed at the variety of services that were transported right to our doorsteps. The delightful indigenous locals served breakfast to us on our bungalow veranda. Papaya, bananas, homemade rolls and lots of coconut milk for the children. Greg unpacked our camp-stove and brewed us a great cup of coffee. We were what we called "happy campers".

One morning we recall a heart-rending scene. A small crippled man toiled slowly down the beach carrying a strange contraption with a stool and a circular stone, which he unfolded in the sand in front of our bungalow. After getting set-up, Isaac, our eldest son was the first to grasp that this little man had come with hopes of sharpening our knives, so he eagerly produced his handy dandy pocketknife, which he always devotedly guarded on his belt loop. We paid the man handsomely for razor-sharpening our four knives then watched curiously as he sat amusing the children by whittling sticks, coconut shells and every other challenge they could produce.

After the kids would fall asleep at night, we would be able to slip away and sit on the balcony restaurant above our bungalow enjoying a drink and the illuminations twinkling around the shoreline. Here we met such extremely interesting

travelers and shared stories until it was time to retire. Even with our six children, this was like a second honeymoon.

Besides exploring the island and gathering mounds of coconuts, we befriended many of the islanders and got ourselves invited to a festival. To prepare I bought the girls little orange bikinis for $1.50 each and colorful sarongs (wrap around skirts) and the boys equally colorful shirts. We would now fit in with the locals. The festivities started in town and several hours later ended up as a parade down to the beach where men, women and children sang, danced, ate and played games late into the night. This was such a rich cultural experience that we shall never forget.

One of the highlights of our island experience was my 34th birthday party organized by the children. They creatively designed party hats for all eight family members from palm leaves, and wrapped homemade whittled gifts

and a sarong from Sabong from my dearest love, Greg. We were having such an enjoyable family time, very relaxed very laid back, daily enjoying fresh lobster, calamari, or some other exotic tropical treat. We had no inkling this peacefulness could vanish within a few hours.

We had just two days remaining when we noticed the tide began to rise higher and higher. We learned from the locals that there was a typhoon at sea. Around noon it was clear that the eastern horizon was amassing dark purple and blue cloud coverage. Now the wind was picking up, the sea had risen and the waves were crashing into the front steps of our peaceful little bungalow. The kids were in their swimsuits

enjoying the wild breaking of the waves on the porch. Greg and I agreed it was time to get off the island. In a hurry we gathered our things into our packs and called for a jeepney. Hopefully, we'd make it to Porta Gallera in time to catch the last Ferry and arrive back on the mainland before the Typhoon would hit.

With no time to waste, our driver gave us a thrilling ride over the hilly terrain. We gripped our possessions and one another to keep from flying out of the jeep, it had begun to sprinkle and a dark foreboding sky frightened many into wanting to flee the island, thus we knew it might be hard purchasing tickets for the Ferry. It was first come, first serve. I desperately prayed for help from the Lord to prevent us from being stranded on this paradise island during a typhoon.

We were the last passengers to purchase tickets on a Ferry that was packed to capacity. Once on board we sensed a strong rocking of the ship due to the high seas. We had had to leave a day early but at least we were out of danger of a Typhoon that became very destructive to the island very quickly.

We returned to the infamous Manila with one day to spare, very grateful to be there. News reports of the conditions on Mindoro Island were serious; many people lost their homes and there were reports of extensive flooding, intense rescue operations were in effect. Forests and vegetation were shredded from high winds and mudslides buried whole towns rapidly. This storm claimed many lives in the South Pacific Islands. Once again, we knew the Lord was watching over us and delivering us out of all kinds of troubles. We departed with sweet and bitter memories, all of which we are grateful to the Lord.

"But I am the Lord your God, Who divided the sea whose waves roared —
And I have put My words in your mouth;
I have covered you with the shadow of My hand,
That I may plant the heavens, Lay the foundations of the earth,
And say to Zion, 'You are My people.'"
Isaiah 51:15,16

Chapter 25

Crossing the Egyptian Border With $2

After 364 days of travel, we waited at the Egyptian border preparing to cross back into Israel. We were returning home after backpacking around the world by faith. My wife and I and our six children, ages four through twelve, had amazingly been to the ends of the earth and back, having spent three and a half months traveling in North America, two weeks in Egypt (all the way down to Aswan), a month in Thailand, two weeks in Hong Kong, a month in China, two months in New Zealand, three months in Australia and two weeks in the Philippine Islands.

We had flown to each of these exotic destinations with airline tickets that we had purchased from Bangkok, Thailand that were open-ended at every location for up to a year. After arriving in each country, we would get out our guidebooks, speak with other backpackers who were 'in the know' and head out with a pre-determined budget to whatever adventures that awaited us.

Several volumes would need to be written to describe all of our experiences, and I'm not sure that I myself would believe all those stories if I hadn't witnessed them unfold first-hand. We had trekked through dense jungles, rain forests, savannahs and deserts; and had hiked on some of the most beautiful trails in the world. We had met and experienced the hospitality of peoples of a great many different cultures and languages. During the year, we had bought and sold three different vehicles, and had traveled thousands of more miles in trains, boats, taxis, buses, and tuk-tuks (Tailand taxis); not to mention riding on elephants and camels. We had experienced more in 364 days than most people do in a lifetime, and we had grown extremely close together as a family as a result.

Refund checks from the United States Internal Revenue Service (I.R.S.) for varying amounts and at irregular intervals had been coming into our bank account throughout the year, and we had miraculously witnessed God's provision and protection at every turn. Heading out a year earlier by faith had been difficult, but once we were on the road so to speak, we never needed to look back – for I believe that the Angel of the Lord who 'encamps about those who fear Him' had been assigned as one of our body guards. During the entire time, we lacked for nothing and the doors that opened in every place occurred as if we were expected before we arrived.

But as I said at the beginning of this story, here we were on the last day of our trip at the Egyptian border getting ready to return to Israel, our adopted homeland. We didn't actually have an apartment or home to live in, or jobs to return to, or any real plan for what we would do when the bus pulled into Tel-Aviv, but then again we weren't very concerned about these things either, as God had always been our provider and had taken care of us.

It was Friday morning and althought we only had eighty-two dollars left to our names, we had a wealth of experiences and faith to sustain us. Basically, we had planned to check into a youth hostel in Tel-Aviv, buy some food from an outdoor market called a 'shuk' and continue on with our adventure in Israel. We knew everything would be closing down at around one o'clock in the afternoon for the short Israeli 'weekend' but would come back to life again on Sunday morning once the Sabbath was over.

It was at this point that I tripped over the finish line and lost it completely. The Egyptians were demanding a ten dollar exit-visa fee from each of us. We had never paid an exit-visa fee in any other country and I felt that our Arabic cousins were just trying to rip us off, so I lied, and at that moment all faith deserted me. I simply said that we didn't have the eighty dollars, which none of the Egyptian officials believed, and so we held up the entire bus for an hour before having to fork over the money in the end.

With literally only $2 to our names, I sat on the bus burning with shame. And if I was not feeling low enough already, I had to sit and listen to the other Israeli passengers and the bus driver speaking about us in Hebrew in a most disparaging manner, assuming that we were just American tourists that couldn't understand them. Now I had no excuse for my behavior back at the border, so I didn't bother to interrupt the fun they were having at our expense.

As I sat there dreading our imminent arrival into the sprawling metropolis of Tel-Aviv and the mass of confusion that masqueraded itself as the central bus station, the Lord began to speak to my heart. I knew that He was asking me to answer the following simple questions," Haven't I taken care of you each day over the past 364 days? Why would I abandon you now?" I repented in silence, realizing that I had genuinely grieved the Holy Spirit, for "without faith it is impossible to please God".

Humbled by the events of the past few hours, I mentioned to the other passengers in fluent Hebrew as we were getting off the bus in Tel-Aviv that they each one of them should be ashamed of themselves for talking about other people behind their backs. Without looking into their faces, I can only imagine what color they were turning.

Because of the delay that I had caused back at the border, it was later than we had anticipated when we pulled into Tel Aviv, so everything was closing up. Immediately I had to leave my family at the central bus station and make a dash for the nearest branch of the bank where we held a checking account. I thought that possibly I had left a few shekels in our account before we departed but wasn't all that hopeful that this was really the case. I was the last one to slip into the bank as they locked the door behind me, and then the teller informed me that the computers were already shut down for the Shabbat and that he didn't have any way to check our account balance until Sunday morning. He did however call our branch and confirm that we indeed had an account, and so he agreed to give me a hundred shekels ($20) to carry us over for the next day and a half.

Well, that was good enough for me as I now had ten times the cash that I had had in my possession only a few minutes earlier. So feeling a little better, I returned to the bus station where my family was now waiting with a friend who worked in the vegetable market. Things were starting to feel surrealistic and I just decided to go along for the ride and see what would happen. Our friend, Eli, drove us all in the back of a borrowed vegetable truck to the one-star guesthouse we had stayed in years earlier. The Russian immigrant owner, Alexander, not only remembered us but also gave us two rooms at a rock bottom price. Eli got us a bunch of fresh vegetables and other necessities and we all settled in for the Shabbat, thankful to be back home. I'm sure the children weren't aware of our financial predicament and were simply trusting that everything would continue 'to work out for the good'. I guess I could have learned a lesson from them at that point in time.

On Sunday morning as the bank opened its doors, I was standing there desiring to be one of the first in line. I didn't have any expectations whatsoever because we hadn't really planned ahead for our return to Israel when we had left a year earlier. When the teller handed me a printout of our bank account balance, I had the shock of my life. There was over two thousand dollars in our account! I nearly cried as I drew the money out, knowing that God had somehow miraculously put it in there for us. The Lord had been far more merciful with me than I had ever imagined He would be. I felt that what I needed to do from now on was to simply believe the promise that Jesus had made to His disciples when He declared, 'I will never leave you nor forsake you'. That promise has sustained us through many more trials of our faith, and has safely kept us to this day.

Ahava hiking along the Sea of Galilee

Greg worked helping a friend with his airconditioning business that summer and we missed hiking so much that we found time to hike and camped around the Sea of Galilee before the Lord took us on another journey back to the US.

"Come now, and let us reason together," says the LORD,
"though your sins are like scarlet, they shall be as white as snow;
though they are red like crimson, they shall be as wool.
If your are willing and obedient, you shall eat the good of the land."
Isaiah 1:18-19

Chapter 26
Start the Engine

If your vehicle is going to break down in the middle of the desert somewhere between New Mexico and Arizona then a thirty-six foot deluxe motorhome is the vehicle to be stuck in. We had just crossed a fruit inspection station somewhere on a desolate stretch of the southernmost Interstate Highway 8 and the deisel engine of the motorhome shut off without warning. When we tried to restart the engine... nothing, just the eerie quiet of the vast desolate wilderness around us.

We were traveling to Los Angeles in comfort with our six children in one of the finest homes on wheels ever built, which we were renting for only four-hunded fifty dollars a month. The only drawback was that a breakdown could be a major expense and delay, as most mechanics would  take one look at our vehicle and quote their 'luxury-overtime-stuck-out-in-the-middle-of-nowhere' rate.

I asked my wife, Bev, and our children to keep a spiritual attitude of prayer and praise while I went into the back bedroom and shut myself in with the LORD. I spread myself out prostrate before the Spirit of Holiness and began to read out loud from the book of Isaiah, beginning with chapter fifty-four. When I finished reading chapter fifty-seven, the Word of the LORD suddenly came to me clearly and I spoke with authority to Bev, "Start the engine. She turned the key and immediately the engine roared to life as all the family began to rejoice. I then told her that under no circumstance was the engine to be turned off again until we reached our destination in Los Angeles, some five hundred miles away.

When my wife pulled up in front of our home in L.A., the motorhome died. Nothing that anyone could do at that point would make it come to life. It would take several mechanics to rebuild the engine, replace the starter and nearly a week of work to ressurect it from the dead, but for five-hundred miles it had run by faith, and had gotten us home according to the spoken Word of God.

> *"And He shall say, Raise up! Raise up! Clear the way! Make the stumblingblock rise out of the way of My people."*
> *Isaiah 57:14*

Chapter 27

The Word of Knowledge

"The Holy Spirit has revealed to me that you will be returning to Israel on August 11th, ten days from now", Reverend Loren Helm boldly proclaimed from the platform of the small church where we were sitting in the front row. My wife and I and our six young children had driven a long way to meet this man of God, and now he was saying something that seemed to be an impossibility at the time.

If it had been anyone else but Bro. Helm who was making such a statement, we probably wouldn't have taken the announcement too seriously. The Biblical test as to whether a man is a true prophet of the Lord or not is that his prophesies must come to pass one hundred percent of the time. We knew very few prophets who could pass such an acid test, but Rev. Helm was one of them. For this was a man of God who had faithfully followed Jesus completely by faith for over sixty years, and who daily proclaimed that to do so was 'thrills, romance and adventure'.

Still, there were quite a few problems that needed to be addressed for this 'word of the Lord' to transcend the spiritual realm and become reality. The most significant of which was that we didn't have the finances to buy even one ticket, let alone eight tickets to Israel, and didn't have any idea where we could get such a sum of money in so short a time. Even if we did, we didn't have reservations on any airline, and all flights to Israel this time a year were full and certainly sold out by this late a date. Finally, even if we did return to Israel in ten days, we still didn't have any means of support or a place to live. After selling our computer business two years earlier, we had traveled to the ends of the world and back again with all of our children, but this called for a much greater measure of faith than usual.

Now we know that 'faith comes by hearing, and hearing by the Word of God', so immediately upon hearing the 'word of knowledge' spoken by this servant of the Lord, we called El-Al to make reservations. When I told the man who answered the call that we needed eight reservations, he said that it wouldn't be a problem and that we could even purchase the tickets and pick them up at the J.F.K. airport in New York a couple hours before the flight on the eleventh of August. Well, we had been flying back and forth to

Israel and the United States for over fifteen years, and that seemed very strange indeed, and especially out of character for any airline, let alone El-Al, Israel's national carrier.

With the reservations out of the way, we got in our station wagon and started to drive back to Maryland to pack up our belongings and say good-bye to relatives. As soon as we arrived, the Lord put it on my heart to call Bill, a fiend who we had met recently in Kentucky. I asked him if he would like to buy our station wagon because we were going back to Israel sooner than we had originally planned. To my amazement, he said that not only would he like to buy it because he really needed a large vehicle for his family, but that he'd pay the full book value of $3000, even though we had gotten a deal on it for half that amount less than a year earlier through my sister who lived in New York. The next day, he wired us the money with an extra $1,000 on top of that, which he said the Lord told him to give us! When I called to thank him, he said that we were welcome to use the car until we left, and that he was fine with the arrangement that my mom would drop it off with him after taking us to the airport on her way back to Michigan where she lived.

Now even though the first two of those huge obstacles were out of the way, we still knew we would by flying back to Israel with no money, job or other means of support, and no place to stay. In spite of this, we were excited because we were assured in our hearts that the 'word of Lord' would come to pass in a most marvelous way. The evening before we were to leave Maryland, a couple whom we had never met, called and said that they would like to drive up from Alexandria, Virginia and visit with us. They said that they were friends of the Helms and had heard that we would be returning to Israel the next day. We gave them directions to the home of Bev's parents and they arrived an hour or so later.

My wife's parents, like most people that loved us, were very concerned about us flying back to Israel with a little more that $100 to our names, but they knew better than to try and talk us out of something that we were sure that we had heard from God about. When this precious brother and sister in the Lord arrived at their home, they told us that they wouldn't stay long but that they just wanted to give us this gift they had received from Reverend and Mrs. Helm that was meant for us. After a few minutes of prayer and fellowship they drove off, and we opened the envelope. Inside was a check for $1500. Now everyone, including my wife's mom and dad were crying with joy at the goodness of God's provision. We quickly went and cashed the check and did some last minute shopping.

When we boarded the jumbo five hundred passenger 747 El-Al airliner the next evening, things started to get surrealistic. The plane was half empty! Each one of us had as many seats to stretch out in as we wanted. When we asked the stewardess why the plane was so empty in the middle of the summer, we were told that it was Tesha B'Av, a day of prayer and fasting for the religious Jews. This was the historic day, according to the Jewish calendar that both the Temples built by King Solomon and King Herod had been destroyed. In commemoration of such a catastrophic event, the orthodox Jews who make up a large percentage of the passengers on El-Al's flights were forbidden to travel. Bev and I both knew that Rev. Helm couldn't possibly have known this and even we, who had lived in Israel all those years, were unaware of the date. If he had said the 10th or the 12th, it would have been impossible because all flights on every airline were sold out for the whole month. Only on the 11th were planes flying to Israel half empty.

When we arrived in Israel the next day, we called our rabbi friend in Jerusalem, the same one I had met at the Jaffa Gate twelve years earlier. He asked where we were staying, and when I said I had no idea, he said, "Why don't you talk with Grant and Barbara, they have a rented home in Metulla that is vacant. Immediately, the Holy Spirit bore witness that Metulla would be our new home. Within an hour we had the keys, and Grant and Barb's blessing to stay in it as long as we wanted.

Metulla is the northernmost town in Israel, and one of the first settlements built over a hundred years earlier by Baron Rothschild. It sort of reminds you of Switzerland at times with its quaint guesthouses and European architecture. It is nestled in the mountains, surrounded on three sides by Lebanon, and has a spectacular view of the snow capped Shauf Mountain range to the north, the Hula valley to the south, and biblical Mount Hermon to the east. The cottage that we were to make our home in over the next five years was in dire need of repair as it was nearly fifty years old, but it had a beautiful backyard full of olive trees, and was only a short distance from the Ayoun Nature Reserve. From our bedroom window, we could actually hear the water flowing over the cliffs of one of the most beautiful waterfalls in Israel.

Since we were willing to do the repairs and fix up that cottage ourselves, the owner didn't charge us any rent for the first six months. We had only been there a few days, when we had a visitor come over one evening while I was trying to cement up a hole in the living room ceiling. He introduced himself as the principal of the regional high school at Kibbutz Kfar Blume. He mentioned that his school had over 1,400 students and was located about five miles south of Metulla. As it was getting late, he came right to the point and asked, "I heard that you're a teacher, and I was wondering if you can teach mathematics?"

I told him that I had studied math for four years in college, but had only taught English and Computers. I added that although I didn't have any experience teaching math, I was sure that it wouldn't be a problem as by that time my Hebrew was nearly fluent. He seemed relieved and explained that he was desperate because school was starting in two days and he didn't have anyone who could teach five of the upper level classes. We quickly arranged for me to have an interview the next day with the head of the math department, and immediately afterwards I was hired.

Now, no one but the LORD and Brother Helm could have anticipated that Bev would spend the last of that $1500 check at the grocery store on the very day that I received my first paycheck from the school.

"For to one is given the word of wisdom through the Spirit, to another the word of knowledge through the same Spirit."
1 Corinthians 12:8

Chapter 28
Adventure in Ashkelon

The green Volkswagen was packed. I was inside doing a last minute check - mosquito repellent, charcoal, bandages, sunscreen, plastic cups, sleeping bags, it always seemed like we were leaving for a month when it would only be a week's vacation. This was our first trip in the Volkswagen since Henrietta had purchased it for us several months earlier. Henrietta now waved goodbye to our jolly family as we headed south toward our destination, Ashkelon.

We had our hearts set on a certain campsite in the park high on a ridge on the edge of the cliffs overlooking the sandy beaches and frothy white waves breaking on the shoreline below and the brilliant sparkling blue Mediterranean Sea beyond. We had visited the park briefly about a year ago and determined it would be a great place for family adventure. The park itself was a massive archeological site of the ancient city where, 3,500 years ago, the mighty Nazarene, Samson, had single handedly destroyed the temple by pushing the central towers down with his bare hands.

We arrived early enough to set up camp and have time for our first cookout. The kids, now tired of sitting in the van for hours, just wanted to run through the park and explore, so we had to coax them into helping carry all of our equipment from the parking lot to the idyllic site we'd hope for and could see was empty and just waiting for us. The park rangers said it was good we'd arrived early and we could have our pick of campsites. They expected a packed out end of the year summer crowd of Israeli's over the weekend. They warned us to be careful with our things because they had had trouble with thieves. The rangers said they'd be keeping a close eye on things. These thieves, they explained were usually young men from the slums in town looking to steal cash from vacationers to support their drug addiction.

Ashkelon is only few kilometers from the Gaza Strip, but in 1989 terrorism had not yet caused the area to be policed, so we didn't really have any hesitations about our welfare or for our security.

You can use your imagination to compare Ashkelon Park to ancient Karnak in Egypt. There, as here, the ruins lie unburied on the surface of the ground. The ancient pillars and towers are still toppled on one another in the open fields gathering weeds and wildflowers. Some massive pillars still defy time and stand as memorials to what was once the glory of an ancient society. After exploring the excavations over the week we enjoyed telling stories about this location at night; how Delilah had enticed Samson to learn of the secret of his strength and how Samson had tied three hundred foxes tails together, set them on fire and sent them out to destroy his enemy's crops.

Our campsite had a soft carpet of grass, an oversized picnic table, a barbecue grill and a place for a campfire at night, a few shade trees around the perimeter and the right amount of space for our three tents. We had not set them up since camping on the shores of the Galilee after our trip around the world. The best part about our campsite was the spectacular view to the west of the setting sun. The park access to the beach meant walking around a large area to the park gate that opened to where there were a couple café restaurants, beach facilities, and lots of umbrellas and chairs along the sandy beach. We had our own private access – a steep thrilling, slid on your rump, straight down a sandy crooked path access and in seconds you were on the beach. Climbing back up that way was the determination of the kids over twenty times a day.

It took a few days to settle down. The kids had a delightful time swimming, hiking and building sand castles until they were all rosy cheeked and bleached blond from the sun. This was our paradise for the week.

The boys were up at daybreak, begging to go fishing. They positioned themselves adjacent to few other local fishermen way down the beach standing out on some rocks in the shallow water, which we could view from our campsite. The sea was calm and the girls enjoyed hunting for seashells while the boys continued fishing for hours, not a thing was caught. I sent the girls out with brunch but the diligent fishermen took only a brief break before continuing on their quest to haul in a big one.

It was high noon when our fishermen returned huffing about some big fish they wanted to buy for twenty shekels from one of their fellow fishing companions. Greg quickly handed Isaac the money more to amuse them than think we'd really have fish for dinner. Shortly, an excited group of kids came dragging a huge three-foot tuna fish up the short cut to our campsite. Greg had to help them carry it up. It was so big we'd have to cut it in half just to fit on the grill. We had such a happy afternoon together preparing and grilling our fish. We thanked the Lord for a lovely day and for our diligent fishermen as we watched a magnificent sunset. The campground had filled up that day with other campers but despite the extra noise and low music coming from the beach, we drifted off to sleep shortly after sunset.

Before the sun had fully risen, I opened my eyes in disbelief. I was lying in the tent in my sleeping bag and just in front of my head was a hand. A hand groping around! A hand protruding through a slit at the base of the tent just two feet from my head! My fanny pack was tucked under my sleeping bag; otherwise this "hand" could have grabbed it.

I shot up out of the sleeping bag, unzipped the tent while half-whispering to Greg, "There's a hand in the tent!" My immediate reaction when I saw a young man with a T-shirt wrapped over his head dash away from our tent was to yell, "Gunnav, gunnav!" which means "Thief, thief!" in Hebrew. I took off barefoot as fast as I could, running after him and yelling as loud as I could, "Gunnav, gunnav!" While in hot pursuit I momentarily wondered what I would do if I caught him or if he pulled a knife on me. He had to have a knife, because he had just cut a hole into our tent. The thought didn't stop me from bounding after him. He was like a gazelle leaping away. I stopped when I could go no further and had come to a high thorny hedge of blackberry bushes along the borders of the campground. There seemed no need for a fence here due to the severity of the natural barrier, but I had just witnessed a crazy guy leap right into the thick of those torturous thorns and somehow disappear. I turned around to see Greg in his shorts right behind me and quickly I realized I was still in my nightgown.

A group of campers were now awake and gathering around. The ranger, having been alerted by my yelling, "Gunnav!" asked a few questions. This thief had been busy cutting open four or five other tents looking to steal wallets or whatever he could get his "hand" on. The rangers assured everyone that it was unlikely that there would be another incident, as they would be keeping a watchful eye out on our campsite. I thanked the Lord for awakening me and protecting us, nothing of ours had been stolen.

Greg and I prayed for our "gunnav" with the kids. We knew he would be a few days recuperating and pulling briars out of his flesh and asked the Lord to humble him and work in his heart and deliver him from his drug addiction.

Ashkelon still remains one of our favorite places to camp, especially knowing that the Lord our God will intervene for us. It was our week of adventure in paradise.

> *"In the houses of Ashkelon they shall lie down at evening. For the Lord their God will intervene for them."*
> Zephaniah 2:7

Chapter 29

Our Sealed Room

This was the second phone call in the middle of the night, this time from Dr. Axtell in Texas. He had seen us in an interview on CNN headline news along with news of the first Scud missile landing in Tel Aviv. After calling international information, he acquired our phone number. We were excited to hear from him and assured him that we were safe and not to worry, just keep us in prayer.

The first phone call minutes before had been from my Dad. I knew his eyes were filled with tears when he said," I want to buy tickets for all your family to come on home." I peacefully tried to assure my precious dad that the Lord was going to protect us.

In 1991, Desert Storm operations were in full swing. American troops were kissing their sweethearts goodbye and heading out to a strange land. Not like other wars, this war, with the madman Sadaam Hussein at the helm, had the world on edge because he was threatening to use chemical and biological warfare. Our little country, Israel, was his first target, which he claimed he would annihilate. Now the world watched in horror at the first news of a Scud missile landing in downtown Tel Aviv.

We had been living a peaceful life over the past two years in the pastoral town of Metulla on the Lebanese border of Israel. Despite the fact that there was seldom a 24-hour period that went by without hearing a katusha rocket land or a round or two fired from a submachine gun or the hum of a drone slipping under radar to spy out terrorists in the not so distant hills of Southern Lebanon and Syria. Yet, for the Wootton family, now adjusted to this life, it still seemed a peaceful place to live. We not only had what we believed to be the best army and security in the world but our family had the "peace which passes understanding" from trusting in Jesus.

We ate breakfast and had a time of prayer together each morning as a family. Greg taught thirty hours a week at Kibbutz Kfar Blume High School ten miles away in the Hula Valley. Our two eldest boys rode with Greg on the bus there on school days. I usually walked about a mile with the four youngest children to the main street of Metulla where their school was indiscreetly located and well guarded. Schools were terrorist targets so you could always find top security where children were gathered.

Though there was an imminent threat of war we knew we were just where God wanted us to be. We had moved into an old abandoned house that was in dire need of repair and now, two years down the road, the improvements were apparent to the whole village. The landlord had felt guilty asking for rent, but now, after we'd turned it into a respectable place, he wanted $200 a month, which we gladly paid from Greg's $1000.00 a month teacher's salary. We were thankful to be raising our family in such a pleasant location with equally pleasant inhabitants.

Talk of Sadaam Hussein dropping chemical or biological warheads on us had the nation on high alert. The army quickly handed out gas masks to every man, woman and child. They came in what resembled a big cardboard shoebox with a black plastic strap for carrying. In addition, that is what we did, the whole four and a half million Jews and the millions of others in the land, we carried our shoebox around our neck everywhere we went. How do you get a nation to obey? Having a clear enemy helps matters; otherwise, if a child came to school without it, a soldier would take him home immediately to find out why he did not have it.

Soon after the first signs of an attack, school was cancelled for an indefinite period. The entire country had been carrying their gas masks around their necks for long enough. We were now instructed by the famous Benjamin Netanyahu on TV to stay indoors and wait. Ha, all day long? Just sit inside with six energetic kids and do what? Such was our situation.

Each home had prepared a sealed room. Supplies of masking tape and plastic became as costly as gold. We bought ours early enough but had very little left over to spare after we had sealed up the girls bedroom. The girl's room was in the center of our house and there were two windows we had sealed using double plastic and masking tape. Other supplies needed were towels, which we would wet with baking soda to place under the door to help absorb chemicals, in case of chemical warheads, and filled water buckets and plenty of plastic containers of drinking water, at least several days' worth. Of course, lots of food! What do you do when eight people sit around in one sealed-up bedroom hours on end staring at each other with gas masks on? It was hard to imagine, but we obediently followed military orders along with the entire panic-stricken country.

No one could have prepared us for that first real air raid siren. It just roared on and on, and on and on. It struck sheer terror to those elderly people who had lived through the Holocaust, it struck terror to those who had lived through the air raid sirens during the Yom Kippur and 6-Day Wars, and it was striking terror again into the hearts of a people tired of terrorism. There was no mistaking this for a practice drill, many of which the army had made us go through, this one just roared on and on.

It was very early in the morning when the siren first pierced our ears. Each of us had our assigned task. I was to first help Israel, our youngest child get his gas mask on. He was a small seven years old. He was still half asleep and I grabbed him from his bunk in the hallway and sat him on the bed in the sealed room. His mask was different from the others. After securing the monster-like device, which covered his entire face and strapped around his head and chin I made sure the valves were open and he could breath. He looked on the verge of tears and I told him that he should not cry because tears would prevent the seal the mask intended to create. Then, through his now steamy goggles, which I gave a nervous kiss, I had to pull the big plastic bag attached to the top of his mask over his head and tie it loosely around his neck, opposite what every sensible parent teaches their kid – that being never ever tie a plastic bag around your head.

I thought to myself… this is pitiful and I felt like a cruel mother leaving him to just sit there… but I had to attend to sealing the door. Isaiah had the wet towels soaked in baking soda in place and I had started taping when one of the kids yelled out, "Mommy, you forgot to get the cat." Off went the tape and I dashed into the kitchen, grabbed the cat, tossed him into our sealed room, and proceeded to finish taping the door. Greg was busy trying to get the news broadcast on the TV which he had moved into this already small bedroom along with, as they say, everything but the kitchen sink.

Then, the cat, in shock looking at all of these strange outer space monsters with their gas mask "big eyes" went hysterical. Have you ever seen a cat get really scared? Our cat was hissing at all of us, his hair stood two feet high on his arched back, we had never seen our sweet little kitty look so demon possessed. He wanted out! Away from these monsters! The door was sealed, but, oh no, the windows. Now, what is the purpose of sealing yourself in if the cat is going to unseal you? Fluffy went straight for the windows. His claws were digging a hundred holes a second into our nicely sealed windows as he jumped from one to the other. Greg finally caught poor Fluffy and ripping away our door seal once again, tossed the helpless cat out. We all felt sorry for our poor kitty, but the adrenaline rush had helped relieve tension from the blaring sirens. We knew our dog, BJ, had a nice secure sealed doghouse. Isaiah had spent time making sure it was covered in plastic inside and out. BJ could crawl in by a small slit in the entrance.

No one felt much like eating or playing any games. I just wanted to pray. The TV stayed on and continued to give details of the whereabouts of the missile landings. There was a sense of real national unity during this time that I had never experienced. Just knowing that each family was locked up in their homes together experiencing the same thing was unifying. The TV was announcing every ten minutes which areas of the country were safe and could then take their masks off. After two hours, we heard the one long siren that announced that the first air raid was over and we could leave our sealed rooms. Now, we would just have to sit and wait for the next siren blast.

The panic resided after we had gone through several alarms that day. We got our masks on and settle down quicker each time. That first night we grew very weary being awakened several times during the middle of the night by the air raid sirens. It seemed like the longest twenty-four hours of our lives had just passed when the first sunrays shone through the plastic wrap. We had not slept much.

Chunks of plaster falling from the walls in our little house needed to be swept up regularly now that the Hamas wanted to back Saddam and had started shooting katusha rockets into northern Israel. Metulla was getting near one hundred a day and we had a narrow escape with one landing in the field behind our house. Due to the escalated attack on our area a friend who worked for the Voice of Hope Radio station sent a CNN news reporter over to our house to interview an English speaking family several days after the first Scud had landed in Tel Aviv. What a funny way to become overnight celebrities. We were thankful it put us in contact with friends around the world.

In retrospect, we give God all the glory. Not one Israeli was killed by any of the twenty some Scuds that landed in Israel. God truly is watching over His land and His people.

"Behold, He who keeps Israel shall neither slumber nor sleep.
The Lord shall preserve you from all evil..."
Psalm 121:4,7

Chapter 30

The Motorcycle License Tests

I cannot really say why after all those years I wanted to get my motorcycle license renewed; maybe I was heading into a mid-life crisis of sorts, or was having nostalgic yearnings for my younger days. Whatever it was that came over me, getting that license became a very high priority at the time in my life, and taught me more spiritual lessons than I had bargained for in the process.

I had been riding motorcycles since the age of fifteen and over the next six years had gradually worked my way up to a large Honda 750 cc bike, which I sold in order to go to Israel with my fiancée in 1974. Over the next seventeen years or so I renewed my Maryland motorcycle license intermittently but never got around to getting an Israeli permit since I didn't actually own a motorcycle and hadn't up to that point seen the need for going through all the hassle and red tape required to do so in Israel.

When I got it in my heart to go through with this thing, I went to the licensing bureau in the coastal city of Haifa and was told I would first have to take a couple of lessons before I would be allowed to take the test because my U.S. license was expired. Well, that didn't set too well with me because I was sure that I could ride a bike better than any of the Israeli instructors. Furthermore I was convinced that there must be some kind of kickback or corrupt relationship between the driving schools and the Israeli Department of Motor Vehicles. Having no other choice, I reluctantly took the minimum of two rather expensive lessons and then promptly failed the test for "changing lanes too often". I had only changed lanes twice during the test and had clearly signaled my intention both times well in advance.

Convinced more that ever that it was all a scam, I went back to Kiryat Shemona, the closest city to where we lived, hoping that by trying again in a new location I would have better results. The first thing I was told when I went to the DMV in Kiryat Shemona was that I would have to take a couple of lessons locally before I would be allowed to take the test again. I wasn't at my best when I went to the nearest driving school that day and informed the owner that I was more qualified that he to take the test and that I thought it was all a big rip-off. However, later in the day, when I was trying to pray, the LORD convicted me greatly and I had to get up off my knees and go back and apologize for my arrogance and pride. The owner said that he had been sure I was going to get into a lot of trouble with my original attitude but was now glad to see that I had a change of heart.

Two lessons later I was ready for the big test, which again I promptly failed for reasons that are still unclear to me till this day. They mumbled something in Hebrew about going too slow around the required obstacle course before going out to the street test. Anyway, I was in good company because over 80% of all drivers of all ages fail their driving test in Israel the first and even second time around… thus requiring more lessons. Well, I had had it with the Israeli motorcycle licensing system and decided that I would just wait and renew my license in Maryland the next time I was back in the good ole U.S. of A.

Since, in my mind I was such a good motorcycle driver, I hadn't even felt the need at all to pray about whether it was the Lord's will for me to have my license or not. About four or five months later we were back in the U.S.A. and on our way to Alaska by faith when my son, Isaiah, was given a 750 cc Kawasaki motorcycle by a pastor in Ohio. One of the conditions was that I would get my license and insure the bike so that I would be able to teach my son how to ride it.

I was pretty confident that day we drove up to the Maryland DMV to take the test since I had already taken that same test and passed it a couple of times or more over the years. I was a bit shocked at how close the cones were set and how miniscule the testing area had become. After failing the test miserably, I asked the tester how anyone ever could pass the test on that course with a large 750 cc motorcycle, and was told that nearly everyone brought in a small rented 125 cc bike, took the test, and then went back to their big bikes since the course obviously wasn't designed for large motorcycles.

Now when I get something in my mind, I'm like a bulldog and I wasn't about to go out and rent a smaller bike in order to take this dumb test. On the contrary, I wasn't going to give an inch more to these people; so I set up a full-scale duplicate of the test sight in a nearby parking lot and practiced until I could literally take the test blind-folded.

When the big day came for us to head out for Alaska, I knew I would have an opportunity to get the license in Cumberland, Maryland on the way out of the state. So with the Kawasaki securely strapped on the snowmobile trailer hitched to our van, we headed up north. I exuded extreme confidence that day, with all six of my children and my wife on hand to see me take the test in Cumberland. The boys and I unloaded the motorcycle at the testing center and I just sat on the bike appreciating the beautiful day and weather as I waited for the supervisor to call me over to take the test. When he signaled me to drive over to the obstacle course, I confidently started the bike and drove the 20 yards or so to where he had indicated.

As I pulled up to where the examination officer was standing, he made some sort of a mark on the form and told me that I had failed the test. At this point I thought he was joking because I hadn't even started to take the test yet, so I asked him in an off the cuff manner, "How come?". "Well", he said, "you just drove over here with your kick-stand down and that's an automatic failure." I had never in over twenty years driven with my kick-stand down before as far as I can remember, so I looked down with unbelief, and sure enough the kick-stand was in a position it shouldn't have been in.

The general consensus at our campsite that night was that "dad was losing it ...for sure!" No one said anything but I could sense that my teenage children were close to giving up hope on me that day. I was feeling like a deflated balloon myself, and we didn't talk much about it as we roasted chicken on the campfire and set up our tents. Miraculously, the testing officer had had compassion on me and told me I could come back in the morning and have one last try, which was the reason we had stopped for the night and set up camp in the area.

Now, I may have been proud, bullheaded and stubborn, but after flunking the motorcycle test for the fourth time, I knew God was trying to tell me something. I got on my knees in our tent and prayed as earnestly as I had ever prayed before for the LORD to speak to me clearly and let me know what I was supposed to learn from all of this humiliation. About two o'clock in the morning I sensed the Holy Spirit say that I would have to die to the whole thing. With that I felt peace and fell right to sleep.

In the morning the whole family was excited to go back to the testing site and get this licensing thing over with so that we could get the insurance and take the motorcycle up to Alaska with us. My son, Isaiah, was probably the most anxious for me not to mess it up again. After a good breakfast, we headed up to the DMV for my absolute last chance to pass the test. We unloaded the bike from the snowmobile trailer after I made the arrangements to take the test.

Suddenly, I began to shake uncontrollably and I knew I would never be able to pass. I simply walked up to the officer and told him that I wouldn't be taking the exam after all. He seemed kind of surprised, asked if I was sure, and then just shrugged his shoulders and walked off. My family on the other hand was now sure I "had lost it" and urged me to reconsider. I told them that it was just no good as the LORD had told be that I had to die to it.

When we arrived in Ohio, we had to go into the DMV in that State and exchange our Maryland driver's licenses for Ohio licenses in order to insure the church van that we were being given to take up to Alaska. As I stood in line, I felt a strong impression that God was about to do a miracle. When I got up to the counter, I gave the man my valid car driver's license, and as he was issuing me an Ohio driver's license I felt to give him my old expired Maryland motorcycle license as well. He nonchalantly asked me, "How long have you been driving a bike?", and I humbly answered him "Since 1970". With that he simply said, "Alright then", and promptly issued me a motorcycle license with my driver's license.

The whole family erupted in laughter after I walked out with the license in hand. Now, after fifteen years I still carry a valid motorcycle license, although I never did pass the test. I keep it as a reminder that God's ways are higher than mine as the heavens are above the earth. While in Alaska I taught my son, Isaiah, to ride the bike on some of the most scenic roads in the U.S. He passed his motorcycle test on the first attempt.

Isaiah on the Kawasaki 750

"I am the vine, you are the branches.
He who abides in Me, and I in him, bears much fruit;
for without Me you can do nothing.
John 15:5

Chapter 31
Heavenly Places

You can read about it, you can see pictures of it, you can even take a photograph of it, but you cannot really experience the Aurora Borealis without standing in the Artic air witnessing God's ultimate symphony of lights. This little story is about how God's entertainment is the best show on earth.

In 1993, our eldest son, Isaac, soon to be eighteen, was studying and working to be a civil engineer. He tends to be overly organized, if there is such a thing, but we thank the Lord that he is much disciplined. Isaac had bought his first car here in Alaska for $250. He and his brother worked hard rebuilding it getting it in good running condition. We had just returned the dark blue van to the Carter's who had purchased it for our family to drive to Alaska from Ohio and then, three months later, they flew up to drive the van back to their church. God willing we would be flying to Israel.

Greg and I had several invitations to speak in Valdez and Glenallen. We asked Isaac if we could borrow his car for the trip. It would be a three-hour drive to Glenallen and then another three-hour drive to Valdez. We had heard the drive was spectacular and there was a high altitude pass through very narrow mountain ranges only passable if the weather permitted.

Isaac was happy to let us use his car. He told us that he had just had it serviced and had the spare tire filled with 45 lbs. of pressure. He assured us it was in fine working condition and ready for the trip. You do not mess around in Alaska knowing the weather is unpredictable and the wilderness can hold any number of surprises.

Our reception at the morning service in the Glenallen church was a surprise. The congregation just loves Israel and wanted to hear more. They did not want to say goodbye but we had made an appointment in Valdez for another service that evening.

It was a beautiful day for sightseeing and we were in a spectacular area of the world. Valdez is the only place where snowfall is recorded each year at being up to 30 feet deep. Now that would mean you would drive in tunnels and your house would have to be dug out daily in the winter months. Thank God, it was summer time, August in fact, the warmest time of year.

The church was a little storefront building. We parked outside and went in to find the warmest atmosphere and the friendliest people. We had a wonderful time and after the service, we were invited to have dinner at the pastor's house. When we climbed into Isaac's little car there was something smelling very bad. Someone had put a Styrofoam cooler in the back seat. I opened the back door and found the top was not closed because inside was this gigantic Halibut. At first I thought it was a joke, then the pastor said, "Oh, I bet I know who gave that to you." With that, I tried desperately to close the top. Eventually Greg got some string and tried to tie it shut. We would just smell like fish on the drive home.

As we left the town that night, delighted to have met such wonderful people, we caught a glimpse of the Aurora Borealis. The moon was out also but in full view in front of us could be seen the most spectacular dancing lights in the sky. We had a long drive back and we wanted to get the car to Isaac to take to work in the morning so we couldn't stop and just enjoy the light show like I would have loved to do for hours.

In Alaska, once you depart from a town it is unlikely that you will discover anything beyond the town's borders. No houses, no people, no gas stations, until you arrive to the next town on the map, and from Valdez to Glenallen, that is the case. There is absolutely nothing for three hours of driving but certainly the most beautiful scenery in the world and some of the wildest animals too. Bears, moose, caribou, wolves and more abound in the remote area we were traveling and I often caught a glimpse of sparkly wild animal eyes glowing in our car lights.

Greg and I were enjoying our night adventure when we suddenly heard a loud pop and then felt our back tire go flat. Wow, it was challenging to get out into the now cold night air and fumble around with our one flashlight to find the spare tire. To our utter amazement, the spare tire was flat too. How could that be? Isaac had said he had just had the tire pressure checked the day before our trip. Discussing it did not help now. We turned the car engine off, climbed up onto the roof of the car with a blanket from the trunk, and began to pray.

It was not hard to get in touch with the Lord in this environment. First, it was 1 A.M. in the morning and very quiet outside in the vast dark wilderness of Alaska. Second, we had the most powerful smelling fish in the back seat of our car that could catch the most distant nose of any hungry bear. Third, we were invited to the best show on earth; the Aurora Borealis theatre was wide open to us. We lay on the roof of the car watching what seemed to be a thousand angels dancing and praising God in Heaven. A spectacular aura of lights entertained us for what seemed like a trip into a heavenly place.

Our experience was disrupted by the sound of a vehicle in the distance, and then we saw lights. A big jeep pulled up and stopped. The burly fellow called out, "You need some help?" This man seemed to be in a very jolly mood. He had us inspecting under his torchlight the big moose kill he had in the back of the jeep. He bragged to no end over his catch, but then said it would be no trouble for him to drive us back to Glenallen. Thank God, he was in such a good mood.

The gas station in Glenallen was closed. It was 3 A.M., a bad time to wake one up, but this was an emergency. The pastors' wife got up immediately and after we thanked our happy moose hunter and said goodbye, she drove us an hour away to the garage. We waited for it to open at 5 A.M. before getting the tire repaired. Our sister then drove us back to our car out on the wilderness highway and in minutes, we were back on the road with the smell of fish to amuse us. The sunrise was magnificent, but we had been to heavenly places that fine morning. We looked forward to having Halibut for dinner with Isaac and as many as we could invite, we had plenty.

Bev on the ATV   *Our son, Israel, at the Matanuska Glacier*

"But God, who is rich in mercy, because of His great love
with which He loved us,
and made us sit together in the heavenly places in Christ Jesus..."
Ephesians 2: 4,6

Chapter 32
Bruce and The Almighty

Don't get me wrong, we dearly love Bruce. It is hard to explain how such a good-hearted soul could be subject to so many amusing dilemma's. Whenever his name comes up, our grown children laugh and begin to tell 'Bruce stories' until we're all in tears. But let me begin by telling his good qualities, which are many.

First, Bruce loves God with all his heart, soul and strength. He genuinely tries to keep the second commandment as well, as best he can, or any of us can for that matter. Bruce loves the great outdoors, walking in nature, hunting, fishing or anything to do with being under the canopy of God's creation. And Bruce loves to eat, which is the reason that he gets overheated rather easily, so he also loves to be where the temperatures are cool or at least moderate in the summertime, such as British Columbia or Alaska.

Physically, Bruce is not real tall but has a huge frame, and I'm not here referring to his weight, but his general bone structure is stout by nature. His neck is huge and his arms and shoulders massive. He most closely resembles a bear if you were to compare him to one of God's creatures that Bruce loves to hunt. His face often has a reddish glow, like the top of a thermometer that is in a constant state of overheating. Bruce's countenance is very kind, similar in some ways to that of a happy and playful bulldog.

My kids absolute favorite saying of Brucesky's (which they affectionately call him) is "he looked me in the eye and I looked him in the eye", a family joke that refers to one of his famous stories about a big black bear that he was hunting in Canada that had suddenly come upon him at close range. Well, all you have to do in our family is say, "he looked me in the eye", and immediately everyone knows whom you're talking about. By now we've all known Bruce for nearly twenty-five years, and he has told us countless hunting and fishing stories, and we ourselves have been with him on various occasions in the wilderness of Alaska and in the forests of northern Israel near the Lebanese border. To this day, no one has ever seen him actually catch a fish or bag any big game, but Bruce has plenty of pictures of his kills to show to 'doubting Thomases' that need proof of his prowess as a hunter.

Bruce is a positive thinker and that to a fault, and he exuberates a confidence that only those who know him well would take with a grain of salt. The one thing missing in his life is a 'Mrs. Bruce' and its assumed by everyone that God hasn't created the other half of Bruce yet to be his helpmate. Yes, I would say that he's a one-of-a-kind sort of person that would have a difficult time finding as adventurous a mate as he would need to find in order to get hitched and 'settle down'.

I know for sure that God loves Bruce even more than he himself is aware, and that God loves him in spite of himself or even because of who he is. Bruce believes in networking and has a knack for putting people of like interests together. We ourselves have met and been blessed by some of the best people in the world through Bruce. When we get together with any of these precious brothers or sisters in the Lord, and his name comes up, there go the 'Bruce stories' once again.

Take for example the one told by Al and Brenda. It seems that they had a large tree that was threatening to come down on their power lines near their house in Alaska. Bruce got out the old chain saw and decided to 'take her down'. Now Al and his wife were a bit apprehensive, to say the least, about giving a big kid like Bruce carte blanche with such a powerful weapon as a chain saw, and tried everything they knew to talk him out of his plan. But he assured them in his usual overly confident manner that he had been cutting trees down bigger than that one all his life, and that this would be a 'piece of cake'. So the show began, as they watched helplessly from their front porch. Just like a pro, he carefully cut the wedge in the tree to make it come down just perfectly into the clearing he had already prepared for it to fall into. And if all had gone according to plan, it would have landed right in that very spot. But as fate would have it, just as it started to fall in the right direction, the tree suddenly did a complete 180 degree turn, like the hand of the Almighty was pushing it, and it landed smack onto the power lines. In retrospect, Al said it wasn't all that bad because the power company was able to remove the tree and restore electricity to their home within the week.

As I mentioned earlier we were in Alaska with Bruce one summer and had a great time together. It was because of the awesome pictures that he had shown us when visiting in our home in northern Israel that we had felt led by God to make this trip with our six children, now between the ages of ten and seventeen. We had driven up to Alaska on the Alcan Highway through Canada in a very nice church van that had been given to us for that purpose. Towards the end of the summer, the pastor and his wife had flown up to Alaska and had stayed with us for a week before driving the van back down the Alcan to their home in Ohio.

Since we still had a few weeks left to stay in Alaska before we were to head back to Israel by plane, we were a little inconvenienced by not having a vehicle in such a remote place. Anyway, I was praying one morning for God to provide us with a temporary means of transportation, when all of a sudden I got the distinct impression from the Holy Spirit to 'Get Bruce a car'. I've learned that its no good arguing with God once He's given an instruction, so I got up off my knees and began to plan how I could go about getting Bruce a vehicle. I knew we would be going back to Israel shortly so we really didn't need one at that time, but Bruce was an 'evangelist without wheels' and had a much greater need.

Bruce had a lot of friends that had become our friends as well, so I thought I might start by taking up a collection and seeing where that would lead. Some people might even been willing to give just to see Bruce leave Alaska for awhile, but that didn't matter just as long as I got him a vehicle.

The first place I went to was Gary's ice-cream parlor and tackle store just down the road, knowing that Gary was a good brother in the Lord, and one of Bruce's fishing buddies. I told him the story of what God had told me to do, and was making a pitch for an offering to get Bruce a car, when he said, "Hey, you want a car for Bruce, I've got one out back you can have if you can get it started". We went to the lot in back of his place, and sure enough there was an a huge old silverish-grey car that looked like it had Bruce's name on it and had been specially built for him. I said, "That's great, I'll take it!", knowing that this was definitely coming about by the hand of the Lord. It seems that Gary never ever bothered with such mundane things as changing oil or doing any maintenance on a vehicle, he just drove them till they stopped running and then bought a new one. This large old silver battleship of a car was only in need of some fluids, belts, and other minor things, and was running like new within a couple of hours.

It was driving so smoothly down the highway that for a moment I became a bit covetous of 'Bruce's car' and thought maybe I'll keep it for a few weeks and give it to him before we left for Israel.

Immediately the car began to act up and start running poorly, knocking, losing compression, and such. I quickly repented and just as quickly it went back to purring like a kitten. As far as I know from Bruce's testimony, he never had a minute's problem with it in all the tens of thousands of miles that he used it to drive up and down the Alcan Highway to British Columbia and back.

Within a couple of days we had the thing shined up like new. I arranged with the brothers at the local Full Gospel Business Men's meeting to take up an offering so that we could give the vehicle to Bruce from all of us, along with a check for the insurance and travel expenses to get on the road. It was so touching to see Bruce behind the wheel of that 'Silver Thunderbird', for it was surely a match made in heaven.

Now I could go on all day telling 'Bruce stories' but then you might think that I was being critical and un-Christian like for picking on him. The truth is that I miss him and his extended visits more than I care to admit sometimes. Over the years, I've come to realize that it takes all kinds to make the world what it is, and Bruce is definitely one of the Almighty's most special creations.

> *"Assuredly, I say to you, inasmuch as you did it to one of the least of these My brethren, you did it to Me."*
> Matthew 25:40

Chapter 33
Thirty Flights in Thirty Days

In the summer of 1993, our daughter Tehila would be turning thirteen years old, the summer of her bat-mitzvah. As a surprise for her, Greg charged the purchase of two round trip tickets to NY from Israel via London on Delta Airline, which came with a special promotional deal for international travelers, a pass that entitled us to unlimited Delta flights within the continental U.S. for one month. The average person might not know what to do for that length of time but now that the Lord had blessed us with unlimited travel possibilities we could arrange for the things we had only dreamed about before. Amazed at this God-given opportunity we excitedly planned what we would do for thirty days.

My brother was getting married in Maryland and all the family would be together so this would be the time to have a special birthday party for Tehila. In her tomboy way, she fell short of the grace to be the perfect little lady. She loved imitating "mommy" and did her utmost to dress like me, walk like me, and talk like me. She was mommies little informant whenever anything happened which gave me the power to claim that "God always shows me". She was never hindered by her siblings relentless teasing for being a tattletale.

We shared a special empathy and I could see so much of myself in her personality, only she more resembled the boisterous and amusing Anne of Green Gables. This trip would be a grand adventure that would bond us even closer, a bond that exists just as strong today as it did twenty years ago.

Our trip was arranged on the condition that we have the faith that God would miraculously provide the money for the tickets somewhere, somehow, so we could pay off the credit card when we returned. Thus, we prayed, "Oh Lord, cause us to be a blessing where ever you lead and let us never be a burden on anyone." We promised Greg we would not worry about the money for our tickets. Tehila and I would have $200 in cash for this trip.

I baked for days before leaving to fill the freezer with quick meals to help Greg get started caring for the three children remaining with him in Israel. Summer break had just begun so they had no schedule to keep. We were excited about the possibility of attending my brother Rick's wedding. God had truly answered my prayers concerning the travel needs with the addition of the Delta Pass.

My friend and sister in the Lord, Ada, met us at Kennedy Airport. Ada had met our family many times upon arrival or departure in the U.S. She would always make sure we were taken care of before traveling on. It was such a blessing to have such a good contact in a city that could otherwise "devour you." Our first meal was in a Jewish deli. To Tehila's delight Ada went next door and got her a hot dog on a bun, she was beaming from the attention.

Tehila and I waved goodbye to Ada as we breezed through La Guardia check-in with our Delta Pass on our first free flight. We were told seats were available even on stand-by, which does not exist anymore, nor do such unlimited-use monthly passes. Ada promised to see us again on our return flight to Israel.

Next stop was Maryland. My brother's wife, Jan, picked us up from Baltimore-Washington International Airport and to Tehila's delight we went straight to the largest mall in the state. Aunt Jan is a shop-a-holic who was determined to ignore my comments saying, "she doesn't need that" as she went crazy buying Tehila new shoes, new jeans (she didn't have any), new hair clips, and lots of beads for making earrings, the list goes on.

A much-awaited visit with my mom and dad in Melbourne, Florida was next. They had spent precious little time with their grandchildren over the years and cherished this opportunity. Due to the convenience of this Delta pass, we were booking flights to the nearest airport of our destination. This would sometimes mean flying to several other cities to catch the exact flight we needed in order to arrive to the closest airport possible to our destination.

We had been friends of an elderly couple from West Virginia, the Allen's, for years. They were excited to hear that Tehila and I would be able fly into Charleston from Florida to visit them. Now that we were frequent flier's it was a synch jumping on these free Delta flights. We had only a medium sized carryon each and handbags. Remember, whatever I did, Tehila did also. Mr. Allen would be picking us up at the airport while Mrs. Allen was home preparing a very delicious dinner for us. We would be getting in just in time, 5 P.M.

This was a small airport so we had no trouble making our way to the passenger pickup area. Mr. Allen was not there. Finally, the airport was growing quiet. I said to Tehila, "Something must be wrong." She said, "Yeah, mommy, we are in South Carolina not West Virginia." I replied, "Nonsense, that's impossible!" Then she pointed to a taxi parked just outside the sliding doors, which had written clearly on the side Charleston, South Carolina. We dashed to the information desk with our tickets in our hands that clearly stated Charleston and the name of the airport. The cashiers began laughing and replied, "Oh boy, another one. Honey this happens all the time. We are sorry to tell you that the next flight to Charleston, West Virginia will not be until 11 P.M." We had no choice but to book it.

I phoned Mrs. Allen and gave her the disappointing news. She said they did not mind but I was sure it was a hardship on them both and imagined the delicious aroma of dinner waiting on the table that would now be left-overs. It was not until after midnight that I realized how important the delay had been. God had a man he wanted Mr. Allen to talk to about the Lord in the airport that night, a man who had been thinking about suicide, but found Mr Allen, who shared with him the love of Jesus.

Next we flew to Texas where we were treated royally by my friend, Barbara Dunn. We had become acquainted in Israel. She desired to bless us while we were in the states and that she did in a big fashion. In fact, we were treated like royalty all week. She had no kids but borrowed a girlfriend from church for Tehila to befriend. It was a hit. The biggest treat was Fiesta Texas. Barb spent a lot of money, I'm sure the Lord blessed her, and we all had a lot of fun.

Tehila especially enjoyed our last weekend in the states having fellowship with the Biley's and their three children on Bainbridge Island just outside of Seattle, Washington. While at a birthday party on our last day before leaving to fly back to NY, a last minute miracle happened. We had a time of prayer together after the party was over. I was asked to share about Israel and I thanked the Lord for this blessed trip with my daughter for her Bat-mitzvah.

As we were about to leave, the lady of the house requested my presence in the kitchen for a minute. Her husband was digging around in the upright freezer, pulled out an icy plastic bag, and handed it to me. I was bewildered when he said, "Open it! We won't be needin' that and I suppose you will." Inside the plastic bag was cold stiff green money. Still amazed, I thanked them and ran off to the waiting vehicle.

We would be late for the ferry that would get us to the Seattle airport in time to catch our flight to NY. We had to wait for the last ferry and hoped we would still get a taxi and arrive at the airport in time for our flight. Mrs. Biley instructed us to call her if we missed our flight as we ran into the airport. She said she would be glad to pick us up and have us spend the night again if we missed our flight.

We missed the flight! The next Delta flight was at 5 A.M. in the morning. We could not bring ourselves to disturb the Biley's and decided to spend the night in the airport. Seattle has a nice airport; it is the only airport I have ever seen to have soft leather couches in the ladies sitting room. Tehila and I prayed for safety, stretched out and slept amazingly well in the airport.

Wrapped up in the frozen plastic bag was exactly the amount of money we needed to pay the credit card debt for the tickets. God became very real to my daughter through His abundant provisions that summer. I believe it was an experience that helped to shape her future.

Tehila and I were seasoned travelers when we arrived home in Tel Aviv. We had flown thirty flights in thirty days.

"Blessed be the God and Father of our Lord Jesus Christ, who has blessed us with every spiritual blessing in the heavenly places in Christ".
Ephesians 1:3

Chapter 34

Digging for 'The Voice of Hope'

When I was a child, one of the expressions my mom and grandfather would use to keep me studying hard in school was that 'if you didn't get a good education you would grow up and become a ditch digger'. The thought of shoveling dirt all day was unappealing enough to get a little more effort out of anyone who wanted to avoid such a fate. As fate would have it, I ended up doing just that, digging ditches for a living.

Of course I only did it for a few months, and it was by choice. I had volunteered for the job when God put it on my heart to help out 'The Voice of Hope' radio ministry in southern Lebanon. Just the same, it involved digging ditches eight hours a day for the Lord, at the local rate of pay of two dollars an hour.

The Voice of Hope radio ministry broadcasted the gospel, Christian music, and news throughout the Middle East, even reaching down into Africa from a large hill overlooking our town of Metulla. Technically, the radio station and its towers were in Lebanon, but at that time the area was under Israeli occupation, so the workers were given free access to the station without having to officially cross any borders. The African Rift, which runs from Turkey all the way down through East Africa made this location ideal for radio waves to travel much farther than would normally have been possible with the equipment and towers that were being used. Not only were a great many Moslems having access to the Word of God daily, but many Israelis were secretly tuning in as well.

Having left my job teaching mathematics at the regional high school, I had four months of down time with nothing to do before I was scheduled to travel to the United States. One day after Paul Johnson, a fellow American who ran the station, shared his vision to reach all of Africa from this station, I felt that I wanted to help out in any way that I could. He told me that the technical people had devised a way to double the strength of the broadcasting transmitters without having to build higher towers or put in any additional equipment. This was indeed exciting news until I heard about how this miracle was going to come about.

It seems that there is something called 'ground effect' that was the key to the whole thing. Basically underground wires, of the same length as the height of the towers, had to be run straight out from each tower, in a pattern that resembled the spokes on a wagon wheel. When they were all connected to a center ring, the wires themselves acted as transmitting towers, doubling the station's output.

The one snag in the whole plan was that ground effect was only made possible if the wires were buried. They could not just be laid on top of the ground. The entire hilltop where the towers stood was extremely rocky, and this would make the digging unbelievably difficult. Eight young men from the neighboring towns in southern Lebanon had been contracted for two dollars an hour to do the job. Each wire was several hundred feet long, and eighty wires running out from the base of each tower were required to do the job. A rough estimate on my part was that we were talking about burying almost ten miles of wire under this hardened terrain. I wanted to help the cause of the Kingdom of God but this seemed like it might be impossible. Still God's Spirit was moving on my heart so I said that I was willing to give it a try.

The next day I began digging for all I was worth, side by side with the Lebanese. The first day, the eight of us probably got about a hundred feet of wire buried. I quickly realized that it would take at least a year to complete the job. Now these guys were strong young men who were used to this kind of manual labor. They didn't seem to mind that it was going to take so long, but I was beat after two days and the 'voice of reason' told me that God hadn't intended for me to kill myself on this project.

The following day I had an inspiration from above, and asked the Lebanese engineer in charge of the project if the wires had to be buried under the ground or whether they could be laid on the surface and dirt put over the top of them. After considering my idea for a few minutes, he answered that this would have the exact same effect as burying them, and then he smiled. Within an hour we had a bulldozer and an operator from a neighboring farm scooping us loads of loose dirt from a nearby hillside, and dropping it wherever we indicated while we ran alongside, filling our buckets and covering the wires on top of the ground with dirt.

There was still some digging to do, and a lot of manual labor involved, but significantly less than before. As a result of this new system, we were able to increase our daily output many times over. Although my co-workers would be out of a job much sooner, even they were grateful to not have to be digging in that rocky ground all day. I estimated that we still had about six weeks of work left in order to complete the project, but now that we could see the light at the end of the tunnel, our burden became much lighter. After a week or so my muscles stopped hurting and I became like one of them, with one exception. They were only Christians in name, having been born into families that were 'Mariannites', and none of them knew Jesus as their Lord and Savior.

Each day when we stopped for lunch, I would eat quickly and then spend the rest of my break reading my Bible. At first, no one said anything to me about it, but then they became curious as we got to know each other better and asked what I was reading. We spoke together in Hebrew as their English and my Arabic were about the same – very poor. I told them I was reading the book of Acts and asked if anyone had ever read it, which no one had. I gave them my testimony and told them how I had been born into a Jewish family but had found the truth that Jesus was the Messiah by reading the Bible. I then made it clear that you could not be born a Christian, but that each person had to be a follower of Jesus and be 'born again' to actually become a Christian. The men listened so intently to what I was saying that I knew that God was working in their hearts.

The next day I gave each a New Testament in Arabic, and over the next weeks we became close friends. The job was progressing extremely well, and because of that we had at least an hour's lunch break daily in which we set aside part of the time to study the Bible together. These young men were very hungry for God's Word and had never heard the gospel before. The good news of the kingdom of God gave them hope, for each of them had suffered greatly as a result of the many years of war that had embroiled southern Lebanon.

Just before completing the wire-burying project, most of these men gave their lives to Jesus, and after repenting of their sins, asked to be baptized in water. They continued to come to fellowship meetings on Sundays in our home and brought along their families, friends and relatives. Soon we had quite a large group crossing the border at the 'Good Fence,' and then walking a couple of miles to the stone storage barn in our backyard that we had refurbished into a meeting place for worship services and Bible studies.

Over the next months, I was able to take several of those same men who had worked along side me, one at a time by bus to Jerusalem, for a weekend walking tour of the Old City and places where Jesus had ministered. This was a fulfillment of a lifelong dream for them; one that they had never imagined would become a reality.

I praise God that he had laid it on my heart to joyfully dig ditches for two dollars an hour. The benefits of being led of the Holy Spirit cannot be measured by this world's economic standard, and truly it was a small sacrifice to make for such a large harvest of souls.

> *"And you will be secure, because there is hope;*
> *Yes, you will dig about, and you will take your rest in safety."*
> Job 11:18

Chapter 35

Wrong Bank, Right Money!

We would become accustomed to a Shabbat noontime visit from a precious couple, John and Nancy Potter and their two boys who lived in the valley in the mostly Moroccan neighborhood of Kiryat Shemona, a city renowned in northern Israel for the worst police department in the country. They were coming to take us out to eat in our town of Metulla at one of the local restaurants up on the Lebanese border. This was the only time we ever ate out and John always insisted on picking up the tab. The Potter boys loved to hang out with our kids and they preferred to play in the yard rather than listen to adult conversation in a restaurant. We usually brought Israeli burgers and chips home for the eight kids who would be starving after wearing themselves out playing.

Our acquaintance with the Potter's went back ten years to the time we lived in Eilat. John had been hired to a prestigious position as chief electrical contractor to help build the Ovda Airbase in the Negev. John and Nancy rented a house in Eilat. They had twins just a few months old when we first met them. We were just new believers living in Jerusalem when Greg's grandfather sent him a book in 1976 called "Jeshurun I" about End Time Prophecy written by John Potter. We had now finally met the author, Jonh Potter.

At the time we were busy operating our new school, Eilat Christian Academy. It served as the school for most of the international families now stationed here for two years to build the airbase. The airbase was a gift to Israel from America after the Camp David agreement.

By the time the base was completed in 1980, John and Nancy had fallen in love with Israel and settled down in a nice home they bought in the northern city of Kiryat Shemona to raise their family. Nancy was expecting their third child. John was already frustrated dealing with the fact that many of his End Time prophecies were not being fulfilled as he had predicted in his book.

We lost touch with the Potter's and we ourselves moved away to Ra'ananna, a suburb of Tel Aviv. It was not until we moved to Metulla in 1989 that we bumped into them again. We started enjoying family fellowship and had a small house group for bible studies in their home. Our Shabbat meals were important and we felt as if we had become a lifeline for John, Nancy, and their two boys. One of their small twins had died in their house when a space heater caused smoke to asphyxiate Run's twin brother. The Potter's blamed themselves and both of them began to drink regularly. At first the drinking seemed social, it quickly became more than that and we found it hard to address the problem. They were in denial. The bible studies were cancelled and their visits on Shabbat became infrequent. John was often too drunk to drive and was finally arrested by the police and his license revoked.

Their boys were suffering as well. When they started walking by foot all the way to Metulla to visit us, I knew there were fights at home. We began to pray for the Lord's help and direction. One weekend Greg and I went to their home without our kids to see if we could get them to go to counseling. When we arrived, we were surprised to find that a local pastor had come and taken Nancy and John and had them both committed to a mental institution. The boys had been taken to an orphanage in Haifa.

When Greg approached this pastor, he was told that the Potter's were old drunks and we should keep our nose out of things. Immediately, Greg drove to Haifa to the institution where they had been committed and brought them home. They were both heavily sedated but sober from alcohol. We arranged for a couple of sisters to stay with them until we figured out how we could help them.

Nancy told us she thought they had some money in the Bank Ben Leumi (International Bank) but she did not know how much and could not find the account information.

I had tried calling her bank several times but could not get through. The next morning, while busy in the kitchen, I asked my daughter Tehila to please look up the number in the telephone book and call Nancy's bank for me. When she got phone assistance Tehila asked if Nancy Potter had an account there and they said yes, but there had not been any transactions for a number of years. She said Nancy would have to come in person if she wanted to withdraw money. Tehila asked how much money was in this savings account and the lady told her this was confidential. After hanging up, I read what Tehila had written down on a piece of paper - Bank Leumi (National Bank). Nancy had specifically told us she had an account in Bank Ben Leumi (International Bank). Tehila had just mistakenly called Bank Leumi and learned the Potter's also had and account in a second bank, the National Bank.

I immediately phoned Bank Leumi to check if Nancy really did have an account with Leumi as well and, to our surprise, yes, she did! That morning I drove to Kiryat Shemona and took Nancy to Bank Leumi. Nancy had forgotten that they had a savings account there with over $6,000, which they had opened when they had first arrived from Eilat. They thought they had just the few hundred dollars in the Bank Ben Leumi left to their names. We were praising the Lord for Tehila's mistake. Wrong bank, right money!

With the money that Nancy withdrew from the Bank Leumi, which the Lord miraculously provided, Greg purchased tickets for them to travel with him to a deliverance ministry we knew of in Bainbridge Island, off shore from Seattle, Washington. He left them with these good people there who were willing to take John and Nancy in and work and pray with them to restore mental and spiritual health.

The Potter's kids remained in a Christian home in Haifa attending a school they really liked. They are both serving the Lord today. God answered our prayers miraculously with help for the Potter's.

"For the accuser of our brethren, who accused them before our God day and night, has been cast down."
Revelation 12:10

Chapter 36

Trouble in Paradise

There's a proverbial saying in the sales industry, which goes something like this: "If it sounds too good to be true then it probably is too good to be true." I should have known that if the Property and Environment Research Center (PERC) in Bozeman, Montana was going to pay me $5000.$^{\underline{00}}$ and give me professional guidance and other invaluable resources needed for me to write the first part my doctoral thesis in economics, then there had to be a catch in it somewhere. I just didn't see it coming at the time.

Now don't get me wrong, they did everything that they said they would, and more. It's the 'more' that gave me such a headache that summer, to the point that by the end I was ready to pay them to let me out of my obligation. In retrospect, I should've known from the very first e-mail correspondence that there was trouble brewing in paradise. The 'reply' that was sent back to me had all my grammatical and spelling mistakes marked in red, with the pithy comment that I would have to learn the difference between the uses of 'that and which' if I hoped to attend PERC's summer graduate student internship program. Not one professor in three years had ever corrected the content of even one of my e-mails, which are taken for granted to be merely quick correspondences, and not the thing of literary scholarship by any stretch of the imagination.

I had driven up from the panhandle of Florida, which was about as different a landscape from Montana as the barren moon is to the blue-green planet earth. The natural beauty of Montana, the home of the oldest and most famous wildlife reserve, Yellowstone National Park, enthralled me. I pulled up to PERC at the beginning of June of 2002, in an almost euphoric mood brought about in part by the surrounding majestic mountains, and the wildflowers that were blooming everywhere. I had this unrealistic expectation of having a great time, a fun summer of hiking and hanging out with my half-brother who lived in the area, while getting a big chunk of my PhD thesis over with and quickly out of the way.

I give them credit though, Terry and Dan, my professional advisors at PERC. They did an excellent job of getting me out of 'la-la land' and into a serious frame of mind immediately after I arrived in Bozeman. I was handed two books on grammar and writing, and told to read both before I wrote my first sentence. I was almost their age, having gone back to school with my oldest son, Isaac, after a twenty-five year hiatus, and was now being treated like an undergraduate novice. I tried to shrug it off as I sat down to read those horribly boring books as quickly as possible.

If either Terry or Dan is reading this story then I apologize here for my backslidden ways, for I have reverted back to the 'fly by the seat of your pants' writer that I was before they attempted to re-train me. You see, at PERC there was a conspiracy to undo everything in writing that you were taught from childhood. Instead of trying to balloon a hundred words into a thousand in order to complete the requirements of some writing assignment, we were forced to make a page fit into a paragraph, and turn a paragraph into a sentence. Adjectives and adverbs were taboo; you simply had to find the correct verb or noun to begin with and use it instead. Publishers seem to be fanatics about being economical when it comes to page space.

These PERC people were very serious economists and writers indeed. Their main forte was trying to find 'free market' incentive-based solutions to environmental issues while avoiding regulations and government intervention as much as humanly possible. So where does an Israeli Messianic believer fit in here? Like a square peg in a triangular hole, I'd say. I was a bit of a novelty at PERC from all the other economists and interns who were writing economic research papers about forests, endangered species, dwindling natural resources, etc.

I had been studying 'Economics and Property Rights' with Dr. Benson at Florida State University for two years, and it was he who had encouraged me to apply and to attend this internship program. Terry Anderson, one of the directors of PERC and a personal friend of Dr. Benson, had written a classic economics paper early in his career entitled, "Raid or Trade". In his groundbreaking work he analyzed the American Indian wars with the Whites in the light of the economic costs and benefits that each had in either keeping peace treaties or breaking them. He convincingly argued with statistical data and through regression analysis of that data, that it wasn't the one-sided picture that Hollywood had painted. The end of the sovereignty for the American Indian had predictably come about when the economic costs of trading any more land, outweighed the economic benefits that they perceived would be derived from peace.

Prior to the last part of the nineteenth century, the reverse had been the case and they had chosen for the most part to 'trade rather than raid'.

Now if I'm boring you here, I apologize because most people including myself are not all that interested in western movies or the plight of the American Indian, but I recognized in Dr. Anderson's inspired analysis a direct application to nearly all modern wars, especially the Israeli-Palestinian conflict. There was an abundance of data available that supported the fact that the two nations formed by the sons of Abraham through Isaac and Ishmael had lived together peacefully for centuries. Why? In recent times, the whole peace process initiated in 1994 by the late Prime Minister, Yitzchak Rabin and the P.L.O. Chairman, Yasser Arafat, had disintegrated into the bloodiest violence and extreme terrorism that the State of Israel and the Jewish people had ever experienced. I was looking for a way to rationally interpret this chaos in hopes that a peaceful economic solution could be found, and hoped to prove that this was a realistic possibility through my research... utopian expectations at the very least.

The scripture clearly states that 'whom the Lord loves He chastens, and He scourges every son whom He receives." (Hebrew 12:6) It also states that "pride comes before a fall". So between God's love and my pride, I was in for a boatload of trouble that summer in paradise. Although it's been over five years since my baptism of economic fire, I am only now coming to the point of being thankful for the help that was painfully inflicted upon me by my mentors at PERC, and for the way the Lord used them to chasten me.

In the end I did gather all of the pertinent data from the Internet and other resources, did all of the statistical analysis correctly and wrote the thirty page paper required of me. I even got to go on some wonderful hiking and camping adventures in Yellowstone National Park with my wife, Beverly, when she flew up for a week in the middle of my summer internship. Besides that one week of bliss, there are two incidents that stand out above all others that summer in Bozeman, and both were in regards to answers to prayer.

I had been at PERC for several weeks, and had already made it through the first of three scheduled presentations before the staff, which was one of the most grueling one-hour sessions imaginable. You had to give each of about fifteen different economists at PERC a copy of the research that you would going to present, a full forty-eight hours in advance of your presentation. They had plenty of interest and the time to take it apart and be thoroughly prepared for your debut in their economic arena. I had five minutes given in which I could say anything that I wanted without interruption. They then had fifty-five minutes to drill you on every aspect of your research. We were told that what we could successfully defend was ours to keep, everything else had to be discarded, which for most of us amounted to about 50-75% of our masterpieces. One major point that I had to concede (but later took me six more months of study to successfully defend) had to be painfully discarded after Dan jumped to his feet and yelled at me to stop. He said that if I used the term 'constant ratio' to describe the fatality rates between the two sides over the period of study (1967-2002) one more time, that I would be asked to leave PERC immediately!

After that first session, Dan called me into his office on a Friday afternoon and angrily asked, "Do you have any economic theory whatsoever for all this stuff your espousing?" He went on to say, "I want the theory clearly written out and on my desk Monday morning or you can pack your bags and leave." Now, I had been hoping that as I collected the data and did the research, the economic theory behind it all would become self-evident. Obviously this was not the case, or they simply didn't have the faith and patience that I possessed. Whatever the case, I was under extreme pressure and knew that I was in big trouble.

That was one of the longest weekends of my life. I prayed and meditated, read my Bible, prayed and cried… and got absolutely nothing from God or anywhere else. Monday morning, I realized that it was time to admit defeat and start packing. I had less than an hour before Dan would be looking for my 'economic theory', and I didn't have even the beginning of one that explained the seemingly irrational behavior behind the Middle East madness that was overrunning the nation of Israel at the time. I got on my knees one last time to thank the Lord for delivering me out of this pressure-cooker program, and was on my knees for just a few minutes when a revelation of the answer came to me in a vision that flashed before my eyes. Suddenly it was all as clear as an elementary textbook. I got up, praised the LORD, and wrote it all out in less than a half and hour. That morning, Dan looked it over, gave me a rare smile and said that I should go back to work and prove 'my' theory.

In brief, the model that Dr. Anderson developed didn't hold for the case of extreme values such as were being displayed on the part of the religious fanatics on both sides of the conflict. No amount of money or economic incentives would prevail in a climate where each side felt that the disputed properties (Jerusalem and the Temple Mount for example) were given by God and of infinite value. The model Anderson used had to be redefined to take into account the 'infinite' values each placed on the territories in dispute.

I believed that the key obstacle to the peace process was that the borders between the two sides had never been defined since Moses had allotted each tribe its inheritance in the Land of Promise in the book of Deuteronomy. In the last century, from the time that the British pulled out after thirty years of ruling according to the mandate given them in 1917, the borders of Israel had been in question and the rights of the Palestinians placed in limbo.

Here, in a rather simplistic analogy, I'll try to explain. Both sides were acting like two small children fighting over a ball, each claiming it was his while neither enjoyed the benefits of playing with it. It was only after one of their mothers or some other authority figure made the call and decided whose ball it was, that order would ensue. The two children could then take turns, or trade riding a bicycle or something similar in exchange for the use of the ball. As long as the property rights of a thing are undefined and remain in dispute, each will claim it as their own and negotiations will break down. Once the rights (borders) are established, compromise can begin and bargaining can take place, with each side bidding according to the value they have placed on acquiring the rights of the object of their desire.

When I left PERC at the end of the summer I still hadn't finished the paper, and would not receive my last sizeable paycheck until I did. It seems that although my theory was sound, with the supporting data and statistical analysis making a fairly strong case, the wording of the final draft of the paper was wrong. They absolutely hated the term 'extremists' that appeared numerous times throughout the paper; a word I had used to describe the unreasonable religious radicals on both sides. Terry said that such a term was not used by economists and would be rejected by every economic journal. He gave me two weeks after my return to Florida to come up with a better word, but had no suggestions as to what that might be.

Just a quick economics lesson here and you'll understand the inspiration that I received on my way home. The term 'marginal' to an economist is what the term 'grace' is to an evangelical, and Torah is to a Jew, in other words sacred. For the economist, the margin is what makes or breaks any cost-benefit analysis. If there is still a profit, however small, being made on the last item sold or manufactured (the margin) then it is still economically viable. It is when the change in costs just begins to exceed the change in benefits that a venture is no longer marginally profitable.

As I was driving home, I knew that I had to find a term for 'extremist' that meant the same thing but was palatable to my fellow Economic Sadducees... and then the Lord revealed it to me in another momentary flash of inspiration. When I got home, I went to my computer and had it replace the word 'extremist' with the expression "extreme marginalist", which I had just coined, throughout the entire thirty-page document. In less than one-hundredth of a second the paper was finished.

Although no letter of congratulations ever came from PERC after I sent them an attached final version of my paper with my last e-mail correspondence, no criticisms came back either. A few weeks later the final check arrived in the mail. It was indeed an 'extremely marginal' blessing in the light of God's love for me and His infinite provision.

"Or what king, going to make war against another king, does not sit down first and consider whether he is able with ten thousand to meet him who comes against him with twenty thousand? Or else, while the other is still a great way off, he sends a delegation and asks conditions of peace."
Luke 14:31-32

Chapter 37

The Bear Looked Me in the Eye

Statistics reveal that mama bears with cubs maul close to a hundred visitors a year, numerous of those children, in Yellowstone National Park. It became imperative that we maintain our rigorous pace and correctly navigate our way out of the forest, as the sun would soon be setting on the horizon. This vaguely marked trail led to the river, where remote bush campsites were the only legal or safe place for hikers to spend the night in this isolated area of the Park.

Fresh in our minds after viewing the required thirty minutes indoctrination film were the images of the wildlife that inhabit Hayden Valley, an area teeming with bears, wolves, elk, and buffalo. The film serves to prepare visitors on the "do's and don'ts" while trekking. Instructions were very clear: "do" set up camp early and "don't" hike at dusk. The majority of the "don'ts" were in reference to the bears, which here, in all likelihood, a hiker would suddenly come across while on the trail. We were about to inadvertently defy the rules!

Late summer brought tourists from around the world seeking a snapshot of a herd of buffalo or a pack of wolves or especially a mama bear and her cubs. Of course, there where less life threatening adventures in the park enjoyed by endless tour buses loaded with people who invaded designated areas. Of the 3.6 million people who visit the park each year, 98% venture less than 500 feet from their vehicle and never see the real Yellowstone. We, the other 2%, intentionally avoid the day-tripper scene.

Located in Wyoming, Montana, and Idaho, it is home to a large variety of wildlife. Preserved within Yellowstone National Park are Old Faithful and a collection of the world's most extraordinary geysers and hot springs, and the infamous Grand Canyon of the Yellowstone. We became increasing aware of the crowds of visitors that descend upon Yellowstone this time of year as we waited for Old Faithful to boast her daily eruption, it being the most popular geyser in the world.

After a leisurely lunch, we commenced our search for a campsite. Of the four campgrounds sprawled about in the vast national park, we were surprised to learn there were no vacancies; all tent sites were booked to capacity. The park rangers notified us that we had only one alternative remaining, and that was a remote campground with two vacant sites, but due to a "first come, first serve" policy, there was a possibility they too would be booked by the time we would arrive to check in.

Time was not on our side as we quickly sped down the narrow windy road to arrive at the ranger's station where we purchased the twenty-dollar permit for one of the last vacant remote campsites. After viewing the required movie at the ranger's station, which would definitely scare off the timid of heart, we set out at a rather late hour, 4:00 P.M., with our foodstuff and gear on our backs for the two and a half-hour scramble to our remote campsite.

About an hour into our stunningly beautiful wilderness trek, panic struck! Tramping uphill, just over a slight ridge and standing before Greg and I, three feet high on two back feet just ten yards beyond my footsteps was the cutest little baby bear cub. For a second I was distracted by her amusing grin when suddenly, rising from behind her to a height of over seven feet, was mama bear. She looked me in the eye, and I looked her in the eye. Although in an alarming situation, I clearly recalled the information from the mandatory film we had just seen warning if such a predicament occurs - don't run, don't yell, don't panic, don't look away - just continue staring the bear in the eye while easing away very, very slowly.

Thus, the slow creep away began, without glancing anywhere but into the mama's dubious eyes, I crept away silently in reverse until I backed into my companion. Upon bumping into him, I jumped trail and took off running for my life. What a rat! How could one ditch their life long partner and mate at such a life-threatening moment? It happened and I am not proud of it, but I am grateful that he remained calm and continued easing backward until he too was well out of mama bears way. Once at a relatively safe distance out of harms way, we motionlessly hid behind trees and waited for mama bear and her cub to slowly wander far-off into a blueberry patch.

Having been delayed more than thirty minutes meant we should make tracks and swiftly move forward. However, this was feeding time for the bears and we were wary after our first encounter. Lo and behold, not having gone more than ten minutes hike below the steep embankment before us, standing in the middle of the trail, was another large mama bear. She had two cubs playing in the tall grass in close proximity to her. She was not cognizant of our company and we intended it to remain that way, as we sat on the ridge watching her for another twenty minutes before she meandered beyond the trail and then, like jackrabbits, we fled into open range.

Before us on the expansive grazing land were the flecked silhouettes of a herd of magnificent buffalo. How could we traverse this territory without agitating these mammoth creatures? Though time consuming, we skirted the grassland and continued to a lower elevation indicating our close proximity to the river, when we first became alarmed at a distressful wailing cry. We were in range of the long wavering howl of the wolves baying at the moon, which had just become visible. The wolves were reintroduced in 1995. They thrived and there are now over 300 of their descendants living in the Yellowstone area.

We had unintentionally arrived at this present predicament, which seemed extremely risky, and knew well of the ridicule awaiting us from family and friends when they would learn of our adventure. Notwithstanding the dangerous circumstances, it is precisely in such events that the Lord wants us, His children, to look to Him. Where was our faith? Was the Lord watching over us or not? No, we were not foolishly tempting the Lord, nor taking the circumstances at hand and running away filled with fear. The most problematical situations in life have cultivated my faith.

It was dark! Cooking would not be wise, as we might attract wolves to pry around our tent. We located the pulley extending from a wire stretched across two tall trees. We hoisted our remaining consumables up beyond the grasp of night prowling bears and with flashlight in hand returned to our slightly moonlit campsite to erect our tent in the dark. Strict park rules forbade lighting of campfires.

We slept well, woke early and enjoyed a great bowl of granola and fruit. Our hike back to our vehicle was exhilarating and we went directly to nearby Mammoth Falls Hot Springs to enjoy soaking our sore legs and shoulders.

> *"Trust in the Lord with all your heart,*
> *And lean not on your own understanding;*
> *In all your ways acknowledge Him,*
> *And He shall direct your paths."*
> Proverbs 3:5,6

Chapter 38

The Shadow of Death

Only one who has walked 'through the valley of the shadow of death' and survived could write such a beautiful song as King David did in the twenty-third Psalm, beginning with the classic verse, "The LORD is my Shepherd, I shall not want." An intimate familiarity to death gives one an even greater appreciation for life. David had come so close to death many times at the hands of the enemies of the Lord, that his love for the Living God brought him to a place in the Bible where God called him 'a man after My own heart'. That heart, which so greatly pleased God, had been formed in the crucible of trials, tribulations and much persecution.

As I lay there on a narrow ledge above the awesome and terrible 'valley of the shadow of death' that I had just hiked through, I reflected on a number of things while awaiting the first rays of morning light. If the LORD who is my Shepherd leads me out of here by His grace and mercy, then you will be reading a story of my survival against the odds. If not then possibly the tragic tale told by someone else recounting how I had died before my time out of shear ignorance, pride and stubbornness.

My first revelation this night was that you can not break every rule of survival and expect to live to tell the tale, so if you are thinking of doing so, please take a moment to reflect on whether or not you are prepared to die prematurely. Soon, you too will be walking through a 'valley of the shadow of death' of ignorance, pride and stubbornness and may or may not come out on the other side alive and wiser as a result. By ignorance, I am here referring to the willful ignoring of known facts that are plainly put before you, not the more common usage of having insufficient knowledge in a certain area.

I should have heeded my own advice that I am so freely giving out here. Truly, I was acting ignorantly when I took off two days ago to hike into the wilderness between the Negev and Sinai Deserts without letting anyone know where I was going. I am not sharing my experience in order to glorify my flesh, but to serve as a warning to anyone who will listen that except for the Grace of God, we are all without hope in this life.

Boredom is a great enemy of the Holy Sprit and the cause of many a servant's downfall. I had over time become very restless with my life to say the least, especially now that my wife was away in the United States visiting our children and grandchildren for two months. Living in Eilat, the southernmost city in Israel on the tip of the Gulf of Aqaba was generally a wonderful experience, except when the temperatures reached the 100-110 degree Fahrenheit range. During the rest of the year, this resort city is crowded with tourists and Israeli's from the north who come to enjoy the beaches, snorkeling or scuba diving among the pristine coral reefs, hiking in the Eilat Mountains, and all of the other tourist attractions that have made this one of the most popular tourist havens in the Middle East. However, in the summertime, a majority of the local residents have enough sense to head north to escape the heat and the boredom of living in a nearly deserted city wedged between two vast deserts.

Hoping to walk the six hundred mile long Israel National Trail in the fall with my wife, Beverly, I knew that I needed to get into shape. Not a bad idea really; just the wrong time of year (July) and the wrong way to go about it. I had been sitting behind a computer screen for twelve hours a day over the past year developing a unique curriculum for teaching English to Hebrew speaking Israeli children and adults. Bev had already completed her contribution to the curriculum for the beginner and intermediate levels on her Mac computer, and I was hoping to complete the advanced course on my PC before she returned in August.

All that typing, translating, and graphics work as well as the highly stimulating mental activities associated with the planning and developing this 'English For Sure' curriculum over the past year, had been at the expense of my health. I was now at least twenty or more pounds overweight and out of breath walking up a couple of flights of stairs to our apartment. That is when I had decided to do something about it and planned a short two-day fifteen-mile hike roundtrip from Eilat to the Netafim Spring and back. The plan was to head north out of the city with a backpack, and two gallons of water, and to return by the way of Mt. Yoash, through Wadi Gishon (Gishon Valley) and up the steep Gishon Ascent at the end where I am now contemplating my fate, before hiking back into Eilat from the south. The trail was well marked as it is included within the last two sections of the Israel Nation Trail itself, which begins at the border of Lebanon in the north and ends up less than five miles south of my ledge, at the Egyptian border crossing at Taba.

The topography of my planned hike was unique to say the least. The Eilat Mountains are ruggedly spectacular and the view of the Red Sea and Sinai Desert from their ridges is beyond description. The course I took had me climbing steadily throughout the first day until my intended destination at Ein Netafim (Netafim Spring) where I had planned to camp for the night. The second day was supposed to be much easier, as it is mostly a downhill trek back to Eilat except for the Gishon Ascent at the end, which I had already climbed once in the past.

From the moment I set out, everything that could go wrong did go wrong, but that is no excuse, for with proper planning it would not have made any real difference. To begin with, I overslept and didn't get going until late in the morning, which is just about the time that the temperatures begin to soar after having dropped down by as much as forty degrees overnight. I had brought way too much equipment and clothing with me for a two-day excursion because I was trying to get used to the weight of the backpack in preparation for the upcoming Israel National Trail walk. I had put all my water bottles in the freezer the night before, and packed them in such a way in my backpack that they remained frozen and undrinkable throughout most of the first day. I did not bring a compass or one of the many Nature Reserves maps readily available as I was sure of my route and was familiar with the area. This bit of ignorance proved disastrous when later I needed to change course in an emergency. I did bring a useless cell phone, which never once worked due to lack of reception in the steep ravines and wadis that I had been hiking through. I did not bring enough food as I was trying to 'lose weight' therefore, I did not have enough energy for the strenuous part of the hike that had overcome me that afternoon. Finally, no one knew I was out here, because I had not let any of my friends know of my plans, fully aware that every one of them would have tried to talk me out of such a foolish idea.

The scriptures clearly warn us that 'pride comes before a fall' and that is what had gotten me here to the point of death. Knowing God's Word should have helped me avoid this 'adventure' altogether but I wasn't really paying attention to all the clear warnings that the Holy Spirit had been trying to give me. Even yesterday began with a 'hamseen', a vicious heat wave that comes in from the eastern Arabian deserts and can last for up to a week or more.

Having resided in Eilat for many years, I had done numerous hikes into the interior of the Negev in the past without incident. Besides this, I had been an officer in the Israeli Defense Forces in the army reserves since 1985 and considered myself well trained in survival techniques. In short, my pride led me to believe that I was nearly invincible. In over thirty years, I had never headed out alone so unprepared or under such extreme conditions, which made this hike for all intents and purposes a suicide mission... only I didn't know it at the time.

I nearly made it to Ein Netafim that first day before sunset, but because I had missed a trail marker for the Israel National Trail, I ended up on another trail that was several times more difficult. I had to climb all afternoon straight up through the steep dry river bed over dozens of ten to twenty foot embankments leading to each successive ledge. Had I taken the correct path I could have avoided that entire section by skirting it from the ridge above. Shortly before sunset, I had to admit defeat and set up my tent. Exhausted and nearly dehydrated, I ate dinner and fell fast asleep. Again, I overslept in this morning, and woke up to find that I had rolled over onto my glasses and had broken them. I knew that now I was going to have some difficulty seeing without them. Of course, I had never thought ahead to carry my spare pair with me.

By ten o'clock in the morning, I had finally reached Netafim Spring, which was now dark green and full of minerals, and is completely undrinkable, as it is just a trickle coming out from the rocks by this time of year. In retrospect, I could have filled my empty water bottles there to use the cold liquid to cool off with, and to boil and drink in an emergency situation like the one I was currently facing but I wasn't thinking too clearly as I have already mentioned. I had believed at the time that I was just a few hours from being back home, so after a half an hour's rest, I had set off for Wadi Gishon, which should be named 'the valley of the shadow of death' for in every respect it was such this day.

If I had known what was awaiting me, I surely would have hitchhiked back from the main road after I climbed out of the canyons at Ein Netafim. Ignorance is only bliss for someone who is safe and out of harm's way, neither of which I had going for me. With great fan fare that morning, I had descended hundreds of yards straight down into the Gishon Ravine, and into the bowels of hell. The jagged black rocky cliffs were so sun scorched that it was impossible to grab hold of them for more than a second or so, and they radiated a tremendous amount

of heat. I estimate that the air temperature in that dry riverbed at the bottom of that descent was over 130 degrees F. Although it was only a couple of hours walk to the Gishon Ascent that led back to Eilat, I had to stop every few minutes because of the unbearable heat and my exhausted condition. I finally reached the Gishon Ascent a couple of hours before sunset, completely out of water and food, and without an ounce of reserve energy in my body.

As I looked up at the 1500-foot ascent on that narrow serpentine trail, my heart nearly stopped. I knew I could not make it. I was having extreme difficulty even walking for more than a couple of minutes on level ground. I was in the final stages of dehydration, as my blood had already thickened to such a degree that my heart couldn't pump it easily, which was the reason that I had been tiring after just a few steps. I did not panic, for what was the use of that, but I realized that this night could well be the end of me, and I had walked right into it with my eyes wide open.

The trail zigzagged straight up in the eastern direction so there had been absolutely no shade to hide under. It would be weeks before anyone might be hiking this trail, or the army would be notified by someone to begin a search for me. In spite of it all, I was at peace, because I knew that even though I had clearly acted very ignorantly, when it was all said and done, God still loved me. I remembered that Jesus had clearly promised that He would 'never leave us or forsake us". Why He would want to be hiking with me out here in this 'valley of the shadow of death' was a mystery to me but I became very familiar with Psalm 23 that night.

I had left my backpack at the bottom of the trail with a note on it for whoever might possibly stumble across it on the trail. I wrote down my plight in general and intentions to try to make it to Eilat, which by direct hike was less than an hour away. When I wrote out my plan, by faith I had said that I would return for the backpack the next day. Normally a good twenty to thirty minute climb, I had only made it up about half-way before it started to get dark and I knew I would have to wait it out until the morning. In my weakened almost delirious condition, it was just too dangerous to try to walk that narrow trail in the dark, even if I had thought to bring a flashlight, which of course I had not.

I had found an area that seemed somewhat safe on a steep ledge, and now without a sleeping bag or anything else to lay on, I was trying to rest on the hard rocky surface and get as comfortable as possible by shifting by body around and away from as many sharp stones as was possible. It had been an awesome and dreadful night, not too cold, but actually quite a refreshing respite from the unbearable heat I had endured all day. I was still extremely thirsty and dehydrated, so I focused on conserving energy as best I could. It was a long night and I did not sleep but for maybe an hour altogether. I knew that I would need every bit of energy in a few hours to make one last ditch attempt to scramble out over this impregnable canyon wall, and onto the dirt road leading to the sea. My life depended on this last ditch effort, and it took God's divine intervention for me to make it.

When I was not dozing off, I prayed and thought about my wife, children and grandchildren. I was a bit sad that I had gotten myself into such a life or death situation, and didn't have a lot of faith that God was obligated in any way to help me get out of the mess that I clearly had put myself into.

Finally, at around 5:00 AM with the first faint glimmer of light making my surrounding somewhat visible, and still a good hour before sunrise, I headed straight up the canyon wall climbing on my hands and knees without even looking for the trail or the serpentine path. I was now using every muscle and last bit of reserves to get out. What exhilaration I experienced when twenty to thirty minutes later I was standing on the top and had a breathtakingly spectacular view of the sea, and the literal hell that I had just climbed out of. My cell phone still wasn't working, but that didn't matter because I felt that now on flat surface without any pack or any extra weight whatsoever I would be able to just keep walking one step at a time until an army patrol or someone spotted me.

I avoided the temptation to take a short cut across the foothills that led directly into Eilat, which was only about a third of the distance. For once, I correctly reasoned that to collapse out there would be sure death. I had to stay on the dirt road that led to the sea which was several miles further to the east but had the advantage of possibly a jeep or someone coming along. I was doing much better than I thought possible a few hours earlier and realized that God was definitely sparing my life for a purpose only known to Him.

An hour later, I saw a bus way up ahead in the distance, which I recognized was the type that were used to carry groups of people out into desert for day hikes. They are ruggedly built and are dependable for taking long distances excursions into the interior of the wilderness. I saw that all the passengers were off the bus and had begun to hike away from me to the south. I could not shout or even hardly whisper by this point as my tongue was stuck to the roof of my mouth. When I finally made it to where the bus was parked, I communicated my situation to the driver who had stayed behind with the group's supplies. He went to the back of the vehicle and got me one of their spare 2 liter bottles of water, which I drank without pause in less than a minute or two. In my whole life, that was the best drink I ever had, and one I will never forget.

Assuming that I was now safe, I thanked him and waved goodbye, as I continued walking east in the direction of the Gulf of Aqaba. I had to stop and wake up a sleeping guard at a desert camel tourist site a half-hour or so later and ask for a refill of my two liter empty water bottle. I was still too dehydrated to make it all the way home, and as a result nearly collapsed within sight of the finish line.

When I got to the sea, I waded in and floated in that refreshing salt water for more than a half hour, until my body temperature finally came down enough for me to continue walking. That early in the morning the water temperature was pleasantly cool, and I cannot remember enjoying a swim more. About nine o'clock, I finally walked back into Eilat and climbed the hill up to the apartment where I resided on the upper end of the city. Once inside, I slept quite soundly over the next twenty-four hours. The next day I rested and ate enough to get my strength back so that I could drive back to the Gishon Ascent and get my backpack that I had left there at the bottom. A day later and nearly fully recovered, it took me less than an hour to scramble down the path, throw the backpack over on my shoulders and re-climb the trail to the car.

Six weeks later, Bev and I began our eighty-six day hike across the length and breadth of Israel on the Israel National Trail. We never ran out of water once, although many times we were hiking in areas where we couldn't refill our water containers for three or four days at a time. The reason for our not running out was that I had learned my lesson, and on more than one occasion, we arrived at a designated resting place on the trail with a liter or more of water to spare. Whenever Bev would question my apparent fanaticism with carrying extra water when we were trying to get rid of every ounce of extra weight from our backpacks... I would smile knowing that she had not been there that long night on the ledge when I promised God and myself that if I lived, I would never again, by His Grace, act so foolishly.

"There is a way that seems right to a man, but its end is the way of death."
Proverbs 14:12

Chapter 39

As the Kinneret Wept

The Sea of Galilee is called the 'Kinneret' in Hebrew, which means 'violin', and she is called so because of her shape and resemblance to the only musical instrument capable of expressing such beautifully exquisite sorrow.

Jesus walked on the waters of the Kinneret, and fed and healed the multitudes near her shores. He taught the 'Sermon on the Mount' while gazing on her brilliance, and commanded her to be calm when her raging waves once threatened to drown his disciples as they crossed over in their fishing boat. From here, Jesus called Peter and Andrew and the sons of Zebedee, these unlearned men who toiled upon her for their livelihood, to leave their nets as He promised to make them fishers of men.

The waters of the Kinneret are fed by the 'dew of Hermon' that flow down from the region of Dan. The winter snows that cover the peaks of the northern mountains melt in the springtime, cascade over the falls of the Banyas at Caesarea Philippi, then form the Jordan River and flow southward for twenty miles before emptying into the Kinneret. As the only fresh water sea in the region, she is the source of life for the Galilee. The Kinneret is solely dependent on the LORD God to send the winter rains to replenish and refill her as she expends herself to quench the thirst of the nation of Israel throughout the rest of the year.

We had hiked for eleven days from the base of Mt. Hermon, and one afternoon in September I laid down beside the Kinneret and cried from the depths of my soul. I wept for many reasons, but mainly for how sad and how empty the sea looked that day, for she was nearly as destitute as I felt inside. I cried out to the God of heaven for deliverance and for sustenance for us both. I acknowledged that I was also completely dependent on the LORD for His blessings from above to replenish me, and that I was nearing at the limits of my human strength. I cried out for mercy and for compassion. As the violin shaped sea mourned with me in the background, God heard the sound of our voice that day and answered us.

I told the Lord so many things that I knew He was already aware of, and yet I needed for Him to hear them from my own lips. I shared my fears and my desperation. I told him that my wife and I had no home anywhere in Israel or anywhere else, and that we were walking across the length and breadth of Israel by faith without the finance to continue on for more than a few weeks more at the most. I confided in him that I was physically and spiritually exhausted, and that I had my doubts about being able to continue hiking much longer without a sign that He was definitely with us on this journey. And I wept for my people, my Jewish brothers and sisters who do not know that our Messiah had walked along these very shores to proclaim the 'good news' that the kingdom of God was at hand.

I felt better after crying out to the only One that I was sure would not chide me for such child-like behavior. It felt as though those tears were not only washing the hurt from my heart, but in some inexplicable way were spilling over onto the throne of grace as well. While lying under the stars that night on the shores of the Kinneret, I was filled with a sense that all would be well. We still had over five hundred miles to walk over the next ten weeks, through the Galilee, along the Mediterranean coast, up to Jerusalem and across the Negev desert, but I knew that we would no longer be walking alone, nor in our own strength.

Numerous miracles would happen over the next weeks and months, many that I can hardly believe now as I recall the emptiness I experienced that day. The LORD would send many precious people to help us, including at times His angelic ministering spirits. Furthermore, we were never without the comfort of the Holy Spirit as God rained upon us such goodness that I am ashamed of myself now for having doubted Him. At the end of November, when we reached the shore of the Red Sea on the Egyptian border, we knew that it was 'not by might, nor by power, but by His Spirit', that we had arrived safely and victoriously.

And yes, that winter the LORD again rained His blessings upon Mount Hermon and upon the region of the Galilee, and refilled that beautiful sea that the people of Israel so lovingly refer to as their 'violin', or Kinneret.

> *"By the way of the sea, beyond the Jordan, in Galilee of the Gentiles,*
> *The people who walked in darkness have seen a great light;*
> *Those who dwelt in the land of the shadow of death,*
> *upon them a light has shined."*
> Isaiah 9:1-2

Chapter 40
Walking in the Spirit

Greg and I had hiked over 400 kilometers, two hundred fifty miles, on the Israel National Trail. Five weeks ago, we started at the foothills of Mt. Hermon of the northernmost border of Israel. Today the climb from Shaar HaGai was intense and very serious, but we would be in Jerusalem this evening and looked forward to resting on Yom Kippur, the Jewish Day of Atonement.

We had taken many breaks all day crisscrossing paths with Hayim and Shlomo during our ascent. Hayim, an engineer, was taking three weeks vacation to hike part of the Israel National Trail. He and Shlomo were two longtime Israeli's friends and they were the first hikers that we had met on the trail our age. At one of our rest stops, we heard them reading and discussing the Psalms in Hebrew, which inspired us and lead us to engage in rich conversations that evening.

All day we had been hiking uphill from the base of the Judean foothills near Latrun, and we anticipated making it to at an ancient Roman pool called Ein Limor near the Arabic village of Ein Raffa that afternoon. Upon arrival around 4:00 PM, we found Shlomo and Hayim already cooling off in the pool just as a herd of sheep and goats arrived. For the next half an hour, we sat around waiting for a herd of sheep and goats to have their drink of spring water collected in the ancient pools while we again engaged in an intense conversation. This time we discussed the book of Isaiah together. Could Isaiah chapter 53 be talking about Yeshua being the Messiah?" We then jumped into the pool!

The hike to Kibbutz Tsuba from the spring was three km (two miles) straight up a very steep mountain road -- exhausting for the end of a long day. We got to the kibbutz as the sun was setting and called our Russian friend, Zalman, who lives in Ramot, a neighborhood of Jerusalem. He invited us to spend Yom Kippur with him and arranged to pick us up at 8:00 PM. In the meantime, we had dinner and a very interesting spiritual conversation with Hayim and Shlomo before saying goodbye to them. We would visit Hayim a month later hiking by his home. We were now very grateful to have a hot shower and sleep in a comfortable bed at Zalmon's.

We spent the next day repairing all our broken equipment: cookstove, flashlight, blow-up pillow, torn backpack, etc. Thanks to Zalman's help we got everything fixed and washed all our clothes and backpacks. After 400 kilometers of hiking, our bodies felt as though they needed a few days rest so we were planning to stay in Jerusalem until Sunday morning.

Erev (evening) Yom Kippur began with loud sirens ringing to announce the beginning of the fast. All traffic ceases and even the traffic lights are turned off. That evening, we enjoyed a walk around the Ramot neighborhood with Zalman observing the many small synagogues packed with worshippers. It was nice to be walking without the backpacks and fun to walk in the middle of the highways normally packed with vehicles. This is a unique holiday experience, which only occurs once a year in Israel when an entire nation quiets itself in reflection before the LORD.

October 13, 2005 was a day of fasting and prayer, Yom Kippur, the Day of Atonement. We took a hike around the city to "Pray for the Peace of Jerusalem." The Jewish fast also involves not drinking water so it was difficult for us in the hot sun and we returned at 1 P.M. and took a nap. We broke the fast in the evening with a light meal and for the first time in a month watched the news on CNN before retiring for the night.

Zalmon had expressed that his sons would be arriving for a few days starting the next day. I had been praying as to where we should go. We knew many people in Jerusalem but we wanted to stay in the will of the Holy Spirit, which meant hearing from the Lord. Our friend Bruce had given me several phone numbers of new contacts in Jerusalem and said to be sure to contact these people.

In the morning, I called John Nunley, and introduced myself over the phone as friends of Bruce. To my surprise, he was very hospitable and before knowing our circumstances, offered us a place to stay saying that he had extra rooms and that he would love to meet us. Zalmon immediately arranged to drive us to John's in Mevasseret Zion, a modern suburb of Jerusalem, just several miles away.

We arrived at John's around 10 A.M. From the first moment of our meeting out on the street, it was as if we had known him for a long time. John was very tall and thin with a white beard that made him look rather distinguished. Then John introduced himself to Zalmon. He said, " Shalom, I'm John Hulley. I'm glad to meet you." Could I have mistaken John Hulley for John Nunley? Were we at the wrong place? This was beyond embarrassment so I kept silent. I figured we would straighten it out after we got inside.

Once settled inside I asked John about his family in the states and how his new organization to sponsor Israeli businesses was going. I had learned this from Bruce, who had previously given me some literature of John Nunley's to read. John said, "Well, I don't know much about that but you're welcome to read the book I've just finished and I'm lonely. I miss my little girl who is living England with her mother."

I had unknowingly contacted John Hulley, a biblical scholar and author of the book "What's the Messiah Waiting For?" Not another word was said about his identity until I went to bed that night and asked Greg how such a mistake could have happened. He said, "I don't know but His ways are above our ways."

John's home is only a few kilometers from the Israel National Trail, which we planned to return to on Sunday morning. Greg and I became engrossed in reading John's book. He loaned us his car to drive to the supermarket and to the vegetable market in the nearby Turkish town of Abu Gush. I enjoyed having a spacious kitchen to prepare the Erev Shabbat fish dinner for John and his three guests from Holland. We had a wonderful time-sharing our experiences with our new friends. One of the Dutch guests, Vincent, an Israeli tour guide, would be meeting us several times over the next few days on the trail and driving us back to John's during a rain storm. He longed to hike the trail with us but do to a life-threatening illness was unable to, so he offered to drive our backpacks to us at the end of each of the next few days of hiking, and then drive back and pick them back up in the morning.

After the meal, Greg got a surprise cake in honor of his 52nd birthday. We would later, after completing the trail, come back to live with John for three months. His home would become one of our "homes away from home," and John Hulley, would become one of our dearest and closest friends.

"If we live in the Spirit, let us also walk in the Spirit."
Galatians 5:25

Chapter 41

Field of Garlic

Up at dawn and hiking by 5:45 AM! We decided to head southeast across the fields for a couple of miles in order to take a short cut and catch back up with the trail. We had taken a side path the evening before in order to find a secure settlement to spend the night on, as we were now close to the West Bank and it was not safe to put up our tent and camp just anywhere. We had now hiked over three hundred thirty miles, half-way from Lebanon to Egypt on the Israel National Trail, which began in the north at the base of Mount Hermon and ended at the Taba border crossing in the south, at the edge of the Sinai desert.

We carried everything on our backs: clothing, camping gear, trail maps, cooking utensils, food for up to five days at a time, and most importantly, nearly a gallon of water each. We had started out on September 5th with a lot more things of course, but had quickly wised-up and gotten our backpacks down to a reasonable forty-five to sixty pounds respectively. Having left Jerusalem a few days earlier, we were now at the southern end of the Judean Hills where David had fought Goliath in the Valley of Elah. Heading south, we turned inland for few miles onto the eastern edge of the coastal plain and into the ancient territory of the Philistines. In a few days, we would be crossing into the barren Negev wilderness, Israel's southern desert that takes up over fifty percent of its geographical area. This month of hiking coming up ahead represented the greatest challenge that either of us had ever faced.

We had dreamed of hiking the length and breadth of the land of Israel since the day we arrived thirty years earlier. However, the Israel National Trail (I.N.T.) did not exist until just a few years earlier. The Nature Reserve Authority had connected forty-four of the most beautiful and scenic trails together into one trail, and had marked them with orange-blue-white stripped markers on rocks every mile or so. Since there were a great many other trails that crisscrossed the I.N.T., we had to make sure every fifteen minutes or so that we were going in the right direction and had not strayed off our trail. The most common question that we asked each other a couple of times an hour for eighty-six days was, "Have you seen a trail marker lately?" A negative reply meant only one thing, we would have to turn around and go back to find the last marker that we knew we had seen for sure. From experience, we had learned the hard way that going forward in hope of finding the trail was the surest way to get turned around and completely lost.

Bev had not been feeling well for a couple of days now, and both of us felt like we might be coming down with the flu or a cold, which greatly concerned us. We had been helping each other to make it this far. In the beginning, we could not hike for a half hour without having to take another half hour's rest, and had only averaged six to eight miles a day. Now we were hiking for an hour or two at a time, and were taking only ten to fifteen minute breaks, while averaging twelve and sometimes fifteen miles a day. Occasionally we had to help each other up and down a steep hill or cliff, or across a narrow ridge. I always lifted Bev's backpack up and down from her back when we stopped to rest, and often we rubbed each other's feet, sore legs and back muscles at night in our small tent before falling to sleep. We had grown so close by this time that whenever we heard the other begin to sing, we would immediately join in knowing that it was better to sing than to complain about the weight of the backpacks, throbbing muscles, sore feat, the blazing heat, the rocky terrain, pesky flies or whatever else would be trying to steal our joy on this marathon walk of faith.

For the most part, we were living a dream and were having the time of our lives. Daily, we would see the hand of God's provision in so many little ways, and we had met some of the nicest people you would ever find anywhere in the world over the past seven weeks. We stopped and prayed over every village, settlement, town, city and army base we came across. One of the special things about this trail was that it took the high ground or scenic route at every possible opportunity, so we were able to pray over all of the ancient 'high places' and the vast areas that could be viewed from such heights. God had commanded Abram in Genesis 13:17 to "Rise up and walk through the land, in the length of it and in the breadth of it, for I will give it to you." We too felt that we were to 'spiritually' possess every place we walked.

Occasionally, we would have to take a short detour off the trail to buy food in one of the nearby towns or cities, as the I.N.T. avoided most of the populated areas of the country. Sometimes, our supplies would run down so low that we would have to dig deep down and scrounge for whatever was left in the bottom of our packs. When we occasionally came across a major supermarket, we would restock our backpacks with essentials, and load up on some extras. Fresh fruits and vegetables would last us only a couple of days, so we had to make do most of the time with canned or dried foods like tuna fish, bread and our own recipe of 'trail mix', which included raisins, nuts, granola, and chocolate chips.

The strain of the hike was beginning to take a toll on our bodies; we had lost at least ten or fifteen pounds each of body weight, and had begun to weaken. Instinctively we knew that we would have to do something to boost our immune systems. With this in mind, we attempted to buy garlic at the small store on the agricultural settlement where we had stopped two days before, but could not find any. Bev had been so worn out that she felt that she just couldn't go on after we rested that afternoon, so we had stopped earlier than usual and set up camp in the middle of Moshav Achuzam.

The next morning, I spontaneously prayed to God quite specifically that we would find a 'field of garlic' during the next twenty-four hours. I do not know why I prayed such a prayer because we had never come across any garlic fields in nearly two months of hiking, and I am not sure I even knew what to look for. The next day, now coming close to the '24 hour' deadline, I had forgotten about the prayer altogether. We were crossing a freshly ploughed field, and the clumps of dirt were so large that the hiking was difficult and quite tiring. Just as we emerged at the far end of a red paprika field, there on the ground were hundreds of cloves of fresh garlic that had surfaced after the rains the previous week had flooded the area and washed them down to where we were walking.

We could hardly believe our eyes. There, all around us were these beautiful cloves of garlic lying there on the ground. Like two kids in a candy store with a twenty-dollar bill, we began take as much as we wanted. We filled one of the pouches in our backpacks, and now had enough garlic to knockout all our cold symptoms, and last us a month!

As we headed into 'Yatir Forest', the second largest forest in Israel, we knew that God was not only watching over us, but listening to our prayers and songs of praise as well. We continued to hike for another thirty-six days, through the forest, desert and wilderness, and never experienced another day of illness... Moreover, come to think of it, we never came across another field of garlic either.

"And all things, whatever you shall ask in prayer, believing, you shall receive."
Matthew 21:22

Chapter 42
$1.85 a Brick

I am a firm believer that "all things work together for good for those who love God and are called according to His purposes." This promise has kept me going despite all odds when I could not make heads or tails out of the circumstances and events in my life, or was clueless as to where they were leading me... And so I found it to be quite ironic that after receiving a masters degree in economics at our state university, I was back there three years later working as a masonry foreman on the university's President's House, just a few hundred yards from where I had studied for four years. As I worked out there in the hot sun that summer, I could only imagine what my professors would think if they could see me now!

I can honestly say that I had little choice in the matter, for God had clearly opened this door in order to prepare me for our upcoming trip to direct a bible college in Kitale, Kenya. Our eldest son, Isaac, and his family were there at the time but needed to come home for six months so that his wife, Clea, could give birth to their fourth child. We were led to replace them after Isaac prayed and felt that he had heard from God to ask us if we would be willing. However, there was one small stipulation, and that was that we would buy our own tickets because no church or other Christian organization would be supporting us.

Now short-term jobs for economists are hard to come by, so we knew we would need God's provision to get thousands of dollars together within a few months. About that time my second son, Isaiah, asked if I would help him with a new branch of his construction business. He had been losing a lot of money over the past several months in the masonry part of his business, although the drywall division was going great. For some unexplainable reason the masons he employed managed to lose him money every week without fail.

I didn't know a single thing about masonry but I agreed mostly because my son needed my help and also because there just weren't any other offers coming my way. Isaiah had just finished the drywall job on the President's House and had done the job so efficiently that it had been completed ahead of schedule and under the bid price.

Well, in the construction business, this is highly unusual, so he was somewhat of a celebrity on the jobsite.

It so happened that the project superintendent was a devout Christian man, named Bill. He was looking to hire a new masonry company to supervise the completion of a huge job that no other company in the area wanted to touch. It involved laying around fourteen-thousand old style tumbled bricks called pavers, on the ground floor of the four story mansion and another ten-thousand or so on the walkways and other areas around the building in a special herringbone pattern. Bill had a number of years experience in the construction business and adamantly stated that masons are by far the most hardheaded of all the tradesmen that he has ever had to deal with. He attributed this to the fact that they breathe in brick dust all day, and because of their general habit of drinking up all their earnings. Bill's advice to Isaiah was to get out of the masonry business as quickly as possible.

Isaiah respected Bill very much and thought that maybe we should not bid on the job afterall. However, Since we already had all the blue-prints for the President's House, I suggested, "Why don't we throw out an outrageous bid and see what happens? If we don't get it, we're no worse off; and if we do – at least you won't lose any money on this job." The advice seemed good to Isaiah; so we calculated what it would take to hire a crew to get the job done, pay workman's compensation and all the other taxes. We correctly assumed that there would be a lot of other unknown expenditures, and we knew we would have to make it worthwhile financially for us to take the risks of accepting this job. We settled on what we thought was the maximum we could ask for without being thrown out of Bill's office – and decided upon $1.85 a brick, which was about three to four times the going local price for regular masonry jobs.

Well, it had to be the LORD that our bid was accepted and that we got the job, because Bill instantly knew after questioning me that I had no experience or any idea what I was doing. Furthermore, he had never paid that high a price per brick before. Deep down inside, I knew God was going to help us in this project, and I was counting on the fact that Bill was a Christian brother and man of prayer.

Nearly all the office buildings in our city are made of red brick and could probably withstand a pretty good size hurricane, the likes of which threaten that area nearly every year. Although there were more masons in our area than you could count, getting a dependable crew together for this job required a lot more prayer and faith that I had anticipated. The deep south in the summertime is one of the hottest and most humid places you'd ever **not** want to be, which was exactly the time of year that we were scheduled to be doing the majority of the outdoor masonry work. We checked around and it seemed that nobody wanted to take the job because, unlike building walls and columns, laying pavers involved working on your knees all day, which is excruciatingly painful even for young apprentices.

About that time a young man, named Josh called us desperate for work. He had years of experience as a masonry apprentice and had just formed his own company. He had a lot of connections and knew most of the masons in several counties around us, so with no other choice, we hired him.

If ever I've seen a motley crew of blue collar working men, our gang was it. I had to learn the 'masonry mentality' and their jargon in quick order to supervise the job efficiently. There were three categories of workers: masons, apprentices, and laborers. Each had his unique role and contribution and each had to be dealt with in an entirely different manner.

Josh wasn't as skilled a mason as most those he hired to work under him, which was alright as long as he remained humble, but became a problem when he tried to assert his authority. He was a young man prone to many vices and thus on more than one occasion couldn't pull himself up out of bed in the morning to come to work, which was a real shame because he set a poor example for the others. I found myself calling him every morning to make sure he was really on his way in to the job site. The problem wasn't his lack of education, because he was intelligent, he just didn't have his focus on his company, his reputation, or his future.

My priority then became to make sure that Josh stayed motivated and focused on the job at hand. At times that meant prayer or just an encouraging word, and at other times it required threats of firing him, throwing him off the job-site, etc. Still in the end, with much prodding and a lot of daily encouragement, Josh did come through and we finished the project together. He told me when we first met that he was a 'backslid' Baptist, so I did my best to love Josh so that he might find his way back to the Lord's amazing grace.

Then there was J.T., a tall, young lanky guy that was never happy with his hourly wage. As a matter a fact, I'm convinced that this was what he had been taught the first day of his apprenticeship – never act like your happy with your pay. J.T. worked hard, when he would get up for work that is, which was not very likely after a weekend of carrousing. He did work harder than the others, but complained louder than anyone else. He was fast but that meant he was also quick to make mistakes as well, and the majority of the bricks we had to pull up and lay a second time belonged to him. By the end of the job we became close, and I can honestly say that admired his fiery spirit.

Then there was Blake who was one of the strongest men on the crew but utterly without any ambition in life. I always felt that he was smarter than most of the others, and could have been whatever he wanted to be in life, but just didn't have an ounce of personal drive. He was heavy-set and a workhorse of a laborer, that is when he was working. He was teamed up with J.T., which meant that he provided transportation for J.T. to the jobsite in the morning. It turned out that when Blake didn't feel like working, we were more often than not two men short as a result.

Now we depended on laborers more than masons most of the time because there is a real hierarchy in the masonry system, which I guess dates back to when bricks were first made thousands of years ago. Masons lay bricks – that's it... they don't pick them up and move them, they don't mix the mortar or cement, they don't clean up and they don't take any talking back from laborers. As a result, without laborers absolutely nothing gets done and that is the weak link in the whole system. Its one thing to lay bricks in stifling hundred degree temperatures for thousand dollars a week, but it's quite another story to be doing twice the work, and be yelled at all day while taking home only half the money that a mason does. Resentment and bitterness ran high on most paydays between the two groups of men. On more than one occasion I had to give out bonuses, especially on weekends, to keep the men motivated.

Everyone was entitled to two fifteen minute breaks per day and a half hour for lunch, but when a laborer is 'give out' he just sits down like he's dying, with full knowledge that he is the vital link in the chain of progress. Of course cursing and yelling at him by other masons is likely to ensue, so most laborers have a way of forgetting to tell anyone when they are running out of cement, sand, water, or even fuel for the cement mixer... in that way they get to take a break while someone (usually me) has to run and get the missing materials.

In order to keep the job going smoothly I had to keep an eye out at all times for every conceivable thing that would grind the brick laying process to a halt. I found out the hard way that laborers were under no circumstance being paid to think or plan ahead.

Apprentices are somewhere in the middle, and are just a heartbeat away from being masons, depending on who has taken them under his wings so to speak. They are paid somewhere in the middle between masons and laborers so they are expected to do everything everyone tells them to do… that is until they become masons, at which point they just lay bricks and do nothing else.

I had thought that the Civil Rights movement in the 60's had brought down the racial barriers in American society, but masons live in a stratum of society that hasn't fully come to grips with that reality. It was great having Dixon on board, as he was a layed back African- American and a fine Christian brother. Our foreman hired Dixon on a whim, because we were extremely short-handed and couldn't really count on anybody coming to work from day to day. Dixon had driven a friend to the job site one morning and was asked if he wanted to work as well. Clearly the LORD had sent him or we would never have completed the job or any of the other side jobs that we were contracted to do over the next few months. Mason Dixon, as his friends lovingly called him, ran a tight crew of black apprentices and laborers and did everything he could to get along with our white redneck crew. He put himself under our foreman's authority but that didn't mean that there wasn't strife between the two groups of men daily, especially if I wasn't around to smooth things out. This would prove to be an invaluable lesson for me in preparation for coming to Africa.

Dixon was a great guy who loved the Lord and loved to fish. He had retired and was living well from the income he received on various rental properties that he had invested in. He clearly didn't need to work anymore, so I guess he really came in day in and day out just in order to help me. Over the next few months we became close friends. We prayed together often, especially for the unsaved men, and I always tried to get him to see what the Lord was saying through all our trials and daily struggles. He mentioned on one occasion that since he had retired, his wife and her mother were worrying him to death at home. In order to regain his freedom and get out of the house, I figure that he came to work for us but went fishing at every available opportunity.

I wouldn't say that the President's House was a job that always went smoothly. Sometimes we had to spend hours of back-breaking work tearing up hundreds of bricks that were laid unevenly or in the wrong pattern. In the end, I believe we really did earn the exorbitant price of $1.85 a brick that we were paid. I worked beside these rugged men, prayed for them and kept them on track until we completed the entire project. Miraculously, we laid the last brick and collected our final check the day before my wife and I left for Kenya.

> *"You also, as living stones, are being built up a spiritual house, a holy priesthood, to offer up spiritual sacrifices acceptable to God through Jesus Christ."*
> 1 Peter 2:5

Chapter 43

Best Friends

We headed out on foot with the ominous Mt. Elgon glowing before us from the earliest rays of equatorial sunlight. I was with Joshua and Fred. We would be going hut-to-hut walking on footpaths, the only accessible way into this tropical area down by the river, to share the love of Jesus with these isolated people and invite them to an afternoon crusade in Joshua's yard.

Joshua, a stocky young Kenyan, the pride of his father, was aspiring to take over the family farm and doing a handsome job of it. He had expressed his concern for the people he had met while farming the fields down by the river. There were several large families running breweries along the river and it was having a detrimental effect on the whole neighborhood.

I was with a team of sixteen bible students on this remote outreach. We were broken up into teams of three and would meet up again on Joshua's farm at 2:00 P.M. for lunch, ugali and sukuma – I have still not learned to enjoy ugali, ground corn mush that is cooked with kale. At 3:00 P.M., we would begin our crusade. It is amazing how densely populated this tropical area is down by the river. Most of the children do not own a pair of shoes and have never seen a "Mazungus" before. I am a Mazungu, a white person. They call me "Madam Mazungu."

Joshua requested that Fred and I follow him to the area down by the river. Our team had been very efficient in going to over 11 huts and had met with several groups of field workers. We had listened to their needs, prayed with them, given out tracts, clothed some of their children and were thinking of heading back when Edna, who had somehow become our jungle guide, insisted on continuing on to one more friend's hut.

Joshua told us it was common to encounter drunkards in these woods down by the river where the illegal breweries were everywhere. So it was with Edna, her breath announced her state of intoxication but her soft eyes and big toothless smile urged us on to follow her big dancing feet as she led us deeper into the jungle. She was insistent that we continue to follow her just a bit more to her best friends hut. She told Fred she knew we were sent to help her friend who was in desperate need. On first glance into the small dwelling, I saw a lady lying on her side. She was wearing badly torn rags and she grabbed at them to try to cover her half-naked body. I backed away and learned from Edna that her friend could not walk and Edna expected me to do something about it.

Pricsea requested Edna's help to reach the adjacent hut where Edna had seated us on doily-covered stumps. After much struggle, Edna managed to seat Pricsea next to me. Her leg seemed stiff at the knee so she dragged it. My team, Fred and Joshua, did the usual introductions in Swahili. I just reached over and began praying for Pricsea. She explained to me thru Fred's interpretation that her knee felt very hot. I learned that this middle-aged lady had been lying around for three years unable to walk. After praying, Joshua told her we would continue to pray for her at the crusade in the afternoon. Pricsea asked if she could attend. I was much challenged at the thought of carrying this more than 160 lb. lady over a kilometer to the Crusade. After some fuss with Edna, we were asked to please come back and get her in half an hour. Edna would help her wash and get dressed.

I did not know quite what we would do and envisioned us struggling to carry her the distance through the jungle. I asked the Lord to honor this ladies faith. We went on to another neighbor's hut along the path while waiting for Edna and Pricsea before returning.

To everyone's amazement upon our return, Pricsea came hobbling out of her yard wearing a clean dress holding onto Edna's unsteady arm. Edna, still too intoxicated to support her, gladly allowed me to replace her and we began the determined walk across the hilly path. We continued to witness to many now following us, as reports were spreading that Pricsea was walking to the crusade – children ran ahead to tell others. At one point, she remarked to me that she had not passed this point since the year 2004. While slowly pacing along, I glanced up into the beautiful blue sky and marveled at the faith of this woman and at the power of a simple prayer for healing in Jesus

Name. I knew to stay focused and continue to praise the Lord for His help.

More than three hundred people showed up for the crusade. The students preached the Word with zeal and ministered through skits and puppets to everyone's delight. There were many testimonies and quite a number were saved and received healings. One very happy lady thanked God for giving her a life back by healing her leg. Edna, now quite sobered up, asked the Lord for deliverance. As often as I reflect on the big smiles of these two best friends I thank the Lord for healing Pricsea, delivering Edna, and strengthening my faith.

> *"Then they cried out to the Lord in their trouble,*
> *And He saved them out of their distresses.*
> *He sent His word and healed them*
> *and delivered them from their destructions."*
> Psalm 107: 19,20

Chapter 44

Empathizing with Bill Gates

"Hey you, mazungus (white persons), give me money," the child yelled from across the road. Now, we have been approached by many different beggars, con-artists, and charlatans asking for handouts here in Kitale, Kenya over the last four months, but this rather unique, straight forward approach to asking was so honest that it made us both laugh. The little girl didn't bother with the usual stories of hunger, father or mother in the hospital, or needs for medicine or school fees – just a plain desire for a taste of a better life that only money or the lack of it stood in her way of getting. In a nutshell, we as 'Mazungus' here in East Africa represented unimaginable wealth to nearly every person we met.

It is normally not a laughing matter because the situation for many is dire indeed, and it is so over-whelming at times that we cannot go to town or think about it without beginning to feel depressed. Five and six year old children carrying heavy water containers filled with polluted water from a filthy stream, young boys with glue bottles tied to their faces like demonic respirators, begging for a few shillings to get a refill, and countless other stories I could relate here would only cause you to want to stop reading this story... so I'll move on to the point.

My wife and I live by faith and have very little materially in this world. No savings account, investments, retirement funds, properties or even a home of our own, yet we are rich in faith and quite wealthy in comparison with most people in the 'developing countries'. We have been trusting the LORD our Provider for as long as we can remember and have been miraculously blessed daily. As He has been our Shepherd, we have experienced no want, and have learned like the Apostle Paul to be content in whatever state we are found, whether blessed with abundance or in a position with little. However, this type of walk is not for everyone. It is too filled with the unknown, with the unexpected, and with a certain utter abandonment to God that is just not realistic in any sense of the word. It requires a level of trust in our Heavenly Father that is difficult in the modern socio-economic climate of our world. I am not here trying to bring anyone under condemnation because according to scripture, there simply is none in Christ.

The LORD once told Elijah, "Go at once to Zarephath of Sidon and stay there. I have commanded a widow in that place to supply you with food." I think that this is a rather amusing story, because the widow that God had commanded to supply Elijah with food was gathering sticks in order to make her last meal for her son and herself before succumbing to starvation and death, when the prophet found her. Instead of empathizing with her predicament, he demanded that she first make him 'a small cake of bread' from her last bit of flour and little bit of oil that she still had to her name. The rest of the story is so remarkable that we might dismiss it, as some sort of made up fairy-tale if it was not the Word of God. For Elijah then promised her that the 'jar of flour would not be used up and that the jug of oil would not run dry' until it rained again, which by the way he had already told King Ahab would not happen except by his word. Her obedience not only saved her and her son, but also provided for Elijah as well until the time for his confrontation with the prophets of Baal on Mount Carmel.

Now the Holy Spirit specifically singles out Elijah, and states in the book of James, 'that he was a man just like us'. So then, there you have it. We are all capable of being fed by a widow woman on the verge of starvation, or for that matter feeding the multitudes with a few loaves and fishes, if we just had the faith as small as a grain of mustard seed. I don't have it and I don't think I've ever met anyone who has that sort of faith, but at least I know it's in the realm of the possible.

Here in Kenya I get a feeling of what Bill Gates, the richest man on earth, must often experience. He has the power to alleviate the suffering of countless multitudes with just the daily interest he receives on his wealth. Even with my limited resources, I too have the power to temporarily alleviate the suffering of those around me here in Kitale howbeit on a much smaller scale, but I do not. We are not 'gods', and none of us are wise enough to know which widow to help out and which ones to ignore, unless the LORD directs us. For Jesus himself said that there were many widows in Israel at the time that God sent Elijah to Sidon, in the country of Lebanon. It's clear that God knew that the widows in the Israel didn't have the faith to obey the 'word of the LORD' and be saved.

I no longer envy the rich, or would want to be like Bill Gates for that matter. On the contrary, I empathize with their daily dilemma and utter sense of helplessness. For Jesus plainly said that those who trust in their riches (and which of us in western society doesn't) will find it indeed difficult to walk the narrow path that leads to everlasting life. He didn't say it would be impossible, just difficult. He went on to say, "What is impossible for man, is possible with God."

Truly His strength is made perfect in weakness, therefore I have come to the conclusion that each of us must only humbly ask for wisdom from above and we are told that we will receive it. Then and only then, will we be able to know whom to give to and to whom to withhold from, so that each may be blessed by our Heavenly Father. Moreover, maybe the giving must begin with those who can afford it the least, like the widow in Zarephath, or my African brothers and sisters in Kenya.

"One man gives freely, yet gains even more; another withholds unduly, but comes to poverty."
Proverbs 11:24

Chapter 45
Raise The Dead!

Ahead, on the paved road, an accident had just occurred. The matatoo (taxi van) doors were flung open and passengers were scurrying over to a limp body lying on the road. I pulled over and began to pray while sitting in my vehicle, "Lord, I do not know why you have brought this to my attention, so please, show me how to pray?" A crowd was quickly gathering but I could still make out men pumping unsympathetically on the chest of the limp body.

While still in prayer, I confidently commanded what I sensed was an angel of death to flee. I then prayed away panic and fear. As I looked on from the car five or six men picked up the lifeless body and tossed it into the overgrown weeds on the side of the road. It was then that I boldly jumped out of the car, instructing Helen, the lady with me, to stay put and remain in prayer with me.

Kneeling down, I immediately checked for pulse in this young mans arm. There was none. I stopped the crowd of men from pounding on his chest and told the dozen or so women standing around screaming and crying hysterically that all fear must leave. They hushed immediately placing their hands over their mouths.

For a considerable time I knelt in the weeds holding onto the unresponsive hand as I sought Jesus to give this boy his life; then, his eyes began rolling in his head. There was a sudden stillness from the on-looking crowd and I could see others were beginning to pray when this boy opened his eyes and looked at me. I began to tell him repeatedly that Jesus loved him. He still had no movement in his body. I cried to Jesus more desperately recalling that I had seen blood on the road as I had stepped over glass from the vehicle headlights that had struck him. Aware that many bad things could have happened to his body, faith welled up in my heart like a torch and I believed God at that moment to make this boy whole.

Several men crowded in to lift him and take him to my car. The young man held onto my arm so tight and whispered to me, "please do not leave me." I pleaded with the crowd not to move his body and just give us time. The young man's eyes never left mine. After five minutes of calling the name of the Lord over him, he said to me, "Jesus is with me" and he stood straight up on his own. I was shocked. The women began screaming wildly, "It is a miracle!"

Several men sought to help him walk but he needed no assistance. They grabbed his shoes that had been thrown out into the road.

I requested of the driver of the matatoo that hit him to please accompany us to the hospital. He seemed stunned but agreed and off we went. On the drive, I explained to this young man named Isaac that God had a very special plan to use the rest of his life for His service. "It is no accident that you are alive right now," I said, "Jesus loves you so much and He wants you to know that you belong to Him. He wants to use you in a powerful way to tell of His great love." Isaac answered, "Yes, I believe so." He asked of me to continue talking to him. Once at the emergency room of the hospital, we located the doctor. I carefully explained that this man was found unconscious, lying in the road after being thrust thirty feet by a matatoo. The doctor's attention turned to Isaac who was sitting upright on the table. It was at that moment that I swiftly disappeared.

My eldest son's words kept had been playing heavy on my mind. Before he and his family had departed for the U.S., leaving my husband and I alone in this new environment, he had clearly explained to me not to get involved in accidents on the highways. He had said that when someone hits you or you hit someone it will always be the "mazungu" (white person) who becomes responsible, even if in most circumstances, the mazungu is innocent, he must still take complete financial responsibility. Hospital bills, insurance bills, doctor bills, auto repair bills, etc. My son was very thorough in getting his point across. He warned me to stay away from such situations, even if it meant fleeing an accident and going straight to the police station. His words rang clear, "Get away and quickly." What had I just done?

This incident has sparked faith in my heart to believe God to continue to move mightily in Kenya, knowing that all He requires is that we be available and obedient to the leading of the Holy Spirit. I will always pray for this young man, Isaac, that his restored life will give God glory.

"Heal the sick, cleanse the lepers, raise the dead, cast out demons. Freely you have received, freely give."
Matthew 10:8

Chapter 46
Love Thy Neighbor

"Who sent you?", my wife asked the lady standing outside our locked front gate. The young Kenyan woman, standing there with a baby in her arms and a little girl cowering beside her, surprised us by answering, "Jesus". Well, we were not buying that line, so my wife asked her a second time, "No, who really sent you? Who told you to come to our front gate?" This time, the woman, on the verge of tears said, "Jesus Christ sent me!"

The question we were asking her was a valid one, for out of desperation she had initially lied to the gardener by telling him that the madame of the house had told her to come that morning. We were house-sitting during our half-year in Kenya in a rather exclusive neighborhood called 'Millamani', which lies just outside of the impoverished town of Kitale. As we were about the only 'mazungus' (white people) left in the area because of the rampant violence that had spread throughout Kenya after the impasse in the national elections, we were keenly aware that nearly every Kenyan looked to us for deliverance from their desperate and tragic circumstances.

Now, after the second time that Penina answered that Jesus Christ had sent her, a deep conviction from the Holy Spirit came over us, and with the 'fear of the LORD' in our hearts, my wife softened her tone and asked her, "Well, what do you need?" She said that her daughter needed medication and that she couldn't afford the prescription that the doctor had written for her, which amounted to three-hundred Kenyan shillings (a little over four dollars). We were still a bit skeptical because this ploy was used by the Kenyans seeking money from the 'rich' mazungus, so we continued to interrogate her through the small opening in our locked front gate.

We generally consider ourselves to be 'good Christians' who love God and try to do what we can to help our fellow man, but we were just overwhelmed by the flood of requests we were daily receiving. After awhile, we finally decided to unlock the front gate and at least pray with this woman and her children. Her little barefoot daughter, Esther, had a badly infected swollen knee and could barely walk. This little three year old had been chased by a neighborhood dog a couple of weeks earlier, and had fallen onto a sharp stick. Her knee was not healing as a result of her poor health and lack of proper nutrition. The situation was indeed desperate, and so we lifted up our voices to God and prayed with Penina for her daughter, Esther.

The Holy Spirit witnessed to our hearts that Jesus Christ truly had indeed sent these precious ones to our gate, and we repented for our callousness and unbelief. Penina asked us to forgive her for having initially lied about my wife telling her to come to our gate, and we ourselves admitted to her that we too are only sinners saved by God's grace. After praying outside our gate, we arranged to drive her to a 'tent meeting' in town later that day, and then we went back into the beautiful home that we were living in, while Penina walked away with her two children in tow.

It was ironic that it turned out that Penina was actually one of our neighbors living only a hundred yards from us. In a field across the road, in a one room mud house that measured only fourteen feet by eight feet, covered with a corregated tin roof, Penina waited for us for three hours before we took her and the children to town. Her family was living in a house without running water or electricity, and which did not even have a window, toilet or bathroom. As a result of their extreme poverty, living conditions and other pressures, Penina and her husband, Michael, were also experiencing marital problems that were driving them toward separation or divorce.

Later that day, we did get the antibiotics for Esther, and she has since fully recovered. Over the next week Penina and her children received more help from a local Kenyan pastor and his wife. Through love, compassion and prayer, she was transformed and gave her life to Jesus the following Sunday. A few days later, after counseling together with Penina and her husband, Michael, their shatttered marriage was restored, and Michael broke down and recommitted his life to Jesus. Soon after that, our 'born again' neighbors were baptized at the 'Bread of Life' feeding station, which borders the Kipsongo slum.

None of us know what is in store for us in this life, but we are thankful that the 'God of the Miraculous' opened our hearts by sending Penina to our front gate that day. Our prayer is that the LORD will continually remind us and help us to keep His commandment to 'love our neighbor' as ourselves.

And the second, like it, is this: "You shall love your neighbor as yourself.' There is no other commandment greater than these."
(Mark 12:29-31)

Chapter 47

Grandpa's Yortzite

Morris Shaeffer had an easy birthday to remember since he was born on April Fools day in 1901. However, the date of his death is somewhat more indefinite. I was living in Israel when he passed away, so I think it was on or around October 14th, seventy-nine years later.

He was a very kind and distinguished gentleman who so wanted to be remembered after his death that he had asked me a few years before he died if I would annually keep 'yortzite' for him. The 'yortzite' is a Jewish custom that involves not only the lighting of a special ceremonial candle at home or in the synagogue, but is also accompanied by the reading of traditional prayers in Hebrew. Of course it also involves the remembering and honoring the memory of the dead on the date of that person's passing, which is kept in accordance to the Jewish, lunar based, calendar. Thus, every year the date changes by as much as three weeks when referenced by the Gregorian solar calendar that the majority of the gentile world uses to keep track of dates and events.

Morris Shaeffer

At the time of his request I was just a young man and I couldn't imagine my grandfather not being with me, so due to the petulance of my youth I politely declined, letting him know that I would not keep 'yortzite' for him. I know this made him extremely sad, as I was probably the only one he thought he could count on to pay those last respects and keep his remembrance alive. At that stage in my busy life I just didn't see what the point was in honoring the dead.

Here, I will give only the briefest biographical sketch of his life, because I'm sad to say that I just don't know more of the details so I can't really 'remember' them anyway. From what he told me and from what I've gathered from my mother, Morris was a self-made man who had worked and studied hard and had risen to a very high position in the May Company department store chain. During the Great Depression in the 30's, when my mother was born, he had hardly been affected by the poverty that encompassed the entire nation as he had obtained to a certain state of wealth and prosperity that was independent of the stock market. As a result, my mother grew up in surroundings that in some ways resembled that of royalty.

I've previous mentioned that my grandfather was a self-made man, and that is evident in that he had not inherited wealth from his parents. After graduating from the University of Pennsylvania's College of Business, he had by choice started as a stock boy in the May Company in order to learn the business from the bottom up. Having been a rather good baseball player in college, he had toyed with the idea of becoming a professional and had even been invited to tryout as a catcher for the Pittsburgh Pirates. At one time he had nearly been persuaded by the leaders of the newly established Jewish 'Reform' religious movement to study to become a rabbi.

But, in the end, he chose business management as a career, and rose rapidly in the May Company organization. Through wise financial planning he was able to achieve considerable status among his family and peers. He spoke to me of his having married later in life so as to fulfill the responsibility of the firstborn to take care of his mother after his father's passing. As a result, he was nearly thirty when he met my grandmother, Mabel Herman while on a business trip in Shreveport, Louisiana. They were married after a brief engagement, had three children, and stayed married until my grandfather's passing despite that fact that as far as I can determine they never had a thing in common with each other. For many years, I recall that they didn't even live together but somehow managed to get together for dinner in one of Chicago's many restaurants almost daily. Of course my grandmother was dutifully at his side for every religious or public function in which it was appropriate for them to be seen together. Their love and commitment to each other was definitely not the stuff of Hollywood.

I know from personal experience that Morris wasn't what you would call a big risk-taker, but leaned on the side of caution in making major financial decisions. With this in mind, I have been deeply troubled over the years by the chain of decisions that he made that brought him to a state of poverty by the time I was born. In his late forties he made a series of miscalculations that not only affected his immediate family but many generations after him. He lost his position at the May Company when the owner's heir took over control of the company, and then made a huge gamble by speculating on an oil venture. He went in as equal partner with a group of businessmen who could afford to take a loss if the oil well they were drilling was a bust. However, Morris didn't have the financial reserves the others had in the event of the worse case scenario. With such enormous potential prophets luring him forward, he threw caution to the wind and went 'all in' with his share.

After the oil fiasco, he was desperate to remake his fortune and gambled on some other shaky deals that bankrupted him in a short time. I can only imagine the agony that my mother and the family experienced as they had to leave their mansion and all the servants and move into a small apartment. But as fate would have it, my mom, in a move to get on with her life, married the manager of the restaurant where she was forced to get a job as a waitress in Chicago, and I was born into the world as a result.

Now grandpa was, if nothing else, a planner for the future, and he spoke to me about life insurance before I was even old enough to know what life was all about. He also mentioned his 'will' so often that I had the impression as a young boy that he might have been updating it daily. Anyway, he had taken out and kept a disability insurance policy over the years that would give him a fixed income for the rest of his life in the event that he became physically incapacitated and unable to work. It seems that those who plan for a rainy day usually get rained on, and so quite unexpectedly he had a series of major heart attacks in his early sixties that left him unable to work. Specialists told him that the stress of trying to make money would kill him, and so he was able to live modestly off of his monthly income that he received from that policy.

From then on, God and his doctor became his closest advisors and confidants. In order to stay alive, he had to radically change his lifestyle and heed everything his doctor instructed him to do. He could not get out of bed before 10:00 AM, which is where I would find him reading his newspaper if I dropped into his room on the 29th floor of the Sheridan Plaza Hotel in the morning. He had to stick to a strict diet and could not do anything stressful. The only slack his doctor cut him was that he could smoke his pipe once a day for relaxation but had to cut out the cigars totally. Although he couldn't work for money, he was allowed to volunteer his remarkable talents several hours each weekday to raise money for Israel through the

'Combined Jewish Appeal'. Over the years he single-handedly raised millions of dollars for Israel and every year received a commemorative plaque with the payment of $1.00 inside in appreciation for his services. He stayed abreast of all the news about Israel daily and used every bit of bad news to drum up larger contributions from wealthy donors whom he called on a regular basis from his office in downtown Chicago.

Now this is where I come into the picture. I was a small boy of six or seven, with no other father figure around, and suddenly grandpa had a lot of spare time on his hands. He took me under his wing and began to mold my character one day at a time. He taught me to ride a bicycle, how to play baseball and football, took me to the zoo often, and to theatrical plays, museums, and countless other cultural activities. When he realized that I had an aptitude for numbers he taught me to keep a play by play score card, and the two of us became regulars at Wrigley Field on weekends watching the last place Cubs play the next to the last place N.Y. Mets, or some other team that would beat the Cubs back into the cellar.

Now as much as I loved driving with my grandfather in his car to these events and activities, it's the things that I didn't like doing with him that has had the most profound influences on my life. He would regularly take me to synagogue with him, especially on the Jewish high holidays. Fasting and prayer were not highlights for any boy my age. He enrolled me in Hebrew school and made me go to classes at our local synagogue three times a week after school. I promptly stopped attending those classes when I turned thirteen and was bar-mitzvahed, which is the right of passage into manhood in the Jewish religion. Even my bar mitzvah entailed a year of grueling study with our Rabbi, Dr. Sofer, in order to be able to recite the weekly Torah scripture reading by heart. The Jewish people annually read through the first five books of the Bible (the Torah) and each Shabbat (Saturday) one of the elders stands up and reads the chapters scheduled for that week. My scripture passage was Lech-Lecha, or "Go Out", which was God's command to Abram to leave the Ur of the Chaldees and go to the land that He promised to give to him and his descendants. After a year of study, it only took forty-five minutes to recite and sing my way into manhood.

Well, as bad as Hebrew school was with all the extra study for my bar mitzvah etc., it wasn't even the tip of the iceberg of the things grandpa did 'for my own good'. Beginning at age ten, he had me start planning for my financial future, something that really irritated me to no end at first. He was a great believer that one should invest for the future, so every Saturday I had to drop by his hotel room around noon after getting paid from my paper routes with the News American, and fork over at least half of my salary. When the minimum $18.75 was accumulated, we would walk over to the First National Bank of Chicago together and ceremonially buy a $25.00 U.S. Government bond, fully redeemable in just seven years and nine months! At that time, I just couldn't figure out for the life of me why anybody would want to buy government bonds instead of spending their hard earned money on toys, clothes, bicycles or just having a good time. Furthermore, getting less than $1.00 a year interest on such a huge financial sacrifice didn't seem like such a good deal to a kid who wasn't even a teenager yet. Well it made him mighty happy so I played along with the investing game until around the time I got over $1000 accumulated, and then I began buying $50 bonds almost weekly by myself. Without a moment's hesitation, grandpa sent me all my bonds on my eighteenth birthday. With that small fortune I bought a brand new 750 cc Honda motorcycle that I sold two years later in order to go to Israel.

After I became a 'believer' in Israel by reading the New Testament, I witnessed to him about my faith in Jesus many times through letters. At first he was incredulous and even a bit perturbed by my life changing experience, but as time wore on he became more curious as he witnessed the changes in me. When I came back to the U.S.A. on brief trips, he and I would talk long about the Word of God, and I sensed that he was becoming more Jewish in reaction to my conversion. Still, he went and heard me speak on a couple of occasions in churches in the area and I know he was deeply touched when one of the pastors, Mike Anderson, started singing the 'Shema', the most sacred scripture in the Hebrew faith: "Hear O Israel, the LORD your God is one LORD"

After he passed away, I opened his very worn Old Testament to the 53rd chapter of the book of Isaiah, and read what he had written in red pencil in the margins... "Could this be talking about Jesus being the Messiah?" I don't know for sure if my grandpa ever came to believe in Jesus near the end of his life, but I probably would never have become who I am in the LORD if it hadn't been for his wonderful and loving influence on my life.

I pray that if my grandfather is in heaven reading this story now that he will be well pleased with this yortzite. I would ask him to forgive me if I haven't gotten all of the facts perfectly correct because I have waited far too long to fulfill his wish. Now, as a grandfather myself, I can fully imagine that day in the not so distant future that he and I will be together again.

"Who has believed our report?
And to whom has the arm of the LORD been revealed? "
(Isaiah 53:1)

Chapter 48
When He Speaks

When God speaks things always happen that are beyond our control, or else we would be tempted to view the events as coincidences. I'm sure that those that have never heard His voice will fall into two categories: those who want to know more about how to 'have ears to hear', and those who simply believe that its not possible for people to hear God's voice in this day and age. For those of us that have heard, there is no greater experience in this life, for it instills faith that can literally move mountains. Jesus declared that His sheep hear his voice, and I think He intended for all His followers (dare I say sheep) to hear Him when He calls. The awesome power of God is made perfect in weakness and He has chosen the foolish things of the world to confound the wise. You can never know when He will speak, but it pays to be listening, for miraculous things are then about to happen...

I was driving down the highway with my good friend, Bruce, one day when God spoke to me as we were passing a rather large Gospel Outreach church. The building lies just off the highway that goes from Palmer to Wasilla, which is an hour's drive north of Anchorage, Alaska. God very simply said that I would speak in that church; so I shared the Word that I heard from the Lord with Bruce. His reaction was not altogether uncommon, although he truly believes in 'hearing from God'. Bruce said," That's impossible, I've been to that church and they have their speakers arranged for six months in advance." Well, I didn't really care one way or the other, so I said to Bruce, "Let's go there this Sunday and check it out", and left it at that.

Nothing very dramatic happened in the Sunday morning service as Bruce and I sat there listening to Pastor Mark speak. Toward the end of the sermon though, I had a strong conviction that I was to go up and pray for the pastor. I don't believe I've ever had that same conviction come over me before, but I knew it was the LORD because a few minutes later the pastor in closing said, "If anyone feels led to come up and pray for me, please do." We were sitting in the front, so I was up and praying for him within a few seconds. I can't really remember what I prayed for, but I do remember that when I finished, he looked at me and asked where I was from, as we had never met before. When I told him I was from Israel, he asked if I was available to share with his church the following Sunday. He said, "We generally have our speakers lined up for six months in advance, but next week I've been called unexpectedly to go out of town and have no one to take the morning service." Bruce, who was standing there listening to the whole thing, confirmed with his look of surprise that this was truly the hand of God.

The point is that God did all the arranging, and spoke what was going to take place. My responsibility was after hearing, to confess what I had heard, and then step out in faith by acting upon what He had said as if it was already a reality. I have had many such experiences, which have similarly worked out supernaturally, but I believe in my heart that this should be the norm and not the exception in our lives.

Many of the stories that my wife and I have written in this book involve miraculous interventions by God after hearing His voice, confessing what we've heard, thereby having His spoken Word established by the mouth of two or three witnesses. We are then in the position to become willing participants in the working out of His plans and purposes. 'Thy will be done', often involves us 'being led by the Spirit of God'. I'm fully convinced that it is not enough to just believe and then go forth, but we must also speak faith ourselves if we wish to see the thing come to pass that we have heard God speak to our hearts. This is also marvelous, for it places part of the responsibility upon us for the miraculous to occur. "For with the heart one believes unto righteousness, and with the mouth confession is made unto salvation."

Once while attending the twenty-fifth anniversary celebration of a precious brother and sister who lived near the Sea of Galilee, I stepped outside to get some air and saw another friend's green Volkswagen, double-cabin, pick-up truck sitting outside. Suddenly out of nowhere God said to me, "It's yours." Well, I knew that vehicle well and wasn't interested in it but I went back inside the place where the celebration was being held and said to Baruch, "How much do you want for your truck." He said," How did you know it was for sale, we only spoke of selling it this morning because my fiancée and I have decided to go to Bible College after our upcoming wedding?" He was asking top dollar (literally), and I mean full book value for a vehicle that had a multitude of problems and looked like it had been through a couple of the Arab-Israeli wars to boot. So I put the whole thing out of my mind.

The next day, a dear old eighty-five year old Dutch lady came to our home in Metulla, and unexpectedly announced that she had been directed by the Lord to come right over to our house and buy us a car. We had known Henrietta for a while and this was certainly an unusual thing for her to say. The amount she was instructed that she should spend turned out to be the exact amount that Baruch was asking for his Volkswagen, double-cabin, beat up old pick-up truck. To make a long story short, we bought it at full price, more as an offering to the Lord than anything else, and drove Baruch and his wife to the airport in it the next week right after their wedding. That vehicle was perfect for our family of eight, and lasted us for many years. I believe it blessed us more than any other vehicle that I can remember.

Now there are many difficulties with hearing, with believing, and with confessing, and I'm not trying to say that any of these are easy. There are many voices and we need to become as familiar with the voice of God's Spirit as a young infant is with his mother's voice. Humble and contrite hearts are necessary for us to be in a position to have God speak to us as clearly as He did with His friend Abraham. Hiding the written Word of God deep within our hearts will make us less likely to sin against Him, either through lack of faith or by walking in our own presumptuousness. Honesty, to admit that we don't understand if we have truly heard by asking God for clarification and verification are essential in order not to place our own interpretation on His words. With these conditions met, we should expect to pray with faith knowing that God will speak to us – in His time and in His way, and not necessarily how we might expect Him to speak.

> *"Call to Me, and I will answer you, and I will show you great and mighty things, which you do not know."*
> *Jeremiah 33:3*

Chapter 49
"But Where Sin Abounded..."

Immediately after I walked out of the American Consulate in Jerusalem, the Holy Spirit spoke clearly to me in an almost audible voice,"Go right back in and tell that man that you lied to him." I instantly replied, "Lord, I can not." I was too embarrassed and could not humble myself at that moment.

I had not consciously thought about lying or that the exaggeration that I was telling was a complete falsehood. I had rationalized my behavior by thinking it did not matter to this official one way or another. Nonetheless, it had clearly grieved God's Spirit.

I was trying to get an American passport for my infant son, Isaiah, so that my wife could take our two boys to the United States for the summer to visit her parents. When the passport was delayed by the fact that Isaiah had been born on a kibbutz in the Jordan Valley, an area of the country of Israel that was covered by the Tel-Aviv Embassy, I became impatient. I began pressing the Consul to get it more quickly than I needed to. Finally, he point blank asked me, "When is your wife's flight?"

Now my impatience had put me on the spot. The truth was that her flight was not for a couple of more weeks, but I reasoned that this was the Middle East and who could count on anything here at the last minute. So, lack of faith in God's provision had now entered into the picture as well as impatience. My pride then caused me become too embarrassed to admit that I had been harassing this man needlessly, so I moved the date up ten days or so. In response to my fabrication, he said that if the passport was not there by the day before the date I had given him, he would personally drive to Tel-Aviv and get it for me. I had now gotten this extremely busy, kind-hearted man involved in my foolishness, to the point that he was willing to make a needless trip from Jerusalem to Tel-Aviv and back as a result of my outright lie.

As soon as I left the Consulate, having refused God's clear direction to go back in and make things right, I instantly started to run a high fever, and began shaking, even though a minute earlier I had been as healthy as I had ever been in my life. It came over me so quickly that I felt like I could barely make it the few hundred yards to the bus stop. By the time I got home, I was seriously ill. In an effort to hide my sin, I told no one of what had happened but went to bed where I had plenty of time to 'privately' repent afterwards. The scripture clearly teaches us that whom the Lord loves He chastens, so you would have thought that I had learned my lesson after such a chastening. I regret to say that I had not.

I wish the story had a happier ending, which in a way it does but not till much later in my walk with the Lord. I never did go back to the American Consul and confess my sin, though I wanted to after I recovered sufficiently to return and pick up Isaiah's passport. I also wish that this had been my last outright lie and chastening from the Lord, which was not the case either. No, it would take at least another twenty years for me to understand the words that Jesus spoke so plainly to His disciples, "And you shall know the Truth, and the Truth will set you free." I just did not have 'ears to hear' at that time in my life, and would suffer greatly because of it.

You may be wondering, why I am confessing now, over three decades after the fact. Well, first of all, Jesus said, "For there is nothing covered, that shall not be revealed; neither hid, that shall not be known." He continued this theme by adding, "Therefore whatsoever ye have spoken in darkness shall be heard in the light; and that which ye have spoken in the ear in closets shall be proclaimed upon the housetops."

So, like my grandson once told me when his grandma, my wife, caught me sneaking some of the icing off one of her cakes, "Uhh oh, grandpa, you're busted, big time."

Secondly, and more importantly, the scripture clearly says that 'where sin abounds, grace does abound even more', and that is truly one of the most miraculous things about God. He forgives us and 'remembers our sins no more'. I cannot comprehend how an omniscient God is able to choose to forget my trespasses after I have confessed and repented of them, but there it is in the book of Jeremiah where the Almighty promised to make a 'new covenant with the house of Israel and with the house of Judah'. It is not the sin of lying that was the real problem here. It is pride that brought the sin to the forefront, for the symptoms of an illness are not really the illness itself. It would take decades more for me to see the true root of my sin was pride, something that was so insidiously hidden deep within me. Only by God's grace was it eventually revealed to me by His Spirit, in order that I could know the Truth and be set free.

Now, I am not saying here that I no longer sin, or do not still occasionally succumb to human pride, for that would be as great a lie as I have ever told. No, we are all sinners and have fallen short of the Grace of God. I am just not interested in hiding behind sin anymore, for sin separates us from God's love, as darkness separates us from His light. It is not that our Heavenly Father separates himself from us, mind you; it is that we separate ourselves from Him when we choose to become 'slaves to sin.'

I have felt to share one of what you might here be dismissing as a 'small sin' rather than some of the darker ones that I've committed, which you might consider sufficiently evil to be worthy of bringing out to the light. Nevertheless, sin is sin. Big sins, small sins, they are really all the same, just as big lies, small lies, are all untruths. I have no desire here to glorify my flesh by recounting much worse things that I am ashamed of now, and that God Himself no longer remembers.

When it says that 'naked we have come into the world, and naked we shall leave', I believe that it is in part referring to the those things, both great and small, that we have used to cover ourselves with in order that other's might not see us as we really are. I have pretended for far too long to be someone I am not while not recognizing that all along I was one of the 'heirs of God, and joint-heirs with Christ'.

Through my many weaknesses and shortcomings, I have come to a much greater understanding and revelation of God's grace, love and the power of forgiveness through the Spirit of Holiness. Furthermore, I acknowledge that I had never been good enough (or will be for that matter) to earn the price paid by Jesus at Calvary. Pride had only lead me to believe that I had been, and kept me bound and incapable of being set free for far too long.

To God be all the glory for the great things He has done.

> *"For I am persuaded that neither death nor life,*
> *nor angels nor principalities nor powers,*
> *nor things present nor things to come,*
> *nor height nor depth, nor any other created thing,*
> *shall be able to separate us from the love of God*
> *which is in Christ Jesus our Lord."*
> Romans 38:3-39

The Holy Land Walk of Faith
Wednesday, August 31, 2005

Chapter 50

We packed our equipment into our backpacks in preparation for an estimated seven-week hike on the Israel National Trail. Our immediate concern was the weight of the packs. When we finished packing, and adding food for several days and six liters (1.5 gallons) of water, which we would each need per day, our combined weight was sixty kilograms (132 lbs).

The most important thing will be our spiritual preparation. We will be walking by faith, focusing on the purpose of this hike, which is to pray throughout the land for the salvation of Israel. We are hiking by revelation of God's word spoken first to Abraham in Genesis 13:17 – "Go, walk through the length and breadth of the land, for I am giving it to you." By this, we believe that we must first take spiritual possession of the land so that the promises of God can be fulfilled in His precious chosen ones.

Bev* I am usually in very good physical condition, but having just returned on August 28th from a two month visit with our family in Florida, I caught a viral sinus infection. It has had me flat on my back since my arrival. I decided to fast and just drink water for two days. So today, thank God, I am back on my feet. We just had a big breakfast and though I am still feeling weak, I am not in pain. I keep thinking that this is not the way to start out on such a strenuous adventure. I am again reminded that if this is a walk of faith, then I will have to have the kind of faith required to accomplish this mission. We are putting our new business adventure of developing 'English for Sure' language school franchises in Israel on hold while we do this. We have $600.00 and are not aware of any other income until we set up new franchises with prospective investors. We have a lot to seek the Lord about, please keep us in your prayers.

Friday, September 02, 2005

Eilat

Preparing for our Departure from Eilat

With backpacks fully loaded, we took off for two short day hikes in the Eilat Mountains to test out our equipment and get used to the weight. We have not carried backpacks for extended hikes for many years and are adjusting to them slowly. We both are probably carrying at least five to ten pounds of extra weight but we cannot quite figure out what to take out at this point. Since it will take us about seven weeks (we had no idea we would be twelve and a half weeks!) to complete the 940 kilometers on the Israel National Trail hike, we are trying to make the trade-offs between comfort and necessities. This will probably be much clearer after we have hiked for a few days.

The heaviest item is the most important - water, as we will have to carry four liters each while in the north and double that when we reach the Negev desert in October and November. The temperature in Eilat is now around 35C (95F) but it should be several degrees cooler in the north where we will begin our 'Walk of Faith' on Monday, September 5.

For those who are reading this while we are hiking, please remember to keep us in your prayers daily.

Saturday September 03, 2005	
Destination: Kiryat Shmona - Metulla - Kibbutz Tel Dan	*Today's Miles:* 0.00
Starting Location: Eilat	*Trip Miles:* 0.00

Thumbing a Ride to the Beginning of the I.N.T.

After packing, unpacking, removing items and then re-packing several times, our backpacks are as light as we can get them – we are ready to go. We have our bus tickets for tomorrow morning from Eilat to Haifa (six hour ride) and we will then take another couple hour bus ride to Kiryat Shmona. An interesting fact is that this 8 hour bus ride up to the beginning of the Israeli National Trail follows the same basic route that we will hike coming back, except it will take us six to seven (actually twelve) weeks longer to complete!

We will be arriving in the city of Kiryat Shmona around 7:00 PM, and we plan to hitchhike the eight kilometers (5 miles) from there up to Metulla. Metulla is not only the most northern city in Israel it is also one of the oldest settlements, having been founded in the late 19th century. It has around two thousand residents and is surrounded on three sides (north, east & west) by the hills and mountains of

Lebanon. From 1989 - 1995, we lived in Metulla with our six children and we both think it is one of the most beautiful places in Israel, with a spectacular view overlooking Mt. Hermon and the Hula Valley. Beginning in Metulla, the Nahal Ayoun Nature Reserve has a wonderful two to three hour family friendly day hike that traverses some spectacular scenery and three awesome waterfalls. The best time to view the Ayoun Reserve is in the spring as the water slows to a trickle in the summer and fall, and rages in the winter.

We plan to spend the night in Metulla with one of our dear friends, Izik Koren, who is quite an outdoorsman himself. Now in his late seventies, he has been a wild boar hunter for the past forty years in the Upper Galilee. Since it requires a special government permit, he is one of the few legal hunters in Israel. The wild boar are a problem in the north of Israel as they do not have any natural predators and thus multiply without restraint, and the damage that they inflict on the grain fields and orchards is extremely costly to the farmers on the agricultural settlements in the area.

On Monday morning, the Lord willing, we will hitch a ride to Kibbutz Dan, and begin hiking the Israel National Trail on our 'Walk of Faith'....

Monday, September 05, 2005	
Destination: Gesher Sneer - Nahal Sneer	**Today's Miles:** 5.00
Starting Location: Tel-Dan	**Trip Miles:** 5.00

Day 1: Leaving Metulla, we hitchhiked to the beginning of the INT (Israel National Trail) at Tel-Dan, stopping in Kiryat Shemona for some last minute purchases of food and supplies for the week. After four rides from hitchhiking, we arrived at Beit Ushishkin at the entrance of the trail and at 11:00 AM, we began our 'Walk of Faith', which will last at least another forty-nine days.

The north of Israel is spectacular at all times of year and compared to Eilat we were in a paradise, with green hills, mountains and rushing rivers all around us -- The Dan, Banyas, and Hatzbani rivers are all tributaries to the Jordan river. We walked along outside of the Tel-Dan nature reserve for the first couple of hours, stopping several times to swim in the freezing cold rushing waters, and to pick blackberries and wild grapes that grow along the side of the trail.

Bev tried her hand at fishing in one of the tributaries where trout and catfish abound but only caught two freshwater crabs for her effort.

The Dan River -- Mt. Hermon in the background

We arrived at the entrance to the Sneer Spring Nature Reserve at 4:00 PM and paid fifteen shekels($3.75) each to pass through. We were told we should try to exit the reserve at the south end by 5:00 PM but that there was not a gate or anything that we needed to worry about.

We managed to crisscross the Hatzbani River several times over the next hour and a half through some of the most beautiful scenery imaginable. The hike was difficult weaving through the roots of trees that lined the riverbanks. The water was rushing besides us even though this area has not seen any rain since last winter. The snow melting from the mountains in Lebanon and the Hermon provide for abundant water flow all year round.

Thoroughly exhausted from our first day's effort and only half way to Tel-Hai, our original destination, we decided to pitch camp on the river just a little bit south of the Nature Reserve. Too tired to even cook we had a sandwich and a cup of herb tea. First night in the tent was difficult as we both ached in every area imaginable and so it took a few hours to fall asleep. We slept in late in the morning until 9:00 AM and then after a nice breakfast and bath in the river headed out on our second day of trekking.

Tuesday, September 06, 2005	
Destination: Tel-Hai, Kibbutz Kfar Giladi	**Today's Miles:** 4.00
Starting Location: Nahal Sneer	**Trip Miles:** 9.00

Day 2: We walked across Hwy 99, which runs east to west from Kiryat Shemona to Mt. Hermon. At the Alon gas station, we filled

up our water bottles and bought some rolls and a couple of freshly baked cheese pastries. After sitting at a nice shaded table in the rest area outside and eating our delicacies and reading our Bibles for spiritual strength and encouragement, we hit the hot trail at 11:00 AM.

View from Our Too Short Tent

This part of the INT today was all uphill and mostly back roads that take you through Kibbutz Mayon Baruch and Moshav (agricultural settlement) Kfar Yuval. We stopped for a refreshing break under an old bridge that crosses over Nahal (spring) Ayon. The water is only ankle deep in the fall but will become a raging river again in the winter and spring.

After a long uphill hike up to Tel-Hai, we arrived at the end of the first segment of the trail and set up camp on a beautiful site overlooking the Hula Valley. David Yisraeli, a Kfar Giladi gardener, greeted us and made us feel welcome. There were eight others camping that were also hiking part of the trail though we only saw one other couple again.

Still our bodies were very sore all over, we had a rough night's sleep, but enjoyed sleeping under the starts. Once finally worn-out we fell asleep and we slept in until 9:00 AM.

Wednesday, September 07, 2005	
Destination: Geologic Trail Park	**Today's Miles:** 5.00
Starting Location: Tel-Hai, Kibbutz Kfar Giladi	**Trip Miles:** 14.00

Day 3: We took a short side-trek into Kibbutz Kfar Giladi to buy some gasoline for our Coleman camp-stove, and to mail five pounds

of extra stuff back to Eilat. Starting out at 10:00 AM, we had a rough downhill climb and then misread the trail marker at the bottom and headed south for about 1 km. After realizing our mistake, we hiked back up to the trail and then had a very steep, difficult and exhausting climb to the forest entrance.

Lebanon Straight Ahead

At this point, there are three roads and we managed again to take the wrong trail, which put us two to three kilometers out of the way. Rather than doubling back again, we found a gate in the security fence and climbed straight up through dense forest back onto the trail, which was very difficult. When we finally got back on the Israel National Trail, we rolled out the sleeping bags in a shady spot and took an hour nap! God is good.

A quick snack and a few minutes later we hiked up to the Shepherd's spring, which had a trough that was full of fresh clean spring water for the local grazing sheep. The view from the top of the mountain range overlooking the Hula Valley is spectacular. The trail at this point is a constant ascent for the next sixteen kilometers (10 miles), and is shaded by magnificent pine and cedars. At the time we could not have imagined how different this area would soon become after war with Lebanon would cause most of this area to be badly burnt from fires caused by Katusha missiles.

At 5:00 P.M. we reached Geographic Park about midway through this second section of the INT. We had hoped to make it to Kibbutz Yafit but due to wrong turns, we needed to stop for the evening. With our water supply dwindling, we asked one of the geologists who was preparing to leave his work site if he had extra water and he generously gave us four liters! In the morning when he and his partner returned, they gave us another bottle.

There was a strong wind all night that kept us cool. It reminded us of the scripture that everyone who is born of the Holy Spirit is like the wind which we do not know where it comes from or where it goes. We could also hear jackals howling at night but we had been assured by knowledgeable sources that they are of no threat to humans.

Our bodies are still very sore but much less so, each day, and we feel that we are getting stronger physically and spiritually each step of the way. We have been praying over each settlement and village that we pass for the Spirit of God to be poured out onto the inhabitants and for the believers in the land to be strengthened amidst the persecution they receive for believing that Jesus is the messiah.

Thursday, September 08, 2005	
Destination: Lipa Gal Lookout	**Today's Miles:** 5.00
Starting Location: Geologic Trail Park	**Trip Miles:** 19.00

Mt. Hermon and Kiryat Shemona are behind us now!

Day 4: Got an early start today -- 8:00 AM! Mostly uphill hike today but it seemed easier. We had a crystal-clear view of the surrounding mountains of Lebanon, Syria

and the Golan Heights across the Hula Valley. We could see at least eighty kilometers (50 miles) in all directions. Our packs feel lighter but that is most probably because our bodies are adjusting. We still stop often for short breaks and to glean fruit growing in the surrounding orchards. We loved the sweet nectarines, peaches, and especially figs that are now in season. This fruit is a great source of energy and supplements our trail rations.

There are wild parrots all over the land of Israel, which we enjoy listening to as we hike along this beautiful trail. There was an Israeli living on a kibbutz in the Hula valley and he raised exotic parrots and sold them for a handsome price. It was assumed some of his fanatic bird-loving neighbors sprung open the latches and let all the parrots free, now they have multiplied and can be seen even in the Negev. This evening we found a fabulous lookout, which was an ideal location to set up camp. On the site is a memorial to one of the Israel Nature pioneers - Lipa Gal. It is only a few hundred meters off the INT and is a lovely enclave - too beautiful for words. It was so exciting to talk with family in the USA this evening by cell phone while watching the glorious sunset from 500 meters (1500 feet) up above the Hula Valley! Dinner was delicious - Raman noodles, soup mix and salami, which only took minutes to prepare and tasted like a banquet to us after a day of burning up so many calories. We slept without the tent on a carpet of leaves, in our sleeping bags under millions of stars. Praise the LORD - Hallelujah!

Friday, September 09, 2005	
Destination: Kibbutz Yiftach	**Today's Miles:** 2.00
Starting Location: Lipa Gal Lookout	**Trip Miles:** 21.00

A day of relaxation at Kibbutz Yiftach

Day 5: Slept well, but woke up to the buzzing of mosquitoes, bees, and gnats -- our sleeping bags moist with the mountain dew (not the soft drink!). It did not take long for it to heat up and for us to pack up camp and head up to the trail. A short forty-five minute uphill trek and we reached the main road that leads to Kibbutz Yiftach. After gorging on over ten juicy ripe figs each from a tree on the roadside, we entered the kibbutz Netafim factory where they manufacture drip irrigation water pipes. One of the plant managers and good friend of ours, Yossi, kindly allowed us to use his office computer to update our trail journal but we are unable at this time to upload our pictures -- hopefully we will later today.

Taking care of our laundry and shopping, we plan to set up our camp today here on the green grass of the kibbutz and continue our hike tomorrow. We had a wonderful lunch at the Kibbutz dining hall and then spent the rest of the day at the swimming pool. We now feel refreshed and invigorated and ready to hike again and hopefully we will be at the Sea of Galilee, a seventy kilometers (43 miles) hike by next Friday if we can average ten to twelve kilometers a day. By God's Grace, we will communicate with all of you then, with new pictures, and trail adventure updates!

Saturday, September 10, 2005	
Destination: Nahal Dishon	**Today's Miles:** 6.50
Starting Location: Kibbutz Yiftach	**Trip Miles:** 27.50

Climb to Keren Naphtali

Day 6: We began bright and early at 7:30 AM on Shabbat morning but forgot that the Kibbutz front gate was locked! After a few perplexing minutes we finally figured out how to open it and off we went. There are 44 sections of the Israel National Trail laid out with maps, pictures, and explanations (in Hebrew) in our guidebook. The first goal for today's hike was to complete the last part of trail #2, Wadi Kadesh (the Holy Ravine) before beginning the hike to the Dishon Nature Reserve. On the map it looked like it should take us less than an hour. Turns out that it was an exercise in pure rock climbing straight down 60 meters (180 ft.) to the dry spring bed and then after

an hour of hiking down the river bed another equally strenuous rock climb out of the ravine with our heavy packs. We got out by 10:00 AM completely exhausted.

We had several days food supply with us, and three out of the four eggs we purchased at Kibbutz Yiftach survived the ordeal whole. After arriving at the Yesha Fortress, which marks the end of trail #2, Bev cooked us up a special breakfast of scrambled eggs. We then filled up all our water bottles and headed out toward one of the highest places in the area - Keren Naphtali. From this small mountain you have a commanding view of all the Hula Valley, Metulla, the Upper Galilee and southern Lebanon. This mount may have been one of the ancient high places where the tribe of Naphtali worshipped. After struggling to reach the top, we called our son Isaac and his wife Clea to pray with us over the area. Coming down off the mountain we were both exhausted and within an hour set up camp in a cow pasture under a couple of trees in the field -- we had a spectacular view even though our surroundings were rugged. We ate a light dinner of soup and herb tea and fell asleep almost immediately.

A half hour later, our cell phone rang and woke us up later as we had been so tired we had forgotten to turn it off. It was Yossi from Kibbutz Yiftach looking for us! He had been driving around searching for our tent with some food and provisions that he had brought for us. We finally were able to direct him to a place close to where we were camped and we then hiked up with a flashlight to meet him and bring him back to our campsite. He was our first visitor on the trek and how we enjoyed his company and the food. After eating and sharing for about an hour, Yossi told us that he would meet us again the next evening at the end of the Wadi Dishon reserve.

Sunday, September 11, 2005	
Destination: Upper Dishon Valley	**Today's Miles:** 7.50
Starting Location: Keren Naphtali - Yachmor Valley	**Trip Miles:** 35.00

Day 7: Our best day of hiking yet, we covered twelve kilometers (7.5 miles) and felt great! After a quick paced hike in the morning, we made it to the lower end of the Dishon Nature Reserve around

noon and after lunch took a nice two-hour nap. The Dishon Spring is dry this time of year but it is clear that it can be a roaring brook after the winter rains. The hike through the ravine is not particularly strenuous as the Israel Nature Authority for day hikers designed it so hikers could made it to the camp, our planned meeting point with Yossi by 3:30 PM.

Finding water in a dry wadi (ravine)

We were happy that we made a decision to go to the end of trail #3, another five kilometers (3.1 miles) because our water supply was running seriously low.

This next part of the Dishon Reserve trail is much more arduous and when we reached the Aviv Spring about two-third's of the way through we were ecstatic to find a well with water in it that I was able to climb down the ladder into the well and fill our water bottles.

Refreshed by the water and the blackberries that grow in the area we arrived at the trail's end at 6:30 PM -- with just enough light to set up our camp before nightfall. We called Yossi and gave him our new coordinates and he met us at 8:00 PM with a spaghetti pasta dinner, fresh bread rolls, hardboiled eggs, and salad, humus and chocolate mints for dessert. He brought 5 bottles of water as well and half liter of gasoline for our Coleman cooker.

Even though we have each other for company, at times on the trail it can seem like such a long and lonely adventure. It is hard to describe how much we appreciated this demonstration of love and concern by our friend, and how much it encouraged us. We went to bed with our hearts revived, our stomachs full, and a renewed belief that with God's help we could make it all the way to Eilat -- only 890 kilometers (556 miles) to go!

Monday, September 12, 2005	
Destination: Chorvat Chamemah - base of Mt. Meron	**Today's Miles:** 6.00
Starting Location: Upper Dishon Valley	**Trip Miles:** 41.00

Day 8: All uphill today! First, we climbed to the extreme upper end of the Dishon Ravine where there is very little foot traffic outside of the occasional hiker walking the Israel Trail. Although very scenic and beautiful, the trail is much more rugged and required more rest breaks for us. We found water flowing in the Upper Dishon Spring after we had been hiking for a few hours, so we stopped to bathe and wash out some of our things.

Trail Marker for Nahal Tzivon

We watched a shepherd pass by us with his tranquil herd of goats, sheep, and dogs while we were resting before starting a steep rocky climb into Wadi Tsivon. This section of trail is overgrown with dense vegetation and was almost 100% shaded from the sunlight for the entire hour or so that it took us to traverse it. We then still had another two hours of hiking to go up to the base of Mt. Meron where water re-supply and campground awaited us. The trail at this point looked like it almost disappeared as branches and thorn bushes snagged us and impeded our progress nearly all the way up.

We set up a nice campsite for ourselves within the Chorvat Chamemah that is near the Field School. An Israeli Defense Force (IDF) army troop was camping nearby and they were also hiking to the Sea of Galilee but probably in a third of the time, it took us. They gave us a loaf of bread from their manot krav (K-rations) and we had a big dinner of tuna sandwiches and hot vegetable soup.

It turns out that our army neighbors did not need as much sleep as we did and so with their lights turned on all around their camp, powered by a very noisy generator, they had a party until around 2:00 AM. Surprisingly, we did sleep in spite of all the noise, as our exhausted bodies just could not be denied rest. Overall, it was a hard but good day -- thank you LORD!

Tuesday, September 13, 2005	
Destination: Moshav Meron - beginning of Wadi Amud	**Today's Miles:** 7.50
Starting Location: Chorvat Chamemah - base of Mt. Meron	**Trip Miles:** 48.50

Resting weary feet on top of Mt. Meron

Day 9: We woke up early despite the entire racket from the night before and started the climb up Mt. Meron after a eating a hearty breakfast. Immediately we came across a grove of very ancient and tall olive trees. The climb to the top of Meron took us three hours and seemed much easier than we had been lead to believe, most likely because we were intoxicated by the beautiful view we had while climbing or maybe we were getting stronger. Spectacular red barked trees line the upper ridges of the mount. From the top, we could see into Lebanon, Syria, and the city Sefat, and all the Carmel Ridge. With great visibility, we could see at least fifty miles in all directions.

At the top, we passed two troops of small hiking children ages six and seven, with their guides. Each child was well equipped with water bottles, small backpack, hiking shoes, and a hat. They learn early here in Israel to hike with the proper gear.

After eating lunch and resting on the top, we headed for the southern base of Mt. Meron where we would begin the difficult Wadi Amud descent towards the Sea of Galilee. Mt. Meron marks the end of trail #4 and we also completed the eight kilometer (5 mile) hike on trail #5 which took us past many of the Jewish ancient burial tombs which are scattered around the area.

We set up camp at the park entrance to Wadi Amud and Greg immediately hiked into the Meron Settlement to buy food and supplies for the next several days. Returning with fresh produce and much needed groceries, we had a great feast and stayed up almost to

9:00 PM talking with a fellow hiker named Barry, who seemed very open spiritually.

Twenty years ago, we had done this same hike in the springtime through Wadi Amud with our six small children and our friends Dave and Maede Greenberg and their children. We wondered how it would be now climbing up and down the rocky ledges with our backpacks full and with five liters of water each & food supplies at a max! We fell asleep dreaming about the trek ahead.

Wednesday, September 14, 2005	
Destination: Lower Wadi Amud	**Today's Miles:** 7.50
Starting Location: Moshav Meron - start of Wadi Amud	**Trip Miles:** 56.00

Day 10: The trail started out easy but it did not last long! We were soon huffing and puffing along until we came to an area where we could glean delicious figs, blackberries, and sabras (cactus fruit which is also the name for native Israelis). The upper part of Wadi Amud from Ein Akeem has much water flowing through it and we went swimming several times along the hike.

In the afternoon, the water dried up and the trail became seriously difficult - up and down rocky river beds and steep slippery rock climbing. We used many band-aids this day on our blisters before we reached the road marking the lower Wadi Amud trail. Wadi Amud is spectacular and worth the effort but is not for the timid or those carrying heavy backpacks. We set up camp only moments before sunset, thoroughly exhausted and decided to only put up our mosquito net and sleep under the stars. Today had been an unusually hot and humid day and spiritually very strenuous. We amused the cattle nearby as we drifted off to sleep. Tomorrow's hike should be much easier and we are anticipating swimming in the

Wadi Amud (The Pillar Ravine)

Sea of Galilee in the evening.

Thursday, September 15, 2005	
Destination: The Kinneret - Sea of Galilee	**Today's Miles:** 7.50
Starting Location: Lower Wadi Amud	**Trip Miles:** 63.50

Day 11: We got off to an early 7:30 AM start, crossed the highway and began the last section of the Wadi Amud descent. Immediately we saw a large herd of wild pigs, which is a very unusual sight during the day. In the cool morning air, we were serenaded by hundreds of birds dwelling in the mountain clefts. The trail was excellent, well-shaded and easy going so we were able to finish in a little over three hours! While Bev rested, Greg hitch hiked to Mosha Hakuk to get water and was gone for less than an hour. After eating lunch, we hiked on with the heat and humidity rising in the middle of the afternoon.

The Pillar (Amud)

The Sea of Galilee lies 200 meters (625 ft.) below sea level and the area is semi-tropical. Grapefruit orchards, date and banana groves abound in the area. By 2:30 PM we made it to a beautifully refreshing spring, called Nun, which flows about one and a half kilometers from the Kinneret. There we rested for more than an hour and Bev tried unsuccessfully to catch fish, which were swimming all around the large pool. We then had a real treat and ate lunch in a real restaurant. We were shocked when we walked down to the Sea of Galilee to see how low the Sea level was, as it was much lower than what we had ever seen it in past years. Realizing that we could not camp at such a spot because of the mud and pollution, we hiked back to the restaurant on the highway where we met a very friendly young married couple, Etamar and Liraz, who were still in the army and had hiked from the Mediterranean Sea to the Sea of Galilee in three days. We arranged to hike with them to the Tamar Beach and set up camp at one of the resort beaches, where they convinced the owner to let us put up our tents on the grass for only twenty shekels ($4.50) each instead of the usual thirty shekels. We spent a wonderful night on the Sea of Galilee in a beautiful location. The facilities with showers and bathrooms were very much appreciated as it had been six days since our last stop on Kibbutz Yiftach. Yossi, called to find out how we were doing and was surprised that we had made it on schedule. It is nice to know that our friends and loved ones are concerned for us and are following our progress and praying for us. We were so needy and recognize that without the Lord's help, we can do nothing, and with His help, there is nothing we cannot do. After drinking herb tea and talking with our new friends for a while we fell asleep knowing that we would need all our strength and God's help to climb Mt. Arbel in the morning.

	Friday, September 16, 2005	
Destination: *Tiberias*		***Today's Miles:*** *7.50*
Starting Location: *The Kinneret - Sea of Galilee*		***Trip Miles:*** *71.00*

On the summit of Mt. Arbel

Day 12: In the morning we ate a good breakfast in preparation for an arduous day. We hiked the one and a half kilometers to the highway and sat outside by a kiosk to share a cup of strong Turkish coffee before beginning the 400-meter (1200 ft.) ascent to the top of Mt. Arbel. Passing by the Bedouin village of Chamam at the base of the mount, we saw some of the children playing in the stream with their dog and took their picture before heading up the Arbel Ravine.

For some unknown reason we missed the Israel National Trail marker and hiked about two kilometers up the ravine in the wrong direction. When we finally realized our mistake we decided to take an alternative trail up the mountain, which was just as steep and more or less paralleled the INT. With a colossal surge of energy and effort, we climbed almost straight up to the top of the ridge in less than an hour and then walked for another half hour or so along the ridge to the summit of Mt. Arbel. What a spectacular view we had of the Galilee, the Kinneret, and the entire area that we have been hiking in for days. Sitting under the only tree on the summit, we took a much-needed hour's break for lunch before heading out for Tiberius by way of Kfar Hittim.

The Israel trail at the top of the plateau runs due south and provides a great view of the Sea of Galilee along its entire length. The trail was smooth and an easy walk so we made great time. The only difficulty is that there is almost no trees for shade and again, because of the heat and humidity, we were tiring rapidly. Our water in our bottles was almost hot enough to make tea with and certainly not very refreshing. When we reached the beginning of the village of Hittim just north of Tibrias we stopped at the cemetery where there was a nice drinking fountain and shaded areas with benches and rested. A half hour later, we were ready for the last push into Tiberias. We needed to hurry since the Jewish Sabbath was getting close and most stores and businesses and things shut down from Friday evening until Sunday morning.

We had arranged to spend the Shabbat with a very dear friend and sister in the faith, Irene, in her home in Poriya Illit (Upper Poriya), which is seven or eight kilometers south of Tiberias and high on the ridge above the Sea of Galilee. When we reached the road at the edge of Upper Tiberias, we hitchhiked and caught a ride to the main road, Hwy 77, and then caught a bus to the Poriya junction where we again hitchhiked and immediately got another ride to Poriya Illit. In less than a half hour, we were at Irene's home, and soaking up all the blessings of her hospitality and the things modern civilization has to offer. Having walked from Dan to Beer Sheva twice in the past, Irene had much compassion on us and blessed us greatly with the warmest of Christian hospitality. We showered, washed all our clothes in her washing machine, and then sat down to a feast she prepared for the Erev Shabbat dinner. That night we slept in real beds with sheets and pillows cases which resembled sleeping on soft clouds instead of the hard earth that had been our bed for the past two weeks. We slept very well indeed, with thankful hearts, blessed and at peace.

	Saturday, September 17, 2005	
Destination: *Poriya Illit (Upper Poriya)*		**Today's Miles:** 0.00
Starting Location: *Tiberias*		**Trip Miles:** 71.00

Day 13: A DAY OF REST!

We enjoyed having a wonderful day with our friend, Irene, in Upper Poriya. Bev went swimming with her this morning in the Sea of Galilee and Greg worked on the Travel Journal website and on uploading and editing our pictures. We enjoyed delicious home cooked meals and did not even think about hiking.

Tomorrow we re-supply our packs in Tiberias and then head south for the southern area of the Sea of Galilee and the Jordan River. From there, we hike for two days to the top of Mt. Tavor and then towards the Mediterranean Sea. We hope to update the journal again in Nazareth where we plan to stop in and see Maoz Inon who hiked this trail last spring in thirty-seven days and has encouraged us on our 'walk of faith'. You can find his trail journal in the 2004 journal list for the Israel National Trail.

	Sunday, September 18, 2005	
Destination: *Jordan River, southern edge of the Sea of Galilee*		**Today's Miles:** 7.50
Starting Location: *Tiberias Illit*		**Trip Miles:** 78.50

Day 14: The morning started with an unusual rain shower for this time of year and dark clouds billowing over the Galilee and we faced a dilemma; whether to skip the section of the trail from Tiberias Illit to Poriya and continue hiking the trail from there or backtracking eight kilometers and picking up the trail where we left off on Friday. We prayed while we were standing on the side of the road hitchhiking, and God answered our prayer and sent Rachel, a believer from Poriya, to drive us to the exact spot where the trail

begins in Tiberias Illit. We were so blessed to get this confirmation from the Lord and knew it was a miracle.

Fresh Dates!

Immediately the clouds lifted and we had a beautiful day of hiking along the scenic mountain ridge overlooking the Kinneret and all Upper Galilee and Golan Heights.

We ate fresh dates along the way, which are as different from the dried dates normally sold in the stores as raisins are from grapes -- what a treat! Along the trail, we met a cyclist, Joel, climbing to Poriya who stopped and asked if he could pray for us. What a blessing to have a second confirmation that we were on the right path today.

After a comfortable twelve-kilometer (7.5 mile) hike, we arrived at Kibbutz Kinneret fishponds between the Jordan River and the Sea of Galilee where we set up camp for the night. Surrounded on three sides by water and date palms, this was one of the best campsites so far. Four other hikers joined us at the campsite for the nights and hundreds of birds serenaded us during a spectacular sunset.

The Jordan River

Monday, September 19, 2005

Destination: Upper Plateau of Galilee
Starting Location: Jordan River, southern edge of the Sea of Galilee

Long climb up from the Kinneret

Day 15: After packing up camp, we found a peaceful spot on the Jordan River and fished for two hours (caught four sunfish!) We met a group of very nice Americans that had volunteered for the Israeli army (IDF) and were camped out near our fishing spot.

Having been delayed by the excitement of fishing, we started climbing up to the high plateau, Mitzpeh Alit at 10:30 AM when it was already getting hot out. The climb is very difficult and we were only able to hike about half a kilometer each hour. We reached the spectacular summit around 5:30 PM and camped at an old abandoned meteorological site. The view of the Jordan Valley, the Sea of Galilee, Mt. Tavor, and all the settlements below and around us dazzled us as the sun set. The wind was blowing extremely strong most of the night but we slept soundly in our cozy tent, which was secured on all fours sides with heavy rocks.

Tuesday, September 20, 2005	
Destination: Kfar Tavor (Tavor Village)	**Today's Miles:** 7.00
Starting Location: Upper Plateau of Galilee	**Trip Miles:** 93.00

Day 16: We started hiking at 7:30 AM and immediately filled up our empty water bladders and bottles from an agricultural pipe near our campsite. After a few kilometers, we came across green grass and a shepherd's well, Ein Serene. We lifted buckets of pure fresh cool water out of the well and had fun freshening up. This morning we picked fresh figs, sabra fruit and blackberries to go with our muesli for breakfast. Later in the day, when it was extremely hot, we came across a vineyard of sweet grapes being harvested for wine and

On our hike to Mt. Tavor (in background)

we were a given huge cluster to eat by a local kibbutznik.

We completed the twenty-eight kilometers (18.5 miles) early on this second-day section of the trail and arrived at the road to the village of Tavor around 2:00 PM, and hitch hiked into the center of the town of Tavor. The municipality has a nice park and the guard invited us to camp the night on the soft green grass. There was a supermarket on one side and facilities on the other and there we had a pleasant and much-needed rest in preparation for climbing Mt. Tavor in the morning.

Sabra Cactus Fruit

Wednesday, September 21, 2005	
Destination: Mt. Tavor - Beit Keshet Forest	**Today's Miles:** 5.00
Starting Location: Kfar Tavor (Tavor Village)	**Trip Miles:** 98.00

Day 17: We hiked the kilometer from Kfar Tavor to the Arab village, Shibli, at the base of Mt. Tavor and started the upward ascent. To our shock and surprise, the Israel National Trail goes straight up the mountain with no fooling around. After several necessary rest breaks we made it to the summit and immediately devoured our lunch before continuing the loop around the top. The view is really worth the climb and we had great visibility.

On Top of Mt. Tavor!

The monastery at the top opened at 2:00 PM, so we took the opportunity to take a nap and rest our weary feet and bodies. The bells ring every half hour, and at two o'clock, we were able to go inside where we refilled our water bottles.

The climb back down was even steeper than our climb up and Bev considered wrapping her backpack up in her sleeping pad and rolling it down the mountain, of course we carried it down, but the thought was appealing.

Because the main road to the monastery is so narrow, most visitors to Mt. Tavor take a taxi from the the town of Shibli. We stopped at the taxi station and had a coke before continuing.

We hiked through the pleasant Arab village of Shibli to reach Beit Keshet forest. As the sun was almost setting, we found a great campsite and put up both the tent and mosquito net on a bed of soft pine needles. Just when you think everything is perfect... loud speakers from a surrounding village blared music until the early hours of the morning! We were so tired from the climb up and down Mt. Tavor that, despite the noise, we fell asleep quickly.

	Saturday, September 24, 2005	
Destination: *Tsipori*		**Today's Miles:** *4.00*
Starting Location: *Nazareth*		**Trip Miles:** *112.00*

Looking back on Mt. Tavor

Day 18: With Mt. Tavor in the backdrop we started the last leg of the hike to Nazareth winding through beautiful forest. Our ankles were very sore from the previous day's climb so we took it easy. After having climbing 470 meters (1550 ft.) to Har Devoriya, we decided to stop for the day and enjoy the wonderful view. The Hebrew name Devorah means bee, not surprising there were many bees camping with us. The site is ideal for day campers visiting this Keren

Kayemet National forest. There are many picnic tables and campsites but NO WATER, therefore our supply for cooking and drinking was limited.

We did not bother putting up the tent this night but slept on our pads on top of the picnic tables under a starry moonlit night. Again, some Oriental celebration music serenaded us way into the night from one of the nearby villages.

	Friday, September 23, 2005
Destination: Nazareth	**Today's Miles:** 6.00
Starting Location: Har Devoriya	**Trip Miles:** 108.00

Day 19: We got started early at 7:10 AM without eating breakfast and were at the bottom of the mountain within a half hour. The trail then led us through groves of olives, pomegranates, pecans and figs. This was a very nice section of the trail and very peaceful in the cool morning. We soon started the breathtaking ascent up to Upper Nazareth, which is the modern Jewish city, which lies above the ancient biblical city of Nazareth. The climb was hard but the view got more spectacular with each step.

The Shuk (market) in Nazareth

At the top, there is a nice road and sidewalk around the side of the mountain, and we had our first view of the Mediterranean Sea, which is about fifty kilometers (30 miles) away.

We finished the tenth section (out of 44) of the Israel National Trail at the Arabic village of Mishod and had a cup of Turkish coffee offered to us from a local merchant. We had decided to take a day's rest in Nazareth as we had been invited by Maoz Inon to stay at his recently renovated guesthouse called the Fauzi Azar Inn. Moaz and his wife hiked the Israel National Trail last spring, and opened a guesthouse in the old market section of Nazareth for the specific purpose of blessing fellow hikers.

We had to walk three kilometers (2 miles) along the road to an Internet Cafe in the suburbs of Nazareth at the town of Reineh in order to find the phone number and directions to Maozs' guesthouse. The owners of the Internet Cafe, Jacob and Steven were unbelievably helpful. They served us ice cold drinks and let us use their computers and Internet service without charge! After having sent a few quick e-mails and getting instructions, we set off for Nazareth.

Within a few minutes of hitchhiking, we were picked up by Manhel, a young, very nice local Arab and were driven directly to our destination in the heart of the marketplace in Nazareth. Maoz met us at the White Mosque in the shuk (outdoor market) and took us to a neighbor's (Ramses) because his guesthouse was full with over thirty visitors.

Ramses was an excellent host and provided us with a wonderful room and many amenities. We went shopping in the market to buy meat, potatoes and salad for dinner and enjoyed a feast back at the hostel. After doing our laundry by hand (everything in both backpacks), we went over to the Fauzi Azar Inn to see a slideshow presentation by Maoz of his 2004 Israel National Trail hike. After nearly three weeks on the ground, it was so comfortable sleeping on a mattress!

	Saturday, September 24, 2005
Destination: Tsipori	**Today's Miles:** 4.00
Starting Location: Nazareth	**Trip Miles:** 112.00

The Fauzi Azar Inn

Day 20: We updated our trail journal at the Fauzi Azar Inn this morning, and have uploaded the new pictures from our last week's hike from Tiberias so friends can view them.

The Fauzi Azar Inn is an extremely interesting place and comfortable too, attracting many unique travelers from around the world. It is a beautiful authentic

Arabic styled house, with interesting architecture, fast Internet connection and an inviting kitchen. We highly recommend this place, which you can check out at www.fauziazarinn.com

We plan to continue hiking for a few hours this afternoon to Tsipori, and tomorrow continuing toward the Mediterranean coast. The Lord willing we hope to make it as far as Hadera by next weekend, a little over one hundred kilometers (63 miles).

We left the Fauzi Azar Inn in the late afternoon and after buying some trail supplies in the little shops from the outdoor market, we caught the #30 bus to Meshed, the point where we had left the trail the day before. Fully rested and restocked with food, water and supplies we began a quick two-hour trek of about seven kilometers to the Tsipori forest and foothills. First, we had to hike through the Arabic town of Mished, which was mostly a straight uphill climb. The local people were so friendly and the children were shouting Shalom and running along with us as we hiked through their village. We made it to the edge of a beautiful pine forest in Tsipori just before sunset. We quickly set up our tent and made soup and tea for dinner, and then Yossi, our friend from Kibbutz Yiftach called to see how we were doing. We always enjoy talking with friends and family at the end of the day, and after our conversation with Yossi, we fell fast asleep to the sound of jackals howling in the distant hills.

Sunday, September 25, 2005	
Destination: Tachana HaNazereem	**Today's Miles:** 8.10
Starting Location: Tsipori	**Trip Miles:** 120.10

Day 21: This was a beautiful day of hiking across rolling hills and through pine and cedar forests. We completed the eleventh part of the trail to the Yiftachel Intersection where Highways 79 and 77 cross by 11:00 AM, and had a break under the Eucalyptus trees. We have begun eating four small meals a day as the trail is quite demanding energy wise and the rest breaks are necessary for allowing sore muscles and tired feet to recover. We usually take a ten-minute break each hour and a longer one every two to three hours. There has been a big improvement since our first days of hiking when we needed to stop every twenty to thirty minutes.

Exhausted at Tachana HaNezareem (The Priest's Station)

We met three hikers on the trail today who are intending to go all the way to Eilat. They seemed to be hiking in a very different manner than us, and not just because they were all less than half our age! First, they hike only in the early mornings and late afternoons and take a six-hour break from 10:00 AM to 4:00 PM every day. They also are wearing long sleeve shirts and pants to protect their arms and legs from thorn bushes and overhanging branches. Another major difference is that they make a campfire every evening which they cook over, whereas we only use a small gasoline Coleman burner to quickly and efficiently cook. Although we love camp fires as much as anyone, we have learned that without the hassle of making a fire we stay cleaner and don't have the smell of smoke in our hair and on our clothes all the time. Anyway, their system was working for them and ours for us and we were able to keep up with their pace for two days and met them a few times along the trail during the week.

At Ein Yivkah we met a Bedouin cattle herder from the village of Caaveyah who was bringing his herd of cows down to the stream and large pools for an evening drink. Earlier we had hiked through his village of Ca-a-vee-ah and had stopped at a small market and bought cold drinks, ice cream and some peppermint tea bags. Immediately afterwards we hiked for a couple of kilometers horizontally across a steep grove on a very narrow path that makes up this part of the Israel National Trail (INT) This was unusual in that it is difficult to hike horizontally along a steep slope and all the trees were growing at the same angle as the hillside and not straight up as most trees will.

We arrived at a small oasis called Tachana HaNazereem (The Priest's Station) around 5:30 and stopped for the day. There is an old large two-story stone farmhouse there with a beautiful stone bridge that crosses the Tzipori Stream. The area is very green and fertile, and just a hundred meters (110 yards) or so from the farmhouse and bridge where there is a cistern with fresh drinking water flowing up from underground. The local friendly Bedouin women came there in the evening to refill their water jugs. The owner of the Tachana HaNazereem spoke with us briefly and said we could camp anywhere along the stream that we wished. Around nightfall, our three hiker friends arrived and after coordinating plans for meeting the next day on the Carmel Mountain range, we went to bed and fell asleep immediately.

Monday, September 26, 2005	
Destination: *Carmel Mountains above Haifa*	**Today's Miles:** *10.00*
Starting Location: *Tachana HaNazereem*	**Trip Miles:** *130.10*

Day 22: Today was our best hiking to date in that we covered sixteen kilometers (10 miles) for the first time. In order to finish the Israel Trail before the winter rains, which will make hiking the gullies and caverns of the Negev extremely dangerous, we must be able to hike between ten and twelve miles per day. Finally, we feel that our bodies have adjusted well to the physical exertion and we are really enjoying the trail and making good time. We still stop often to just explore, take pictures, or just rest but we are improving.

On Top of the Carmel Mountains

We often sing and pray while walking along the Trail and have enjoyed growing closer to each other every step of the way. After thirty-one years of marriage, we are surprised at how much richer our friendship and our relationship has become because of this 'walk of faith'. We have begun to massage each other's sore muscles and feet, and have been helping one another in difficult areas such as steep climbs and slippery slopes. After three weeks of no television, newspapers, or contact with the hussle and bustle of the world, we have found a completely new realm of love, joy and peace in the Holy Spirit. The valleys today were extremely gorgeous and quiet and we walked for hours without seeing a soul. At around 2:30 PM we arrived at the foothills of the Carmel Mountain range outside the northern end of the city of Haifa, and stopped for a couple hours to rest and buy groceries and supplies from an Orthodox Jewish supermarket in the Hassidic village of Recesseem. At 4:30 PM, we began a short two to three kilometer hike to Kibbutz Yagur, which marks the entrance to the Carmel Mountain Trail. At the kibbutz, we met some nice people, one who gave us a half-liter of gasoline for our cook stove, and another named Boaz who works on the kibbutz but lives in Haifa. He offered to assist us in anyway we needed at anytime during our hike and even offered us a lift in his car to the top of the mountain -- which of course we declined! He and others were concerned that it would be getting dark in a couple hours and that we might not have enough time to make it to the campground at the top of the mountain range. After exchanging cell phone numbers with Boaz, we started a very quick uphill climb on the Carmel Trail. God's grace was greatly upon us and the trail and view are unbelievably spectacular. The first half is a very steep climb and the second has a series of switchbacks, which makes it a bit easier. Still it is a challenge that is well worth the effort, and we would say that it is one of the nicest parts of the Israel National Trail that we have hiked so far. Amazingly, we made the 4 kilometer, 500 meter (1500 ft.) vertical climb, in one hour and forty minutes, and got to the campsite about fifteen minutes before it became too dark to safely hike. Our three friends were they are waiting for us and concerned that it had almost become dark and we had not yet arrived. This campground is a very nice spot with picnic tables, a bathroom and fresh water faucets. We were almost too exhausted to appreciate the view or to eat after such an effort, so we decided to just have a hot drink and cold snack. After sitting with our friends around their campfire for a few minutes, we crawled into our tent and into our sleeping bags and were fast asleep within minutes.

Tuesday, September 27, 2005	
Destination: Oren Campground - Carmel Mountains	**Today's Miles:** 7.50
Starting Location: Carmel Mountains above Haifa	**Trip Miles:** 137.60

Scaling Cliffs on the Carmel Mountain Range

Day 23: Our three hiking friends, Matan, Shy, and Doe, left the campground around 6:00 AM but we did not get going until 9:00 AM, partly because we were still recuperating from the previous day's climb and partly because it was a great place to wash and to reorganize our things. Since we only had twelve kilometers (7.5 miles) to hike this day, and we were up in the mountains so mid-afternoon heat would not be a factor, we were not concerned about getting an early start. This we later found out was a major miscalculation as this part of the trail is as difficult as it is beautiful.

Within an hour we arrived at a memorial to the soldiers fallen in the War of Attrition (1967-70) along the Suez Canal. This is probably one of the better war memorials that we have ever seen and is a real educational site. We were both deeply moved with emotion after walking around the complex and reading the names of those who gave their lives so that we could have the freedom to live in the Eretz Israel (Nation of Israel) and hike this beautiful trail.

We next reached the Druze Village of Eisphiyeh at the highest point in the Carmel range (546 meters) and stopped for a cup of coffee and to buy some groceries from the market. We walked through some fantastic woods, riverbeds and ravines and each time were awestruck by the magnificent views and spectacular scenery. From the mountain peaks you can see all of Haifa and as far away as Nazareth, with an inviting view of the Mediterranean Sea coastline. The trail reminded us of parts of the Appalachian Trail that we have hiked in the state of Georgia in the U.S.A.

By 3:00 PM we were only a few kilometers from the Oren campground, our destination for the day and were unconcerned about the time or pace, but were a little sorry that we would probably miss our friends who would begin hiking again after their six hour rest at 4:00 PM. Well each kilometer became more difficult from this point and it took us a very long time to make progress down the mountainside. At the end, we could see the campground directly below us -- 350 meters (1140 ft.) -- but were horrified to see the steepness of the descent off the rock face that it would take to get there. Slowly, slowly, helping each other every step we made steady progress with our fully loaded packs, and at 6:15 PM, we reached terra firma! Hallelujah! Looking back at the summit from below, it was hard to believe what we had just done, and knew that it had only been possible because God had strengthened us and helped us every step of the way.

Since it was middle of the week and a full week before the Jewish New Year, the campground was empty and we had all the facilities to ourselves and chose the nicest spot next to the restrooms. We quickly set up our tent, cooked dinner, washed our socks and ourselves and then massaged one another's legs, knees and feet so that we could fall asleep.

Wednesday, September 28, 2005	
Destination: Mitzpeh Other (Ophir Overlook)	**Today's Miles:** 8.10
Starting Location: Oren Campground - Carmel Mountains	**Trip Miles:** 145.70

Day 24: Having now hiked 217 kilometers (141 miles), we finished walking the breadth of the land from Tel-Dan to Haifa (see Genesis 13:17), and now have the length to go! We head south now for the next couple of days, hiking along the Carmel range about 3 km (2 mi) east from the Mediterranean coast. We began with a one hundred fifty-nine stair-step climb (exact number) to a lookout point on the most northwestern

Carmel Mountains - Southern range and caves

section of the Carmel Mountains, and from there, another twenty minute climb to the summit. We now had a view north and south as far as fifty kilometers in each direction and since there had been an early morning light sprinkle, the air was crisp and clear.

Today we are sore from the previous three day, fifty kilometers (31 miles) hike from Nazareth but we are spiritually rejoicing and mentally preparing for the remaining 723 kilometers (452 miles) we have left to hike to Eilat on the Red Sea. We climbed up and then back down over five mountains in this range today and the rocky trail is taking a beating on the bottom of our feet. At 1:30 PM, we arrived at the visitor's center of the Caves' Stream National Park and immediately bought two ice cold drinks. This is a beautifully scenic area, which reminds us of the western United States, with huge prehistoric caves high in the rocky cliffs.

Anat, one of the park attendants that runs the visitors center was very nice to us and allowed us to make use the facilities while we took our afternoon lunch break and a short nap. After lunch, we met an Israeli woman, Ayana, whom we had not seen in eighteen years. While we were on our trip around the world with our six children from 1987-1988, she had moved into the house that we rented on Moshav Tsde Varburg near Kfar Saba. We did not recognize her at first but she immediately recognized us and over the next half-hour or so, we were re-acquainted.

Having taken a long afternoon break, we realized that we would not make it to our destination of the city of Zichron Yaakow, so decided to stop at an amazing overlook and campsite called Mitzpeh Ophir. This place is not only located at a very high elevation on the Carmel Mountain range, but it also has a five story lookout tower on top. The facilities are very nice and well maintained, and again we were the only ones camped there and we had the whole campground and picnic area to ourselves. What a tremendous 360-degree panoramic view we had from the top of the lookout tower! It was hard to believe that we had driven along the coastal highway within a few miles of this spot dozens of times and had never known it existed.

With our tent pitched on a sandy spot facing the Mediterranean Sea, we turned in for the night knowing that God had altered our plans to allow us to enjoy this wonderful place this night.

	Thursday, September 29, 2005	
Destination: Ramat HaNadiv		**Today's Miles:** 8.10
Starting Location: Mitzpeh Ophir (Ophir Overlook)		**Trip Miles:** 153.80

The Pools at Ein Tsur (The Rock Spring)

Day 25: A week of hiking up and down mountains has been taking its toll and today our feet are sore and we had difficulty just getting to Zichron Yaakov, which is a city just eight or nine kilometers (5-6 miles) south of Mitzpeh Ophir. The trail is nice along this mountain ridge, and the hike not very strenuous but physically we were in need of a break.

At 1:00 PM, we reached Hwy 70, which marks the end of the 14th section (out of 44) of the Israel National Trail. From there, we had the choice to hike along the highway and then south along the power lines or hitchhike into Zichron Yakow and get some much needed groceries and supplies. We had gone through most of our groceries and supplies over the past several days and were out of just about everything. Anyway, we decided to hitchhike into the city and within five minutes, a young lady named Morine, who lives in the village of Binyaminna, picked us up and drove us to the supermarket in Zichron Yakov. She was sweet and did not mind that it was out of her way and seemed anxious to learn all about our journey. She gave us her cell phone number and highly recommended a campground not far away (which happened to be right on the Israel Trail), and said that maybe she would come to visit us in the evening.

Zichron Yakov (Jacob's Memory) is one of the oldest cities in modern day Israel, founded in 1882 and is a beautiful community nestled in the foothills in the southern end of the Carmel mountains. After buying all the groceries we would need for the next few days as well as a fresh supply ingredients for our trail mix which we eat while hiking (almonds, walnuts, raisins, muesli, etc.) we sat down in the park and had a picnic lunch of baked turkey wings which had been on sale. Invigorated from our rest and our lunch feast, with happy hearts we proceeded to hike the four kilometers (2.5 miles) to the Ein Tsur (Rock Spring) springs and Ramat HaNadiv campground. The Ein Tsur Spring is the only 1st century BCE Roman aqueduct and spring that has water still flowing! The cold water comes out of the ground, and runs along the aqueduct and into a series of several pools. The water is crystal-clear and delicious. The name Ein Tsur is very close in sound to "I'm sore" and the cold water really helped heal our sore fee, which we soaked in the pools for about fifteen minutes. After filling our water bladders from the spring, we hiked the last kilometer to the campground and set up our tent and mosquito net. Since we were so tired and sore from the Carmel Mountain hike, we gathered a mound of pine needles from around the area and put them under the tent. We could now appreciate a comfortable bed of pine needles to sleep on that night.

At 8:30 PM Morine and her boyfriend, Shlomi called and let us know that they had driven up to the campground. After a few minutes, they located us and we sat and talked with them for about an hour and a half. They brought us some homemade herbal soap for the hike and some dried figs, dates and almonds to snack on. Morine had just lost her job this day and when she stopped to pick us up and heard that we were hiking all across Israel on the INT, she became encouraged again, realizing that there was much more to life than just material things. We had a wonderful time, sharing and speaking with them both and felt that we had now made two new friends. We hope they can join us for a couple days of hiking when we reach the Negev Desert. It is so wonderful meeting people and making new friends as we hike this trail on our 'walk of faith'. One can never know what God has in store tomorrow until you let Him lead, guide and direct, but you can always rest assured it will be thrills, romance and adventure.

Friday, September 30, 2005	
Destination: Caesarea & Hadera	**Today's Miles:** 13.20
Starting Location: Ramat HaNadiv	**Trip Miles:** 167.00

Day 26: We began the day in the pine forests on the Carmel Mountains to the south of Zichron Yakov and we ended the day on the Mediterranean Sea along the archeological site of the ancient Roman city of Caesarea. Overall, we had

2000-year-old Roman Aqueduct

the best day of hiking yet, going 21 kilometers (13.2 miles) and arriving in Hadera just before sunset.

For the first few kilometers this morning we walked through the scenic forests of Ramat Nadiv, south of Zichron Yakov and quickly reached the rocky cliffs, which mark the southern end of the Carmel Mountain, range. These cliffs are 140 meters high (455 ft.) straight vertical drops that run from north to south parallel to the coast, which is only a few kilometers away.  The rocks on these cliffs are extremely sharp and we felt like they were tearing up the soles of our shoes with each step. Along the cliffs are several very interesting archeological sites, which we stopped at to take pictures and explore. One such site is an ancient Jewish settlement at Chorvat Ekev that dates back twenty-one centuries and was later inhabited in the Byzantine and Medieval periods. There were also ancient tombs in the area called Tumuli, which dated back 4500 years.

When we reached the southern most edge of the Carmel Mountain cliffs, we had a view as far south as Tel-Aviv around sixty kilometers (37.5 miles). From this point we begin hiking on flat terrain until we come to the Judean hills and the mountains around Jerusalem. We slowly and painstakingly hiked down the rocky cliffs for about a half hour and reached the outskirts of the village of Bejaminna. From this point we walked westward towards the coast along an ancient Roman aqueduct that runs from the Carmel mountain foothills to the ancient Roman city of Caesarea. We were amazed that this engineering marvel was in such relatively good condition after twenty centuries. Three kilometers (2 miles) later we reached the coastal Arabic village of Jesr- Al-Zarka and hiked through its length until we came to a small outdoor cafe near the beach where we stopped to have coffee and a pastry. After another kilometer of hiking in the sand, we reached the Caesarea beach. Having anticipated this moment for over a week, we jumped into the sea and played in the waves like two kids for over an hour. This beach is pristine and beautiful, without any people around, only two fishermen fishing from the shore.

We changed out of our normal hiking clothes into sandals and beachwear and proceeded to walk along the shore for the next eight kilometers (5 miles) parallel to the ancient Roman aqueduct which lies about one hundred meters inland. Along the way, an Israeli couple, Avi and Nurit, stopped us and inquired about our backpacks. They were so excited about what we were doing that they even offered to pick us up wherever we would be next weekend from the trail and take us to their home in the village of Pardes Hanna for the weekend. After chatting with them for about an hour, we exchanged telephone numbers and promised to keep in touch. The warmth and sincerity of these total strangers towards us touched our hearts.

In the late afternoon, we finally reached the Caesarea National Park and as we walked around the outskirts of the park we kept looking inside with fascination at the ruins of the city where the Holy Spirit was first poured out upon the Gentiles (Acts 10). What could have been a hot and boring part of the trail turned out to be an exciting spiritual adventure. As the week came to an end we were looking forward to reaching our destination city of Hadera for a Shabbat rest, we now began to make very good time, hiking four kilometers per hour!

After we passed the Caesarea amphitheatre, we stopped at a Paz gas station rest area and rested for about an hour. During which time we had a wonderfully encouraging cell phone conversation with our youngest daughter Tehila who is finishing her undergraduate degree in political science at Florida State University in the USA. We also spoke with a group of tourists who were sightseeing all the highlights in Israel in just eight days -- what a contrast from the way we were seeing the country!

We hiked the last five kilometers (3 miles) along the Hadera River, past the Caesarea Electric Power Plant and along a road parallel to the coast into the outskirts of Hadara in just one hour and twenty minutes. Exhausted but exhilarated from a week of hiking nearly one hundred kilometers (60 miles), we called our friend Rena who lived in Hadera and she drove out to where we were at the Olgat Interchange on Hwy 2 and picked us up so we could spend the Shabbat with her.

We are amazed at the contrasting environments we have seen and hiked through this day, from forests and mountains, to rocky cliffs, fertile plains and vineyards, from very poor Arabic villages to beautiful sandy beaches then along an ancient Roman aqueduct and ruins and finally into a modern skyscraper city all in just twenty kilometers (12.5 miles). There is probably no other trail in the world that would take you through such diversity in just one day. We have now completed over a fourth of the trail, 278 kilometers (174 miles), and only have 662 kilometers (426 miles) to go! We are thankful for God's grace, provision, and strength this week and for His protection and blessings that have been upon us each step on this 'walk of faith'. "It is God who arms me with strength and makes my way perfect. He makes my feet like the feet of a deer; he enables me to stand on the heights... You broaden the path beneath me, so that my ankles do not turn." II Samuel 22:34-35, 37.

Saturday, October 01, 2005	
Destination: Hadera	**Today's Miles:** 0.00
Starting Location: Caesarea & Hadera	**Trip Miles:** 167.00

Rena blows the shofar for Rosh HaShana

Day 27: A day of rest at Rena Kalina's apartment in Hadera. We are thankful to be able to put up our tent in Rena's backyard and have some great fellowship with her, wash all our clothes, eat well, upload our pictures and update our trail journal. Rena is a gifted musician and blew the shofar (ram's horn) for us.

Monday, October 03, 2005	
Destination: Hof HaYarok – South of Netanya	**Today's Miles:** 7.50
Starting Location: Yinai Beach - north of Netanya	**Trip Miles:** 180.80

Day 29: We walked all day along the coastline, stopping to swim, relax and nap several times on the beach. The coastal cliffs,

which are very steep, run parallel along the shore and the view is awesome. Words alone cannot describe the beauty of this part of the

Hiking the coast from Netanya to Tel-Aviv

trail. The Jewish New Year - 5766 - begins at sundown today, thus the eve of the holiday Rosh HaShana so there are thousands of people on the beaches walking, sunbathing, fishing, paragliding and just enjoying the beautiful weather and the Sea. As we were getting close to the Netanya beach, a young man named Ori came ran up to us waving his arms and handed us two apples saying "Happy New Year, trail hikers". He as well had hiked the entire Israel National Trail last year and had spent six months in the Negev exploring off the Israel National Trail all on his own. We exchanged great stories and determined to stay in touch with this young man. Towards evening we completed the 17th section of the Trail and arrived at Hof HaYarok (The Green Beach) just south of Netanya where we camped the night. Our spirits were soaring after such a beautiful hike and a nice hot bowl of soup and a sandwich, which prepared us for a good night's sleep.

Tuesday, October 04, 2005	
Destination: Acadia Beach - Hertzelia	**Today's Miles:** 9.40
Starting Location: The Green Beach - Hof Yarok	**Trip Miles:** 190.20

On the cliffs overlooking the Mediterranean

Day 30: Today is the first day of the New Year (a two day holiday in Israel) and as expected the beaches filled up quickly. In between towns the beaches were nearly deserted and the scenery inspirational. People were all day stopping us and asking about our hiking. We met two more young men, Tal and Gil from Nes Zion, who having completed their army service were hiking the Israel National Trail as well. About mid-day the trail took a surprising turn upward to the cliff heights about one hundred meters (325 ft.) above the shore. For the next several miles, we hiked along the most dramatic trail with the most spectacular view imaginable. We could see from Caesarea in the north to Tel Aviv in the south as well as the Samarian Mountains to the east. We even found a wonderful picnic area under some eucalyptus trees where we enjoyed a tuna and garlic sandwich with halva (a sweet sesame roll) for dessert. We passed through some of the beaches that we were familiar with from the time we lived in Ra'ananna, which brought back many memories of enjoying the sun and sand when our children were small. We set up camp at the exclusive Acadia Beach in Hertzelia, famous for the rich and famous who visit Israel regularly.

Wednesday, October 05, 2005	
Destination: Joshua Gardens - Yarkon River & Park	**Today's Miles:** 7.00
Starting Location: Acadia Beach - Hertzelia	**Trip Miles:** 197.20

Rosh HaShana (New Year) -- Yarkon Park

Day 31: With only eight kilometers (5 miles) of shoreline remaining to our trail before arriving in Tel-Aviv, we decided to take it easy and enjoy one last dip in the sea and rest at Tel Baruch before turning inland to hike along the Yarkon River. After lunch on the beach, we hiked around the Sde Dov Airport between Ramat Aviv and Tel Aviv and marveled all the progress that the city has undergone since we first came to Israel over thirty years ago. Today there are bicycle trails everywhere and the city's skyline is an architectural marvel. We arrived at the Yarkon Park around 2:30 PM and found it was swarming with families picnicking and barbequing everywhere. We hiked for several more kilometers through this beautiful park completely amazed that you could be unaware that we were in the largest metropolitan city in Israel. We arrived at the Joshua Park in the Yarkon Reserve and found a great campsite on the lake. We called an old friend, Eli, whom we had not seen in over ten years. Eli immediately came out to visit with us and brought us dinner and a bottle of wine. We had a great time catching up with our friend and slept very soundly in our tent on the soft green park grass that night. Holidays stir sentimental memories and for us we were missing all of our precious family more than usual. We hope to hike the best parts of this trail with them someday in the future.

Thursday, October 06, 2005	
Destination: Moshav Elishema	**Today's Miles:** 8.00
Starting Location: Joshua Gardens - Yarkon River & Park	**Trip Miles:** 205.20

Hiking along the Yarkon River

Day 32: We hiked all morning along the Yarkon River and although we crossed through Tel Aviv and three suburban cities (Ramat Gan, Bnei Brak, & Petach Tikvah), we were hardly aware that we were in the largest city in Israel. Our view had been only of the gorgeous green park and the gentle winding Yarkon River. It was no coincidence that we once again met up with Yuval, a young man just out of the army, who was reading his Tenach (Old Testament) while he walk the land he loved in search of God. He was hiking with his parents for a short distance through Tel Aviv on the trail because they lived close by in Petach Tikvah. Around noon, he caught up with us and we hiked together to the Adanim intersection where we parted company as he was going on to visit friends in the area. We hope this young man finds the answers he has in his spiritual quest from the New Testament we gave him. We then called Yair and Darit Erez who we had become acquainted with at the Fauzi Azar Inn in Nazareth. They lived very nearby the Israel Trail. They had invited us to stop in for coffee but it turned out that they had a surprise luncheon feast

prepared as well as their guest room for us to stay in. Without hesitation, we decided to take an early Shabbat rest and enjoy their warm hospitality. They took us to the MEGA supermarket, which is similar to the Wal Mart in the USA and we restocked all of our supplies and provisions and are especially grateful to once again have clean laundry. Yair and Darit know the land extremely well and have hiked extensively throughout Israel. They gave us some great tips and we were happy to have new friends. We hope to be in Jerusalem, a hike of around 80 kilometers (50 miles) by Wednesday evening, which marks the beginning of Yom Kippur, the Day of Atonement. Since many in Israel will be praying and fasting on this day, we will take a break from our hike and join the nation in prayer. The weather continues to be ideal, in the low 80's F (high 20's C) and great visibility. We have really enjoyed the sea breeze all week long but look forward to the fresh mountain air in the Judean hills as we start our ascent to Jerusalem. "Pray for the peace of Jerusalem: May those who love you be secure." Psalm 122:6

	Friday, October 07, 2005	
Destination: Eucalyptus / Pine Forest (El-Ad)		**Today's Miles:** 7.50
Starting Location: Moshav Elishema & The Baptist Village		**Trip Miles:** 212.70

A day of rest at the Erez family's home

Day 33: We awoke early in the morning having slept so soundly on nice comfortable beds in the home of our new friends, the Erez family. After completing our updates on-line for the trail journal, we will first finish the Yarkon trail and then start hiking south and parallel along Israel's first toll highway, Kaveesh Sesh (Hwy 6). We will be walking very close along the borders of the West Bank, which should be an interesting experience. We are told it is a highly patrolled area and should be safe, though it is not recommended that we spent the night camping anywhere in the area. Hwy 6 is Israel's newest attempt to alleviate the city congestion as the original highways were designed and built for about one tenth of the current traffic. There are no tollbooths but each license plate is photographed on entry and exit from the highway and a bill arrives in the mail for the number of kilometers that you traveled. It is super fast, efficient and expensive! After a twenty kilometers (12.5 miles) walk along this area we will be heading southeast into the Judean foothills toward Latrun and then onto Jerusalem. We have uploaded twenty-five new pictures on our 360.yahoo.com/gregandbev2004 website in an album called "On the Coast - Hadera to Tel-Aviv," and thanks to Yair and Darit we have been able to update our trail journal today. Yair and Darit took us back out to the Israel National Trail near the Baptist Village and we continued to hike from there to Afek National Park. Since we arrived relatively early (around 1:30 PM) at Afek Park which marks the completion of section #19 of the 44 sections of the Israel National Trail, we decided to continue onto section #20. We hiked for several hours parallel to Hwy 6 and reached a eucalyptus and pine tree forest eight kilometers (5 miles) south of the city of Rosh HaEin (Head of the Spring). We found a group of four picnic tables in the middle of the pine forest and just a couple hundred meters (yards) from the trail where we set up our tent on top of a thick cushion of pine needles we had gathered. The pine needles make a wonderful mattress when sleeping on the ground especially with our rubber sleeping mats on top. After setting up the tent, we went to greet the people picnicking near us who were speaking Russian. They immediately invited us to have a toast to the New Year and share their barbequed meal with them. Once again, we made new friends, sat around their bonfire, and talked for hours. They gave us two full bottles of water when they departed which really helped us, as there was not any water source nearby.

Saturday, October 08, 2005	
Destination: Tel Chadid - the Ben-Shemen Forest	**Today's Miles:** 7.50
Starting Location: Eucalyptus / Pine Forest (El-Ad)	**Trip Miles:** 220.20

Day 34: We woke up well rested on this beautiful Shabbat morning. After breakfast, we headed out towards the Ben-Shemen Forest, which is about twelve kilometers (8 miles) south. From our campground, we had a great view of hiking in this week. It was very hot and humid all day with little shade for us as we hiked through open fields and several desolate looking marble quarries. Our water

supply was very low and we thanked the Lord when we passed a large construction site we saw a water tank with a faucet! We filled up our water bladders and another bottle for the road. Now, with extra water we were able to have a nice cup of coffee and some chocolate on a break before hiking the final four kilometers to Tel Chadid on the northern edge of the Ben-Shemen Forest where we planned to set up camp for the night. It had been a very hot, long and dusty day.

When we got to Tel Chadid, which was in the forest, a couple was driving by on the dirt road and stopped and asked if we had found a scarf and then asked us if we were hiking the Israel Trail. Sageev and Galit had hiked the trail last year and had just returned from

Tunnel-Crossing under Kavesh Shesh (Hwy. 6)

a three-day hike in the Negev. After talking with them for several minutes, they insisted that we spend the night in their home in Hod Ha-Sharon and they assured us they would return us to the same spot in the morning. What a blessing they were and we needed cleaning up and to be refreshed before our ascent to Jerusalem this week. This couple had such a warm heart for fellow hikers and we know we will surely remain friends. We added the seven new pictures for the last two days onto the 360.yahoo.com/gregandbev2004 website and into the album named 'On the Coast - Hadera to Tel-Aviv'. Please take time to enter our GUEST BOOK on this site and leave us a message and we'll get back to you next time we log on. The LORD willing, our next journal blog entry will be from Jerusalem!

Sunday, October 09, 2005	
Destination: Kibbutz Shaalabim (near Latrun)	**Today's Miles:** 9.00
Starting Location: Tel Chadid - Ben-Shemen Forest	**Trip Miles:** 229.20

Looking back on the Tel-Aviv area

Day 35 (30th day of hiking): In the morning Galit drove us back to Tel Chadid and we began hiking from the exact spot where they had picked us up the evening before. The first two-kilometer were great and we quickly got to the Ben-Shemen forest and a lovely picnic area where we had breakfast. From that point the trail got difficult as it was hot and there was practically no shade as we hiked along quarried limestone fields. We were running very low on water when we reached a construction site where we were able to refill our water supply!

Our goal today had been to walk nineteen kilometers (12 miles) to Latrun but somehow we missed one of the trail markers around 2:30 PM and it took us an extra hour to backtrack and then reconnect onto the Israel Trail. After several more kilometers of hiking in the heat, we reached an Orthodox Jewish kibbutz (agricultural settlement) called Shaalabim and decided to stop at their small grocery store to buy some cold drinks and a few supplies. One of the residents saw that we were tired and offered us a ride to the kibbutz store, and a few minutes later, we were picnicking on a grassy lawn. Since it was getting late we decided to spend the night and a nice lady that we met, Tsipi, had tea with us and made us feel welcome to camp the night there on the kibbutz. Tsipi lives in Ramla and works three days a week on the kibbutz. She spoke very highly of the love and spirit of cooperation on this orthodox settlement and wished all of Israel could be like this community. We certainly felt the peace and slept well.

	Monday, October 10, 2005	
Destination: Shaar HaGai		**Today's Miles:** 8.10
Starting Location: Kibbutz Shaalabim (near Latrun)		**Trip Miles:** 237.30

Climbing up to Jerusalem is difficult even with a jeep

Day 36: Without eating breakfast we started hiking at 6:15 AM in the cool fresh morning air towards Latrun and quickly crossed Highway #1, which is the major thoroughfare up to Jerusalem. Walking along large plowed fields, we had a view of

Tel Aviv behind us and the fast approaching Judean Hills ahead of us.

We made it to Latrun around 8:00 AM and stopped at the Monastery on the site where we had breakfast. Unfortunately, our Coleman gasoline cooker caught fire and we had to shut if off and empty the fuel from it, hoping to repair later when we get to Jerusalem. From Latrun we began the mountainous climb up to Jerusalem twenty-eight kilometers (17.5 miles) away. The first part of this trail to Shaar HaGai is not very steep and was very easy to hike. We arrived at the park campsite early and set up our campsite in a beautiful pine forest. Because our camp stove was broken, we had to make our first wood campfire to cook soup and tea. Bev made a delicious fresh broccoli soup and shared it with a fellow hiker, named Hayim, who was camped nearby.

The trail from Latrun is very important historically and there are many markers indicating the heroism in battles fought for the conquest of Jerusalem during the war of Independence in 1948. This area was also a key to a massive project to bring water to the city after the war. Only after this hike have we been able to appreciate the difficult challenges that were faced by the pioneers who established the State of Israel.

Tuesday, October 11, 2005	
Destination: Kibbutz Tsuba (13 km S.E. of Jerusalem)	**Today's Miles:** 12.00
Starting Location: Shaar HaGai	**Trip Miles:** 249.30

Looking Down on Hwy. 1 to Jerusalem

Day 37: Hayim had a friend, Shlomo, join him for a few days on the trail. He brought him some fresh supplies and they shared fresh borekas (pastries) with us for breakfast. The climb from Shaar HaGai was intense and very serious. We had to take many breaks over the next few hours and criss-crossed paths with Hayim and Shlomo several times. Hayim is an engineer who was taking three weeks off to hike part of the Israel

National Trail. He and his friend were the first hikers that we had met that were our age. At one of our rest stops together, we heard them reading the Psalms in Hebrew and discussing them, which inspired us and lead to some rich conversations that evening.

All day hiking uphill we anticipated arriving at an ancient Roman pool called Ein Limor near the Arabic village of Ein Raffa. Upon arrival around 4:00 PM, we found Shlomo and Hayim had already cooled off in the pool just as a herd of sheep and goats arrived. For the next half hour, we all sat around waiting for all the animals to have their drink of spring water before we could jump in and cool off.

The hike to Kibbutz Tsuba from the spring was three kilometers (2 miles) almost straight up a very steep mountain road -- exhausting for the end of a long day. We got to the kibbutz as the sun was setting and called our Russian friend, Zalman, who lives in Ramot a neighborhood of Jerusalem. He invited us to spend Yom Kippur with him and arranged to pick us up at 8:00 PM. In the meantime, we had dinner and a very interesting spiritual conversation with Hayim and Shlomo before saying goodbye to them.

We were again very grateful to have a hot shower and sleep in a comfortable bed.

Wednesday, October 12, 2005	
Destination: Jerusalem	**Today's Miles:** 4.00
Starting Location: Kibbutz Tsuba (S.E. of Jerusalem)	**Trip Miles:** 253.30

Sharing the Ein Limor pool with goats and sheep

Day 38: Today is the day before the Jewish Day of Atonement, Yom Kippur. We spent the day repairing all our broken equipment: cook stove, flashlight, blow-up pillow, torn backpack, etc. and thanks to Zalman's help we got everything fixed and washed all our clothes

and back packs. After four hundred kilometers (250 miles) of hiking over the past five weeks, our bodies felt as though they need a few days rest so we are planning to stay in Jerusalem until Sunday morning.

Erev (evening) Yom Kippur began with loud sirens ringing to announce the beginning of the fast. All traffic in Israel ceases and even the traffic lights are turned off. That evening, we enjoyed a walk around the Ramot neighborhood with Zalman observing the many small synagogues packed with worshippers. It was nice to be walking without the backpacks and fun to walk in the middle of the highways normally packed with vehicles. This is a unique holiday experience, which only occurs once a year in Israel when an entire nation quiets itself in reflection before the LORD.

Thursday, October 13, 2005	
Destination: Jerusalem	**Today's Miles:** 6.00
Starting Location: Jerusalem	**Trip Miles:** 259.30

Jerusalem - No Traffic in Israel on Yom Kippur

Day 39: Yom Kippur - The Day of Atonement. It was so quiet that we slept in late, almost to 8:00 AM. Since we were fasting, we decided to take a hike around the city and "Pray for the Peace of Jerusalem." The Jewish fast also involves not drinking water so it was a little difficult in the hot sun and we returned quite tired at around 1:00 PM and took a much-needed nap.

The city itself was strangely quiet and still with a look of being almost deserted as everyone is either in synagogue or inside his or her homes. Children love riding their bikes, scooters and skateboards on the empty roads.

We broke the fast in the evening with a light meal and for the first time in a month watched the news on CNN before retiring for the night.

Friday, October 14, 2005	
Destination: Mevasseret Zion	**Today's Miles:** 0.00
Starting Location: Jerusalem	**Trip Miles:** 259.30

Celebrating Greg's 52nd birthday with friends

Day 40: We contacted John Hulley, a biblical scholar and author of the book "What's the Messiah Waiting For?" who invited us to his home in Mevasseret Zion, a modern suburb of Jerusalem. His home is only a few kilometers from the Israel National Trail, which we will be back to on Sunday morning. He loaned us his car to go to the supermarket and to the vegetable market in the nearby Turkish town of Abu Gush.

Bev enjoyed having a spacious kitchen to prepare the Erev Shabbat fish dinner for John and three guests from Holland. We had a wonderful time-sharing our experiences with our new friends. One of the Dutch guests, Vincent, is an Israeli tour guide and hopes to join us in the Negev on part the Trail with his wife, Tabitha. After the meal, Greg got a surprise cake in honor of his fifty-second birthday, which will be on Saturday.

Saturday, October 15, 2005	
Destination: Mevasseret Zion	**Today's Miles:** 0.00
Starting Location: Mevasseret Zion	**Trip Miles:** 259.30

View of Jerusalem from Mevasseret Zion

Day 41: Saturday - A Sabbath day of rest at John Hulley's home in Mevasseret Zion, and Greg's fifty-second birthday. We updated the journal and uploaded this weeks pictures to our website. The new picture album in Yahoo is called "Climbing up to Jerusalem."

Tonight we have been invited to

a spiritual evening of song and fellowship, which we are looking forward to. Today has been a very relaxing day and we enjoyed reading John's book "What's the Messiah Waiting For?" Contact us if you are interested in getting this book on CD, either by leaving us a message in the Guest Book on this site or e-mailing us at gregandbev2004@yahoo.com

Tomorrow morning we go back to Kibbutz Tsova, only a few km from here, and begin hiking southwards toward the cities of Beer-Sheva, Dimona and finally Arad where we embark into the Negev Desert. We still have five hundred and forty kilometers to go to get to Eilat and by God's grace and help hope to arrive in five to six weeks. Remember us in your prayers!

Sunday, October 16, 2005	
Destination: Mevasseret Zion	**Today's Miles:** 0.00
Starting Location: Mevasseret Zion	**Trip Miles:** 259.30

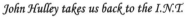

John Hulley takes us back to the I.N.T.

Day 42 (Sunday): Having gotten thoroughly spoiled at John Hulley's home, we decided to take one more day's rest before starting the second half of our hike from Jerusalem to Eilat. We spent the day reading, relaxing, and catching up on correspondence. Early tomorrow morning, we plan to return to the Israel National Trail from where we left off last Tuesday night at Kibbutz Tsuba.

Monday, October 17, 2005	
Destination: Tsur Hadassah	**Today's Miles:** 13.10
Starting Location: Mevasseret Zion	**Trip Miles:** 272.40

Day 43: We were so blessed to hike this day without our backpacks as our Dutch friend, Vincent, offered to drive out and bring them to us at our campsite tonight. The daypacks feel so light

Yad Kennedy Lookout (The Kennedy Memorial)

that we can hardly stop from running. John took us back to the trail early in the morning and we immediately had to climb down a steep mountain trail and up an equally high mountain on the other side of a narrow Wadi to reach a spectacular overlook at Ein Sataf. With light packs, we made it in less than an hour (about half the usual time) and stopped to have a cup of coffee at the beautiful cafe overlooking all the mountains and forests in the area.

Even after getting rid of or sending all the unnecessary items we had back to Eilat over the past six weeks, our backpacks still weigh approximately fifteen and twenty kg (33 and 44 lbs.) respectively when we are carrying three and a half liters of water and a three days food supply. All day we were so thankful to be hiking without our backpacks and made great time as a result, even though the terrain was mountainous and very rugged. The southern Judean mountains are gorgeous but rather steep with many archeological sites along the trails dating back to the Roman & Crusader periods. We pasted a current archeological dig where remains of artifacts dating to John the Baptist have been uncovered. This area is proposed to be a major tourist site soon.

After having hiked twenty-one kilometers (13.1 miles) by evening, we decided to set up camp in a beautiful park outside the town of Tsur Hadassah. Vincent and his wife, Tabitha, met us a half-hour later at our campsite with our gear, several gallons of water (there wasn't any in the park) and a hot meal they prepared for us at home! After eating, we made a campfire and sat around talking for a couple of hours, enjoying the warmth of the fire and a beautiful full moon. Tonight is the eve of Succoth, the Feast of Tabernacles. Most Jewish families in Israel celebrate this seven-day holiday by sleeping in their homemade shelters (booths) near their homes and apartments.

We turned in to go to sleep in our tent late this night (10:00 PM), but not until Vincent had convinced us to allow him to drive back out in the morning to take our backpacks and gear so that we could hike another day with only the light day packs! It was so wonderful of our new friends to join us and keep us company, and we really appreciated their love and kindness in a way that words cannot express.

	Tuesday, October 18, 2005	
Destination: The British Park - Tel Azeka		**Today's Miles:** 15.00
Starting Location: Tsur Hadassah		**Trip Miles:** 287.40

The Caesar Road -- looking over the city of Beit Shemesh

Day 44: We woke up late at 5:45 AM and had to pack up our tent and backpacks quickly because we needed to meet Vincent at the start of the next trail at 8:00 AM. We had hiked the day before without the backpacks, and although we only had to hike four kilometers (2.5 miles) with all our equipment to where he would meet us, it seemed to take us such a long time. We hiked as quickly as we could for an hour and forty-five minutes without a break and just made it in time! After having a great breakfast and filter coffee which Vincent had brought from home, we quickly repacked our day packs and headed off on the Caesar Road, having agreed to meet again with Vincent at the British Park at 4:15 PM, twenty one kilometers away. The Caesar Road was built by the Romans to bring one of the Caesars to Jerusalem from the Mediterranean coast and was in surprisingly good condition in certain sections after two thousand years.

Again, without the packs we hiked quickly and in just a couple hours crossed the length of the Valley of Elah where David had fought Goliath. We passed the city of Beit Shemesh by lunchtime and after a quick break made it to the base of Tel Azeka by early afternoon. "Tel" means mound and signifies an area where there have been layers of settlements built up over many centuries and because of one generation building on top of the ruins of previous generations, it forms an archeological mound. The ancient city of Azeka had, at the time of King Hezekiah, been the third largest city in Judah outside of Lachish and Jerusalem. It was captured and sacked by the king of Assyria, Sennacharib when he came up in a failed attempt to conquer Jerusalem. It is a huge site and one of the highest mountains in the area with a spectacular 360-degree view of the entire region. We reached the summit of the Tel without any difficulty but immediately began having a spiritual struggle, as we were feeling tired, frustrated and stressed. As will happen in these situations, we immediately missed an Israel National Trail marker and walked a couple of kilometers out of our way even though we had gone back and looked for the marker. In the end, we just followed our map and we just made it to the pick-up point at the last minute, but were exhausted from the effort. This was our longest day yet and we had managed to hike twenty-four kilometers (15 miles) of the Israel Trail which transverse the southern Judean hills and mountains. The absolute beauty of this area and its historical and biblical importance was something we had never known about or experienced in our twenty years of living in Israel. We made a nice soft mattress of leaves from the carob trees growing in the British Park and set up our tent on top of them. Again, we had a great hot meal that had been prepared by our friend and benefactor, Vincent. We really appreciated his thoughtfulness. While eating, we noticed a very friendly white Labrador in the picnic area, which apparently did not have an owner. He enjoyed our company and we enjoyed sharing some of our dinner with him before retiring early for the night.

Wednesday, October 19, 2005	
Destination: Mevasseret Zion	**Today's Miles:** 0.00
Starting Location: The British Park - Tel Azeka	**Trip Miles:** 287.40

Day 45: We woke up to a beautiful morning under the carob trees in the British Park. There was a lovely fresh breeze blowing from the sea, and our new friend, whom we nicknamed "Dogly," was lying on a blanket at our feet. Today would be an easy day as trail #26 is only eleven kilometers (6.9 miles) and it was actually rated as "kala"

meaning "easy" in our Israel Trail book, which is in Hebrew.

Vincent came to our campsite at 8:00 AM with a friend of his, Gertjan, and we had coffee and breakfast together. As we were eating, the skies started to darken and threatened rain, which is unusual for this time of year. We drove back to Tel Azeka as Gertjan had not been there and Vincent is an Israeli tour guide who knows all of the historical and biblical background of this ancient site.

Bev makes a new friend on the Israel Trail

After driving back up to the Tel, we walked around it exploring the site and praying during which time the storm clouds and winds gathered force. As we were leaving the mountain, it began to drizzle and by the time we got to the car it was pouring. The heavens opened up and we could see that this downpour would not let up anytime soon. Actually, the weather reports that we do get from the occasional hiker (since have no radio, TV or newspapers) had been informing us that the rain would continue for two days. Faced with the prospect of hiking in the cold rain on slipper and muddy trails or going back to our friend John Hulley's home in Mevasseret Zion, we chose the later and are thankful we did. The thunderstorms persisted and it rained on and off all day throughout central Israel. It would have been a very miserable day had we gotten up and just started hiking at 6:00 AM instead of returning to Jerusalem.

We have God's assurance in our hearts that He is watching over us, and we are so grateful that He has been preparing our way each step and every day since we began this 'walk of faith' -- 450 kilometers (281 miles) ago at Tel Dan on September 5th. Tonight we are enjoying the warmth and love that is not only in John Hulley's home but is coming through to us from all our friends and loved ones. Many precious new friends that we have met along the Trail or who have been following our hike on this journal have called us to see how we are doing and to encourage us.

Thank you all, we really appreciate every one of you. Please remember to "pray for the peace of Jerusalem" (Psalm 122:6) and for us as we continue toward the Negev Desert and Eilat.

	Thursday, October 20, 2005	
Destination: Mevasseret Zion		**Today's Miles:** 0.00
Starting Location: Mevasseret Zion		**Trip Miles:** 287.40

John, Mel, Lynn, Suzzana, Jesse, Suzan & Gertjan

Day 46: Cloudy, but it did not rain (at least in the Jerusalem area). Things will be drying out for hiking tomorrow. Since we still have a several mountains to hike up and down in the lower Judean Hills, we do not want to be slipping and sliding with mud caked on our shoes so we do not mind waiting another day. John was awaiting a group of five visitors from Pennsylvania expecting to stay with him for a few days. Bev prepared a very nice dinner for twelve persons and we had a great evening of fellowship. John's guests were very encouraging and have promised to pray for us as we continue our 'walk of faith' on the Israel Trail.

	Friday, October 21, 2005	
Destination: Tel Lachish		**Today's Miles:** 12.50
Starting Location: Mevasseret Zion		**Trip Miles:** 299.90

Day 46: A beautiful morning and great day for hiking. After breakfast and a time of prayer with our friends, Gertjan drove us back to the Trail at the British Park south of Tel Azeka and we continued from where we left off on Wednesday morning. The air was so fresh and clean that we could literally see several times further than we had been able to before the thunderstorms. We quickly re-adjusted to hiking with full loaded backpacks and arrived at the summit of Mitzpeh Massua within an hour. At the top, there is

a fire tower and lookout as well as a small kiosk and picnic area where we ordered a cup of Turkish coffee. We could clearly see the coastal cities of Ashdod and Ashkelon to the west on the Mediterranean Sea, as well as the Hebron Mountain range above the Dead Sea to the east.

Since this week is the holiday of Succoth or the Feast of Tabernacles, children are out of school on holiday and many families were visiting the park. In addition, hundreds of children were hiking along the trails in the area in individual age groups with scout leaders. Israel is one of the only places we have ever witnessed this phenomenon of children of all ages hiking in the nature reserves. Each year every school has one to three day class trips to various nature, historical or archeological sites throughout the country.

Even though we did not start hiking until 9:00 AM, we arrived at the end of trail #26 at Beit Govreen at 2:15 PM and stopped at the gas station rest area for a short half an hour break. We had originally thought that we would stop here for the day but felt strong enough to continue the six to seven kilometer (4-5 miles) to Tel Lachish where we set up camp at the National Park.

The landscape dramatically changed as we left the last of the Judean Hills and we now hiked through the southern plains towards Beer Sheva. Near Lachish, we passed hundreds of acres of vineyards, and each vine was loaded with delicious grapes. After eating several clusters, we continued on to Tel Lachish but at one point had to run while we held our breath through an area that was being sprayed with chemical pesticides. There was no way around this situation and I'm sure that the farmer did not realize that there were hikers on the trail because it was getting so close to sunset.

Fruitful Vineyards growing near Lachish

Although we didn't breath in very much of the chemicals, the residue was on our clothes and skin for the next several days.

At sunset, we arrived at Tel Lachish. It took us nearly a half hour to walk around the Tel to the campground, and on the way around,  we rescued a small kitty that was crying in the vineyards. This cat followed us to the campground and stayed with us all night. The kitty was almost dehydrated and was extremely hungry, but rapidly improved after we gave him some water and food.

The Lachish National Park is a very small area and is situated in a pine forest between the modern moshav (agricultural settlement) of Lachish and the Tel, which marks the site of the second largest city in ancient Judea. It was rather chilly out and so we made a small campfire to keep warm as we ate soup and drank a cup of hot herbal tea before retiring for the night.

	Saturday, October 22, 2005	
Destination: Moshav Achuzam		**Today's Miles:** 8.75
Starting Location: Tel Lachish		**Trip Miles:** 308.65

Day 48: At this point we have reached the halfway point of our 'walk of faith' on the Israel National Trail, having hiked 470 kilometers out of the 940 total! After breakfast, we took 'kitty' to the moshav and left him on the doorstep of someone's house with part of a can of tuna. This was such a friendly and nice cat and we hoped that someone would quickly adopt him. Afterwards, we climbed up the Tel and prayed over the site and the entire area for fifteen minutes or so before continuing on the Israel Trail.

Again, we hiked past many acres of vineyards before reaching an area where the high northern desert plains above Beer Sheva stretched out before us. For the next several hours, we hiked along a dirt road beside enormous plowed fields without shade of any kind to be found. Every few miles there would be a small grove of either pine or eucalyptus trees (like an oasis) where we would stop to cool off and rest, otherwise the area was quite barren. We both were feeling flu or cold coming on and by 2:30 PM were very exhausted and decided to stop for the day at moshav (agricultural village) Achuzam. We put up our tent near the moshav's youth center next to a children's playground and spent the remainder of the afternoon resting. Toward evening as we were getting ready to eat our dinner, about a dozen youths came us to us in a group to ask us many questions about what we were doing. They were very excited to hear about our hike across Israel and made us feel both welcome and at home on their moshav.

Israel Trail Map -- We are 1/2 way to Eilat!

Sunday, October 23, 2005	
Destination: Kibbutz Beit Kamah	**Today's Miles:** 11.25
Starting Location: Moshav Achuzam	**Trip Miles:** 319.90

The landscape changes drastically!

Day 49: We woke up early but waited for the moshav store to open at 8:00 AM in order to buy some supplies. Already everyone on the settlement knew about us and about our hike from the children's report the night before. After purchasing a few things for the trail (they didn't have any fresh fruit or vegetables), we quickly hiked to the end of trail #27, which is at Tel

Keshet. It was good that we had stopped at the moshav for the night because there was no water at Tel Keshet, and outside of a few trees, there was nothing else there in the way of camping facilities. The landscape here again changed dramatically and we now hiked up and down low barren hills that were occasionally dotted with a small grove of trees. At 3:00 PM, we arrived at highway #40, which is a busy thoroughfare to Beer-Sheva. At this point, we decided to leave the Israel Trail and walk two kilometers (1.25 miles) parallel to it southward. On this section of the Israel Trail, there is not any water available. We had not felt strong enough that morning to carry eight liters (2 gallons) of water each that we would need for the next two days. Instead, we walked along the western side of Hwy. #40 toward Kibbutz Beit Kamah and arrived there just at sunset. The people on the kibbutz were very nice and allowed us to put up our tent on the grassy lawn in front of their dining hall. We had a nice dinner at the picnic table near the children's playground. We wanted to buy some supplies at the kibbutz grocery but were told that it was for members only and that they could not sell anything to outsiders. However, Rivkah the store manager gave us some rolls and some fresh garlic which we both wanted to help fight our colds. Although the sound of the traffic from the highway (which was less than a half kilometer away) was very loud, we both were so tired that it did not disturb us in the least and we slept very soundly all night.

Monday, October 24, 2005	
Destination: Kibbutz Lahav - The Lahav Forest	**Today's Miles:** 13.10
Starting Location: Kibbutz Beit Kamah	**Trip Miles:** 333.00

Holiday Feast at Kibbutz Lahav

Day 50: Up at dawn and hiking by 5:45 AM! We decided to head southeast across the fields for a couple of kilometers to catch back up with the Israel Trail. We crossed through several freshly plowed fields and nearby a red paprika field; we found dozens of cloves of fresh garlic that had surfaced after the rains. The amazing thing is that the day before we

had prayed specifically that we would come across garlic in a field! We now had enough garlic to knockout all our cold symptoms. For most of the day, we skirted several pine forests before reaching the southwestern border of the West Bank. Here the area was a vast contrast to the earlier part of the day as the landscape was barren and treeless. We climbed a couple of very steep hills in the middle of the day before finally reaching the Lahav Forest. Our goal for the day was to reach Kibbutz Lahav and set up camp in the picnic grounds outside the settlement. Since we arrived early at 2:00 PM, we decided to go to the adjacent kibbutz and try to buy some supplies from the store. What happened next was surrealistic as we walked for nearly two hours around almost the entire perimeter of the settlement looking for the entrance, which was not marked on our map. Finally, after we were at the point of exhaustion, we reached the front gate, which was locked. Now at the point of desperation, we prayed and immediately a car drove up and the driver asked us what we wanted. We told him that we were hiking the Israel Trail and that we needed some water and a few other items from the store. He informed us that the store had closed at 2:00 PM as this was the evening before the holiday of 'Simchat Torah - the Giving of the Law', which is the day after the seven day holiday of Succoth. He offered us a ride in his car and then drove us to another store several miles away which was still open. He then asked where we planned to spend the night and offered for us to stay in his home.

It turned out that our benefactor, Moshe, is the manager of the kibbutz and that his dream has been to hike the Israel Trail! This fifty two-year-old agricultural settlement has some unique industries and innovative technologies. They raise pigs for consumption (highly unusual in Israel because they are not kosher), grow cactus for the 'kobo' fruit, and have a cosmetic industry with products made from camel milk. Their waste treatment ponds are very efficient and they are exploring the possibility of capturing methane gas for power usage. Moshe drove us to his home where we he and his wife treated us royally. We had hot showers and coffee and they offered us their son's room that was away for the holiday. That night we were invited to have a holiday meal with Moshe and Pnini and their children in the kibbutz-dining hall. What a feast -- baked salmon, stuffed potatoes, every kind of Middle-Eastern salad and Bavarian crème cheesecake for desert! We so appreciated being in a home with this great family for the holiday.

Tuesday, October 25, 2005	
Destination: Maitar	**Today's Miles:** 7.00
Starting Location: Kibbutz Lahav - The Lahav Forest	**Trip Miles:** 340.00

The Partition Fence -- A New Border?

Day 51: The holiday of Simchat Torah was so peaceful especially on the kibbutz as it is similar to the Shabbat when most Israelis sleep in. After we had a great breakfast with Moshe, he drove us back to the Israel Trail, which was only a few kilometers from the kibbutz. We could tell that in his heart Moshe wished that he were hiking with us. We know that we will have a lifetime friendship with him and his family because of this divine appointment.

We began our hike very close to the new Partition Fence that Israel is building between the West Bank and Israel, and could see how this may one day become the defacto border of Israel. The fence is not very high but has an area cleared between it and a small parallel wall that may be monitored both electronically and by IDF patrols. After hiking for a few minutes, we came upon a very old carob tree in a Wadi, which is located on the Israel Trail book map for this section. As we now had our exact bearings, we found the trail marker and proceeded to hike eastward into some beautiful pine forests. The contrast here is amazing in that to the north in the West Bank the area is without vegetation. Due to the holiday, it was an extremely quiet day and we did not encounter any people or traffic in the area except for the occasional army outpost with a few soldiers guarding this frontier.

We finished trail #29 by noon and continued on to an outpost high above the town of Maitar called Mitzpeh Yaaranim, which was suppose to have a guest room with showers for hikers of the Israel Trail. When we got there at 2:00 PM, we were disappointed to find it locked up and abandoned. However, there were a couple of picnic tables and a water faucet outside this run down facility. After resting for a couple of hours, it became apparent to both of us that camping for the night on such a high point would be too cold and windy to be comfortable, and that we had better make other arrangements for the night. We called Chaim, who we had met on the Israel Trail in Latrun and had hiked up to Jerusalem with a couple weeks earlier. Chaim lived in Maitar and had told us to call him when we got in the area. Immediately when we called him, he and his wife, Eva, insisted that we come to their home and spend the night.

Within a half an hour, we had hiked off the mountain and into Maitar where Chaim picked us up in his car. Maitar is a large town with very nice homes that is only around fifteen miles from Beer Sheva. Chaim and his wife's hospitality was so wonderful that not only did we have a great meal with them but at 7:00 PM we went across the street to their American neighbors, Marvin and Debra, and had a second meal! After two meals and a great evening, we fell asleep very quickly in a nice warm bed.

Wednesday, October 26, 2005	
Destination: *Mercaz Yaar Yatir (Yatir Forest Center)*	**Today's Miles:** *10.00*
Starting Location: *Maitar*	**Trip Miles:** *350.00*

We climb up and up from Maitar

Day 52: Chaim had to leave at 6:30 AM to go back to work at the Dimona Nuclear Power Plant so we had breakfast with Eva before heading back toward the Israel Trail. Eva was so thoughtful that she even made us some sandwiches to take with us on our hike.

We initially climbed back up on the ridge above Maitar but couldn't find the trail and had to backtrack all that way to the abandoned shelter on the Mitzpeh (outlook) that we had left the previous evening. We finally found the Israel Trail's orange, blue and white marker, which headed straight out of the Maitar forest and up into the steep barren hills to the northeast. For hours we walked up and down these mountains with no shade whatsoever. The terrain was eerie and even more so in that we did not encounter one person or vehicle the entire time that we were in this area. Although we had a great view of the city of Hebron and the other Arabic villages in the West Bank to the north, we were looking forward to the Yatir forest, which was on the horizon to the east.

After arriving at the forest, we hiked through some ancient Crusader ruins at a large archeological site that has not been restored. This pine forest is very beautiful and very well maintained by the Israeli Forestry Service or the KKL (Keren Kayemet L'Yisrael). At the top of a huge mountain in the distance, we could see a tower marking a place where our Israel Trail book assured us that there was a place for hikers on the INT to get a free room for the evening at the forestry center.

The hike up to the Yatir Center at an elevation of 658 meters (2140 ft.) was one of the nicest parts of the Trail that we had been on so far and we kept remarking that this could be anywhere such as New Zealand or in the Appalachian Mountains of the USA. It was so peaceful and the air so clear that the hiking was very enjoyable even with our backpacks and sore feet.

We arrived at the Yatir Forest Center at the summit around 2:30 PM and were immediately greeted by Ahmed who was in charge of the compound. He showed us to the guest room provided for the Israel Trail hikers, brought us a bottle of ice water and made us feel very welcome. Although the showers only had cold water, they were very refreshing and the room was well decorated with posters of various forests and places in Israel. The room, like the entire compound, was very nice and well kept up with nice beds and furnishings. We immediately settled in and after cleaning up took a short nap.

The view from this place is quite amazing and we both remarked that this part of the trail would be ideal to bring visitors, especially since such nice facilities were available for the INT hikers. We spent the rest of the evening relaxing and reading, and after a nice dinner retired for the night.

Thursday, October 27, 2005	
Destination: Arad	**Today's Miles:** 15.00
Starting Location: Mercaz Yaar Yatir (Yatir Forest Center)	**Trip Miles:** 365.00

Day 53: We were back on the trail by 7:30 AM and expected to have a long day ahead of us to reach the city of Arad before sunset. The trail through the Yatir Forest continued to be spectacularly

The Yatir Forest

beautiful and we marveled that we had never heard of this forest before. We sited a few deer but know this forest is a haven for many animals. Outside of the Carmel Forest, Yatir is the second largest forest in Israel and is even better maintained by the Israeli Forestry Service. We walked up and down (more up than down) this forest trail for another three hours and finally reached the end of the Yatir Forest at Kibbutz Ahmsa on the edge of the Negev.

Kibbutz Ahmsa is at an elevation of 800 meters (2600 ft.) and this small settlement was established in 1984 but was abandoned shortly afterwards and resettled in 1993. One can tell that it is going through difficult times today but the people were very hospitable towards us and are very open to all those hiking the Israel Trail. They have a free guest room for hikers to use whenever they pass through this area. We spent about forty-five minutes at the kibbutz recreation room eating lunch and resting before heading out towards the desert.

Never have we seen the topography and scenery change so dramatically within a few minutes. Within a half hour, we were on top of Mount Ahmsa, 869 meters (2824 ft.) looking into the vastness of the Negev desert to the south and east of the beautiful Yatir forest and us to the west. We could see the city of Arad and its high rise apartment buildings off in the distance below us (elevation 600 meters, 1925 ft. and approximately 18 kilometers, 11 miles, to the southeast) and realized that we would have to make good time over the next five hours to reach it before sunset.

The rest of the day was rather difficult as the trail was steep and full of jagged rocks. At one point, we hiked alongside a quarry that was in full operation and became covered in limestone dust. At the bottom of Mt. Ahmsa, the terrain levels off and we hiked along several Bedouin villages on the flat plateau, which is above the Dead Sea and north of the Negev Desert. It seemed to take much longer than it actually did but we made it to Tel Arad, the site of the ancient city of Arad, around 3:30 PM. We were both so tired that we just laid down on the rocky dirt road and rested for about twenty minutes before getting up for the last push across the plain to Arad. We made it to the Park Arad, a small grove of pine trees four kilometers (2.5 miles) east of the city. We called Polly, a friend of Rena's (who we had stayed with in Hadera) and she immediately drove out to pick us up from the Trail. Within a half an hour, we were in her home with her three teenage sons and five foster children, drinking a cup of hot tea and preparing to eat a home cooked dinner! Although Polly has such a large household, she always has room for one more and we both felt loved and welcome. After a hot bath and a scrumptious meal we almost forgot about the twenty-four kilometers (15 miles) we had just hiked as we fell asleep under the stars on her back patio -- not in sleeping bags in our tent but on soft mattresses under several warm quilts!

	Friday, October 28, 2005
Destination: *Arad*	***Today's Miles:*** *0.00*
Starting Location: *Arad*	***Trip Miles:*** *365.00*

Polly and the City of Arad

Day 54: We woke up later than usual for a Friday morning (8:00 AM) and were so grateful to not be hiking today or tomorrow as we both felt we needed a couple of days to recuperate and prepare for the upcoming 383 kilometers (240 miles) hike across the Negev to Eilat.

After eating a great breakfast of fried eggs and toast, we headed out with Polly in her van on a spiritual mission to pray on and around the high places surrounding Arad. There has been quite a spiritual battle raging against the believers in this area for some time and we were more than glad to go out to all of the mountains and high places and pray with our precious host. The 'chess club' and 'outreach center' in the market area of Arad had recently been burned out by vandals, so we went to meet with it's owner and director, Eddie, to pray for him and encourage him in his work. He is currently rebuilding and refurbishing the interior and is fearlessly going forward in this spiritual outreach. For the next couple of hours, we prayed around the city of Arad and for its inhabitants and arrived back at Polly's home exhausted but with the assurance of victory in our hearts.

The rest of the day was spent in updating our trail journal, uploading our pictures, purchasing food and supplies for the continuation of our 'walk of faith', and washing all our clothes and everything else in both our backpacks. We had arrived here in Arad the night before with all our supplies at an all time low as we had only a small packet of one-serving oatmeal and one pita bread left in our food bag!

Monday, October 31, 2005	
Destination: Hwy 258 - 20 km south of Arad	**Today's Miles:** 12.50
Starting Location: Arad	**Trip Miles:** 377.50

Looking east from the Zoar Overlook. The Dead Sea is in the background

Days 55-57: Shabbat (Saturday) was a day of rest and we took advantage of the day to gain strength for the Negev Desert ahead. At 10:00 AM, we went to a messianic service in the morning with Sharon where there were about forty in attendance. Afterwards we spent the rest of the day finishing updating our trail journal and resting. We decided to stay one more day in Arad as we felt we needed to help Eddie refurbish the Chess Club and we still needed to do a few things in preparation for continuing our 'walk of faith' to Eilat.

Sunday was an interesting day as we began by driving twelve kilometers (7.5 miles) out to Tel Arad with a friend of Polly's, Sharon, to the fortress on top of the archeological site and National Park. Ancient Arad has a rich history dating back from the Canaanite period, through the reign of King Solomon, and continuing through the Roman and Byzantine periods. We walked around and prayed over the site for quite awhile before returning to Arad. On the way back from Tel Arad, we stopped at Park Arad that is five kilometers (3 miles) west of Arad and Greg walked into the city on the Israel Trail so that we would not have to backtrack to this spot on Monday, but could start hiking southward from the city center. Although it has been difficult to do, we have endeavored not to skip any of the sections of the trail in that we want to fulfill the scripture in Gen. 13:17 to walk the entire length and breadth of the land. After a little over an hour of hiking, Greg arrived in Arad and spent the rest of the afternoon working with Eddie at the Chess Club.

Monday morning was cold and very windy with the weather forecast predicting rain for the next few days throughout the central and northern areas of Israel as far south as the Dead Sea. We began hiking with only daypacks as Polly offered to bring us our backpacks and water around 4:00 PM on the trail (Hwy 258 - 20 km south of Arad). We began hiking at 8:00 AM and walked from the open market of Arad eastward towards the Dead Sea through Wadi Yaalim for five kilometers (3 miles). We then had a steep mountain climb straight up to the Zoar Outlook, which sits above Arad. From Mitzpeh Zoar we could see the Dead Sea and all the area in over a thirty-two kilometer (20 mile) radius of Arad... What a spectacular view! We stopped and spoke briefly with a group of bicyclists on top of the summit who were touring the area, and then marveled at how quickly they descended the mountain as they were nearly out of site within minutes.

For the rest of the day we were battered by strong winds that howled in our ears and kept us from sweating or even stopping to rest for more than a few minutes at a time. With only daypacks, we were able to hike quickly around the southern Arad mountain ridges with ease and we passed by several Bedouin villages throughout the morning. In the afternoon, we started down off the mountain range on a very rugged trail in the direction of the two-lane highway and reached our pre-arranged site by 3:00 PM. After climbing back up a nearby hill in order to get reception on our cell phone, we contacted Polly and within a half hour, we were together with our friends. She arrived at our campsite with her son, Moshe, her foster son, Aaron, and neighbor, Sharon, just in time to enjoy the campfire and help collect wood. At 4:30, they had to leave and we were very sorry to see our dear friends depart. We continued to sit around the campfire for a couple of more hours while we ate soup and drank herb tea before retiring for the night in our cozy tent. From this point forward, we were aware that except for the LORD, we would for the most part be by ourselves in this vast expanse of the Negev wilderness.

Tuesday, November 01, 2005	
Destination: Massad Tamar (The Tamar Fortress)	**Today's Miles:** 9.40
Starting Location: Hwy 258 - 20 km south of Arad	**Trip Miles:** 386.90

A herd of 'wild' camels crosses our campsite

Day 58: We awoke early to a beautiful sunrise and were surprised by a large herd of 'wild' camels, which crossed the road in front of our campsite. We began hiking early and entered a very scenic area with fabulous views of the Jordanian mountains, the Dead Sea and the mountain range south of Arad. Although it was chilly at night, it quickly heated up and the wind had died down completely. The air was so clear that we could see further than any time previously. We hiked up and down several very steep rugged trails before reaching a plateau at the top where the terrain became rather barren, except for the occasional wandering camel. We saw an unusual structure in the distance, which upon inspection turned out to be a massive conveyor built delivering materials from the Dead Sea to the Arad Chemical works. We arrived at the end of trail #32 at the Tamar Fortress at 2:30 PM. We then hitchhiked to the Arava Junction, which lies six kilometers (3.75 miles) away and one thousand meters (3,250 ft.) below the Trail at the southern end of the Dead Sea. Our Israel Trail guidebook said that the gas station just south of this junction would be the only location to refill water for the next two days. The gas station attendants were very friendly but informed us that there was no drinking water available! After we explained our predicament, they kindly filled all our water containers from their own personal water supply. They then offered us coffee and a room for the night and invited us to watch a movie with them. We had not been watching any television for over two months and their offer was much appreciated. The sunset was spectacular and the outside temperature was much warmer here several hundred meters below sea level.

Wednesday, November 02, 2005	
Destination: Maktesh HaKatan (The Small Crater)	**Today's Miles:** 11.00
Starting Location: Massad Tamar (The Tamar Fortress)	**Trip Miles:** 397.00

On the ridge of the Maktesh HaKatan (The Small Crater)

Day 59: We awoke at first light and after having coffee with our hosts, hiked the half kilometer back to the Arava Junction in order to hitchhike back up to the Trail. Within minutes, we were back at the Tamar Fortress and hiking straight up a mountain on our way to Maktesh HaKatan (The Small Crater). At the top, we had breakfast and then hiked to the crater's rim by 10:30 AM. The rim of the crater has a view as breath taking as the Grand Canyon and we greatly admired the hike before us. Our descent was quick but crossing the length and breadth of the crater took all day. By evening, we began the "Ely Ascent" up the southwestern end of the crater, which went straight up the crater wall. We had calculated that it would take about forty-five minutes but it turned out to take about a half hour longer than that and we just reached the summit as the sun was setting. It was an altogether spectacular experience but an extremely difficult climb up. With one quick look back at the crater, we quickly hiked another two kilometers (1.25 miles) to the campground and set our tent up in the

dark. The temperature dropped quickly and we jumped inside the tent, ate a cold snack and fell fast asleep.

Thursday, November 03, 2005	
Destination: Ein Yorq'eam (The Yorkeam Spring)	**Today's Miles:** 8.10
Starting Location: Maktesh HaKatan (The Small Crater)	**Trip Miles:** 406.00

Day 60: It was freezing cold when the first light woke us at 5:30 AM. A group of young Israeli guides camping near us already had a hot campfire burning and coffee brewing. We immediately meandered toward the delicious aroma to made friends. We enjoyed watching the sunrise as we all drank a cup of 'campfire coffee' together.

It is very important that we spend some time stretching our muscles before hiking because if we do not we tend to get leg cramps throughout the day. We quickly packed up our gear, by 7:00 AM it had warmed up, and we were back on the Trail.

This became one of the most spectacular sections of the Israel Trail and we would highly recommend to all hikers (who are physically in shape). The first part was an hour and a half hike along a beautiful ridge of mountains toward the Tsafir Fortress. We had a panoramic view of the Jordanian mountain ridge on the east, the Desert of Zin to the south, and the Carbolet Mountain Ridge that forms one side of the 'Great Crater' on the west. The area to the north cannot be discussed in detail or photographed for security reasons!

From the Tsafir Fortress the trail just kept getting better and better. We hiked along various ridges for the next couple of hours and then reached a dramatic view of cliffs surrounding Wadi Yamin. The Yamin overlook is several hundred meters above the ravine and is a sheer drop with a powerful waterfall during the short desert rainy season (winter and spring). There were deep crevices in the rocky cliff at the Yamin overlook where you could not even see the bottom (like the glacier crevices in Alaska).

An ice-cold swim in the desert at Ein Yorq'eam Spring

You could only imagine a small earthquake sending huge sections of this cliff into the Wadi below and so might not want to spend the night camping on such a beautiful spot. We rested briefly and began the steep descent to the canyon floor. This is a remote location that would require several hours of backpacking to reach from the nearest road and so is not very well known. It would rank on our list of the top ten spots to return to with our children and grandchildren in the near future.

We had lunch at the bottom of Wadi Yamin under a tall Acacia tree -- smoked tuna, cheese sandwiches and freshly squeezed lemonade (lemons that Chaim had picked for us in Maitar) -- What a treat in the desert! Greatly strengthened by the view and our lunch, we hiked for over an hour through the very hot Wadi's of Yamin and Chatira until we came to a completely blocked canyon. It seemed that there was no way out except for the trail markers pointing straight up the canyon wall. After a good rest, we began the very difficult climb up the 'Palmach Ascent' which included a ten meter (30 ft.) ladder and many metal bars and cables bolted into the canyon wall that were provided to help in the climb out. This is not for the faint of heart or those who are not in good physical shape. Within a half an hour or so, we were back on top of the mountain ridge hiking toward the end of the trail. We had arranged for Margalit Cohen from Dimona to pick us up at Hwy 206 at 4:30 PM but we were ahead of schedule. Just as we were approaching the last five minute climb out of the canyon to the road, two female hikers seemingly came out of nowhere and suggested that we take a three minute detour off the trail to a 'swimming hole'. Having hiked four days from Arad without showers or water to spare, and since the canyon ravine was very hot during the middle of the day; we immediately took their advice. Within minutes, we were at the "Ein Yorq'eam Spring" having a freezing cold swim. The water bubbles up from underground and is just a few degrees above freezing. There are ancient Byzantine steps carved into the rocks indicating that this has been an important source of water in the desert for centuries. Rocks surround the Yorq'eam pool, which keeps the water very cold. What a wonderful way to end such a beautiful section of the Trail. Within a few minutes, we were up on the highway and decided to hitchhike the twenty kilometers (12.5 miles) into Dimona. Even though there was very little traffic out here in the wilderness, we got a ride within a half an hour. Our ride dropped us at the Dimona bus station where Margalit picked us up. Although this was the first time we had met the Cohen family, we immediately felt welcomed and blessed as if we had known them for years. After hot showers, a fabulous dinner, clean laundry, and a nice warm bed -- we slept like we were in heaven.

Friday, November 04, 2005	
Destination: Dimona	**Today's Miles:** 0.00
Starting Location: Ein Yorq'eam (The Yorkeam Spring)	**Trip Miles:** 406.00

Shimon Cohen and Greg at the Dimona Overlook

Day 61: After a great breakfast (compared to our normal camp food), Shimon took us on a tour of the Negev Desert city of Dimona. He is a landscaper that has done many city projects and he enjoyed showing us all the lovely blooming gardens and landscaping around town. Shimon has proved that 'anything' can grow out here in the desert. With just the smallest amount of water, the Negev can bloom as prophesied in the Bible.

Dimona now has over forty thousand residents and has really advanced and developed tremendously over the past decade. We also drove by the 'Village of Peace', which is a community within Dimona where the 'Black Hebrews' reside. This group came from the USA into the country illegally thirty years ago claiming to be one of the lost tribes of Israel. After years of negotiation with some persecution, they have recently been granted Israeli citizenship and their sons and daughters, who are eighteen years old, will begin serving in the Israeli Defense Forces this year. They all speak English and Hebrew and maintain a strict Vegan dietary code.

We spent the day uploading all our new spectacular pictures from Arad to Ein Yorq'eam onto our Yahoo website at 360.yahoo.com/gregandbev2004, and updating our trail journal. The new comments we have received in the Guest Book on this site are much appreciated. We also purchased all of our supplies that we will need for the five-day hike ahead to the Negev Desert city of Mitzpeh Ramon.

In the evening, we enjoyed a Cohen family barbecue with some of their family that was visiting from the desert agricultural settlement of Hatsiva (a major place for organic farming in Israel). We had such a great meal with so many delicious dishes and plenty of grilled meat. This was appreciated very much as the strenuous nature of our hike requires that we get enough protein in our diet to maintain muscle development.

We have been invited to spend the Shabbat (Saturday Rest) here with the Cohens in Dimona, and have taken them up on their gracious offer. Among other things, our gasoline camp stove is again malfunctioning and in need of some maintenance before we leave on Sunday morning.

The next section of the Israel Trail is rated as "DIFFICULT" that will require all of our strength to accomplish within two days. The trail begins on the Carbolet Mountain Range, where we will be hiking up and down along the jagged ridge of 'The Great Crater' (Maktesh HaGadol in Hebrew). The hike is thirty-two kilometers (20 miles) long with only one water source near the beginning of the trail.

We appreciate all of you who are following our 'walk of faith' and who are supporting us in prayer. God Bless all of you.

Sunday, November 06, 2005	
Destination: Wadi Mador -- Mt. Carbolet	**Today's Miles:** 7.50
Starting Location: Maktesh Hagadol	**Trip Miles:** 413.50

Har Carbolet "The Rooster's Comb"
A jagged mountain range forms the SW rim of
Maktesh HaGadol (The Big Crater)

Day 63: Shimon drove us to the start of the trail inside the Canyon of Colors at 5:50 AM. We were well bundled against the cold in the warm thermals and jacket the Cohen's had generously given us. Immediately after we started a serious climb up the side of the crater. We were up on top for the beautiful sunrise. The magnificent wonder of the view will stay with us all of our lives.

Dark clouds lined the western skyline and we were aware that the weather report predicted probable showers for Monday. As the day wore on the clouds broke up and the high altitudes and intense hiking exhilarated us. Our packs were heavy with food and water. We had not yet needed to carry such a load, but now we knew there was no water source for the next three days. We would have to take as many breaks as we needed but it was necessary to carry eighteen liters (4.5 gal.) between the two of us.

The first ridge up and down the crater took us an hour and a half. We quickly realized we would be camping the night some where along the Carbolet Range (Rooster's Comb) named after the ridge formation. We saw no one all day.

Around 4 PM., we found a lovely valley between four walls of high canyon cliffs. A campfire spot was already set up from previous hikers, so we settled in and kept warm around our campfire. Once the last flame was out, the billions of stars that light up the sky awed us. It had been our most strenuous hiking day so far on the Israel Trail. Much of it was walking sideways along the ridge crest a 30-40 degree angle. We fell asleep quickly.

Monday, November 07, 2005	
Destination: *Wilderness of Zin*	**Today's Miles:** *10.00*
Starting Location: *Wadi Mador -- Mt. Carbolet*	**Trip Miles:** *423.50*

Dark rain clouds formed all day over the crater

Day 64: At first sunlight we peeked out of our tent to see a beautiful rainbow set against some very dark clouds. Yes, rain was on the way. We packed up camp without breakfast and very quickly and began hiking just in time to find some shelter under a cliff for the first rain of the day. It only lasted a few minutes. It was cold enough to see our breath steaming.

Now hiking was more difficult since the sideways rock cliffs were now slippery wet. To complicate things the wind was fierce and howling. We knew we were near the descent to the Zin Valley and were very happy to start the descent off the ridge just before more serious downpours began.

Once in the valley the clouds cleared, the rain was mostly hanging over the crater. We were so hungry now for lunch and had a nice break at the campsite. We found 8 liters (2 gals) of water left behind at the campground. What a treat to wash up and refill our supply. We continued an afternoon hike across the arid basin of Wadi Zin.

Tuesday, November 08, 2005	
Destination: *Ein Shaviv (Oasis Spring)*	**Today's Miles:** *10.00*
Starting Location: *Wilderness of Zin*	**Trip Miles:** *433.50*

Day 65: We woke to very cold temperatures but also very clear skies and a fascinating array of colors from the sunrise over the Great Crater, which lies, to our north and the Zinnim Cliffs to the south.

After a short hike through the Zin ravine, our view opened to a giant flat basin called the Zin Wilderness. This is where Moses and the children of Israel came through on their Exodus from Egypt.

To our surprise, we saw two hikers coming toward us over the vast horizon and eventually enjoyed the company of Amir and Tamir. These were the first people we had seen in three days. We enjoyed sharing our hiking experiences.

Our next surprise and shock was to see the Israel Trail markers going straight up the canyon wall of the Zinnnim Cliffs 244 meters (1400 ft.) above. It was a very dangerous and exhilarating climb. This was no time to panic so we just stayed focused and climbed. We arrived at the pinnacle called Hod Ekev within an hour and marveled at the feat

Climbing up from the Wilderness of Zin to Ekev Pinnacle

of this climb. The flat surface on top was only 100 sq. meters (100 sq. yards) around, quite intimidating if you wanted to gaze over the very steep ledge. We had a spectacular view but after a short rest, we headed down the south face toward the lower Ein Ekev spring pool. Now the desert temperature was rising to over 85F degrees. Our hiking pace picked up over the next six kilometers (4 miles) just knowing we were headed for a swim. At the pools several soldiers we also enjoying the cold pool of fresh water. One of the soldiers offered us some of the cold food supplies he had in the army jeep (cottage cheese, salami, tomatoes, and pudding). We also met a desert guide from Holland named Arthur, who told us where we could find safe drinking water.

We filled our water bottles in the small pools above the swimming hole. This is the only fresh water supply for 160 kilometers (100 miles) on the Israel Trail from Arad to Mitzpeh Ramon.

On our continued journey to the upper Ein Ekev spring two-day hikers, Amigo and Naftali, who were on their way to the spring, joined us. These kind fellows even carried our packs for us for a short distance. Together we sited over twenty ibex. At 4 PM, they left to return and we headed east to our destination at the Ein Shaviv Oasis.

As the sun was setting, we hiked down 640 meters (2000 ft.) the face of a cliff to arrive at the beautiful dense oasis just before nightfall. We set up camp in the dark but it was now much warmer and we enjoyed the star filled night sky.

Wednesday, November 09, 2005	
Destination: Hava Canyons	**Today's Miles:** 9.00
Starting Location: Ein Shaviv (Oasis Spring)	**Trip Miles:** 442.50

Ein Shaveev Spring -- an oasis in the wilderness of Zin

Day 66: We were awakened in the very early morning by rough growling which turned out to be a camel upset that we were camped in the middle of his herds' crossing area. After some snorting and more growling, they decided to pass us by going up over us on a ledge.

While packing up our camp we met two hikers, Miki and Shy, headed on an area day hike. They shared their experiences on the Israel Trail and shared their Oreo cookies with us over hot Turkish coffee.

We hiked south up out of the basin to the top of the cliffs. Once again, a very exhilarating morning experience. For the next few hours we walked along a flat high plateau thousands of meters above the Wilderness of Zin. We decided to camp early at 2 PM. because Greg's ankle was sore and we expected a very intense descent and hike into the canyons which lay ahead.

	Thursday, November 10, 2005	
Destination: Mitzpeh Ramon		**Today's Miles:** 16.00
Starting Location: Hava Canyons		**Trip Miles:** 458.50

On top of the world on the ridge of the Ramon Crater

Day 67: We woke very early and were climbing along, high above the Hava Canyons for a gorgeous sunrise. We again sited many gazelles and ibex startled by our appearance. This canyon is very steep and narrow with rock cliffs several hundred meters on either side. Our voices echoed through the long corridors of the canyons. Our descent only took ten minutes but we are getting pretty good at this cliff climbing and make good time. We had a spectacular hike over huge boulders for over an hour once in the bottom of the canyon. The ascent out was also very amazing. What a morning!

After a short rest on top, we started hiking again and met a group of over thirty day hikers from England headed for the Canyon and the Shaviv Oasis. They were very interested in the Israel Trail and asked us many questions about our journey. We had fun sharing and they left us with candy and water. Within two hours, we were at the Makmal Fortress, which is on the north Ramon Crater ridge.

We hiked until 6 PM across the curving ridge of the Ramon crater over sixteen kilometers (10 miles) to arrive in Mitzpeh Ramon one hour after dark. The moonlight and distant town lights helped guide us to this outback town.

Once in town, we called our Russian friend Alexis, who quickly came out to pick us up and take us to his Zimmer (Guest house) where we spent the night. Oh, how great it was to have a hot bath after five days of intense hiking.

	Friday, November 11, 2005	
Destination: Mitzpeh Ramon		**Today's Miles:** 5.00
Starting Location: Mitzpeh Ramon		**Trip Miles:** 463.50

Philippe and Stephanie Fryman

Day 68: We had a nice walk around the town of Mitzpeh Ramon in the early morning buying supplies for Shabbat dinner and searching for an Internet connection. This town has many new innovative environmental industries starting up, such as organic farming, natural cheese making, clay furniture making, and other interesting businesses. At noon, with no success finding a computer to use, we went back to the Guest House to have some lunch and get our laundry cleaned. We both prayed and asked God to please direct us to a computer so we could get our trail journal updated and get our pictures uploaded.

While having lunch on the porch, a couple came by looking for Alexis. We got into a conversation with them and after five minutes, this friendly couple invited us to come over to their house to use their Internet computers and have Shabbat dinner with them. We offered to bring our chicken and salad for dinner. Phillipe and Stephanie have a company called "Green Systems" promoting natural eco-friendly construction materials. We enjoyed getting to know this very talented and innovative couple

.

	Saturday, November 12, 2005	
Destination: Mitzpeh Ramon		**Today's Miles:** 0.00
Starting Location: Mitzpeh Ramon		**Trip Miles:** 463.50

Day 69: Mitzpeh Ramon is a very quiet town with hardly any traffic and no traffic lights. It is Israel's 'outback' town and lies right on the edge of the Ramon Crater about an hour and a half's drive from Beer-

Sheva. There are less than ten thousand residents, only one supermarket, and a couple of mini-markets in the whole town. Saturday is especially quiet in Mitzpeh Ramon, and we walked over to the Frydman's at 10 AM to finish our Trail Journal update. We had a nice lunch with them and then returned to the Guest House to enjoy our day of rest.

It is great getting phone calls from our family who are all enjoying our new pictures for the week. We know our six children are all a little jealous. They all love the outdoors and will someday really enjoy hiking the Israel Trail themselves.

Mitzpeh Ramon

Sunday, November 13, 2005

Destination: Mitzpeh Ramon	**Today's Miles:** 0.00
Starting Location: Mitzpeh Ramon	**Trip Miles:** 463.50

Ibex on top of the Ramon Crater

Day 70: Last night it rained in Mitzpeh Ramon! We woke up early and realized that the trail down to the Ramon Crater basin would be very slippery and that we would not be able to start hiking before 9:00 AM when the sun would have time to dry off the rocks on the steep path that winds downward. We also realized that leaving that late would make it difficult to reach our destination of the Bedouin campsite 'Beerot' before dark. Instead of getting under pressure and hurrying such a magnificent section of the trail, we decided to stay one more day in Mitzpeh Ramon and leave very early on Monday morning. This gave us a chance to finish getting all our supplies for the next five days and to take a leisurely walk around the entire town of Mitzpeh Ramon. We

started out by hiking out to the northern most end of town and climbed up to the 'Camel Lookout', which is a very high overlook of the entire town, and the Ramon Crater. As we were coming down from the overlook, we saw a herd of ibex lying around the rim of the crater. While photographing the ibex, a fellow Israel Trail hiker, Ronny, called out to us and we sat and spoke with him for about a half hour. He is hiking the trail in a zigzag manner in that he does whatever section he feels like in whatever order or direction that is convenient. Ronny lives on Kibbutz Maagan Mica'el on the Mediterranean coast, west of the town of Zichron Yaachov, and he has taken two months off from his work farming the kibbutz's fishponds to hike the Israel Trail. Due to the heavy rains in the northern part of Israel at this time, he was doing many of the sections of the trail in the south and taking a bus home every second or third day. He is an interesting and spiritual guy and we enjoyed sharing our experiences with him. We did not know it at the time but we would meet him again on the Trail.

We spent the rest of the day getting ready to hike eastward across the Negev, forty-six kilometers (29 miles) to the Arava Valley. In general, our equipment needed some repairs and our feet, legs, shoulders and many other muscles just needed a little more time to fully recover. There are no other towns from Mitzpeh Ramon to Eilat and so we used our time this day to spiritually and physically prepare ourselves for the last leg of our walk by faith -- through the awesomely beautiful wilderness of the southern Negev Desert.

Monday, November 14, 2005	
Destination: Beer'ot Campground - Ramon Crater basin	**Today's Miles:** 10.00
Starting Location: Mitzpeh Ramon	**Trip Miles:** 473.50

Day 71: We were back on the trail at 6:00 AM, and what a beautiful morning as we began the winding climb down into the Ramon Crater. In just over forty-five minutes, we reached the basin and began the fabulous walk across the crater, which we thought had been formed by a 'meteorite'. It turns out that all five craters in Israel were uniquely created by water erosion. All of them started as mountains with a crack on the summit with only one opening for water to escape. Over millions of years the erosion process left these

spectacular craters which rival in beauty to God's work in the Grand Canyon, in the western U.S.A.

Climbing up Shen Ramon (Ramon Tooth) from the Ramon Crater basin

After a couple hours of walking in a southeasterly direction we began a steep ascent to the top of Shen Ramon (Ramon Tooth), a mountain in the center of the crater. What a view from the summit! The descent down was very difficult and exhausting. We finished crossing the crater by 2:00 PM and arrived at a campground without water, which marked the end of this section of the trail. There we met Yoram and Mali, two directors who were in charge of an eleventh grade school trip. Over one hundred and twenty students, eight teachers, four guides and several guards and medics were traveling for four days on this section of the Israel Trail to Sapir in the Arava. Yoram invited us to join them as they had plenty of water and supplies that were being prepared for them at each campsite ahead.

We continued hiking northward off the trail for a couple of kilometers toward the Bedouin campsite called 'Beerot' where there is water and a unique Bedouin encampment. On the way, a jeep stopped and Chanan, a desert guide, offered us a ride to Beerot. Since this hike was off the Israel Trail, we did not hesitate to take him up on his offer. At the Bedouin camp, we enjoyed tea and hospitality. It turned out that Chanan was working with the school group we had just met and was delivering their evening meal. He offered to take us to their campsite in the jeep and he gave us a grand tour of the area.

We had a great dinner at the campsite with the group and again we met Ronny who was from the same kibbutz as this school group. What a coincidence! He had already hiked from Sapir to this campground, in the opposite direction that we were headed, and was very happy to meet up with us again. This campground is nestled in a gorgeous canyon, which was clearly visible all night, by the light of

Tuesday, November 15, 2005	
Destination: Gev Chuleet campground	**Today's Miles:** 12.00
Starting Location: Beer'ot Campground - Ramon Crater basin	**Trip Miles:** 485.50

Camping at Ein Chuleet with students from the Maagan Micha'el regional highschool

Day 72: We put everything into one backpack and put it with the student's gear that would be delivered to the next campground. With only water and food for the day, we set out for a fun day of hiking. We met up with Ronny after about fifteen minutes and continued to hike and share with him for four kilometers, which was the section of the Israel Trail that we had not hiked the previous day. From Mt. Saharaneem, we parted company as Ronny was continuing south and we were going east to catch up with the school group, which were hiking rather slowly. We stopped for a break at the Saharaneem Springs, which is a lovely oasis that crosses the Carbolet Mountain in the area, and then we quickly caught up and passed the school group while crossing some beautiful canyons. We arrived at the Gev Chuleet campsite about an hour before our hosts. Gev Chuleet is a spectacular canyon with almost 360 degrees of cliffs dropping into a deep and lovely Wadi.

That night, after dinner, Yoram invited us to share with this group around the campfire our Israel Trail experiences. These teenagers were very attentive and asked many questions. Most Israeli young people seek to travel abroad to India and the Far East after serving in the army for two to three years. We challenged them to first see their own country and do the Israel Trail before going abroad in the future. Afterwards we all baked delicious pita together in a Bedouin stove. The group was very exhausted and fell asleep much earlier this night.

Wednesday, November 16, 2005	
Destination: Sapir Park -- The Arava Valley	**Today's Miles:** 10.00
Starting Location: Gev Chuleet campground	**Trip Miles:** 495.50

Park Sapir – in the Arava Valley

Day 73: After having coffee and breakfast with Yoram, Chanan, Mali, and all our new friends, we said good-bye and parted from the school group. They intended to hike only eight kilometers (5 miles) this day and we would be going twice as far to reach Sapir a settlement on the Arava Valley, which is very close to the Jordanian border.

We started out hiking through the Nekorot valley and around the side of Mt. Yahav. From the northeast corner of the mountain we began a steep upward climb that took us to the summit in three stages. From the plateau at the top, we had an unbelievable view of the entire Ramon Crater area and all of the surrounding valleys and mountains. From Wadi Nekorot there was no path eastward except up and over Mt. Yahav. The descent from the opposite side of the mountain was very gradual and we quickly hiked into the basin and through an area of several canyons.

After we hiked for another couple of hours, we reached Nahal Tsavera and began a several hundred-meter climb up out of the valley to the top of the cliffs at the southeastern end. This turned out to be the highest point in the entire area and we could see for over fifty kilometers (30 miles) in every direction around us. What a sight as we could not hardly believe how the view from the Israel Trail just kept getting more spectacular each day! After having lunch we began what we thought would be an uneventful eight kilometers (5 miles) hike to the Arava Valley and our destination at Park Sapir. Just the opposite was the case, and each kilometer of hiking brought us another breathtaking view. When we were less than a kilometer from the Sapir settlement we had one last shock as suddenly we realized that we again had been hiking on a high plateau above the Arava Valley and had one more descent to reach the settlement and park ahead. As the sun was setting, we walked into the lovely oasis at Sapir Park at sunset. The park has a large pond in the center, which is fed from deep underground springs that are underneath this area. The entire park is covered with date palms and trees with picnic tables and areas for campfires set up throughout. As we were setting up our tent, Shy and his two-year-old son, Dodo, came up and greeted us. He asked us if we needed anything and then invited us to breakfast on his agricultural settlement (moshav), Zofar, which is six kilometers (3.75 miles) south of Sapir. He agreed to pick us up the next morning at 6:30 AM. We made a nice campfire, had hot soup and tea, and turned in for the night feeling like we were camping in the Garden of Eden.

Thursday, November 17, 2005	
Destination: Chadod Cliffs south of Ramat Tsofar	**Today's Miles:** 17.50
Starting Location: Sapir Park -- The Arava Valley	**Trip Miles:** 513.00

Ancient Nabaetian fortress on the 'Spice Route' that went from Yemen to Gaza

Day 74: Shy picked us up and took us first to his fields on the Jordanian border. He farms forty-five dunams (11 acres) of organic sweet peppers under net greenhouses. This is very hi-tech farming and seeing the desert "in bloom" impressed us. After breakfast at his moshav, he drove us to the beginning of the trail at Sapir. We were hiking with day packs, as Shy offered to pick us up at the end of our hike and bring us back to his home to have a hot shower, dinner, and spend the night. This motivated us to hike our longest day so far, twenty-eight kilometers (17.5 miles) in just over eight hours.

The trail was flat and did not take us up and down the mountains all around us. We were traveling along two very ancient routes - the Spring Route and the Spice Route. The Spring Route obtains its name from the series of deep fresh water wells in the area. The

Spice Route was the ancient Nabatian camel caravan route from Yemen to Gaza, thousands of years old.

After sunset, as dark approached, we reached our trail marker indicating the road to the Arava Hwy. and phoned Shy. He was already on his way and within minutes picked us up on the 4x4 trail two kilometers from the highway.

He drove by a natural desert hot spring on the way back to Zofar. This spring bubbles up boiling water only once a day at different times. It is possible to enjoy a hot soak here if you arrive at the right time.

We were treated to a great dinner, hot shower (first in five days), and a good bed. We are so blessed to have met Shy and his wife, Orly. They are world travelers and sailors who plan to purchase a boat in a few years and sail around the world with their children. We will pray for their success in all they put their hands to do.

Friday, November 18, 2005	
Destination: Moshav Zofar	**Today's Miles:** 0.00
Starting Location: Chadod Cliffs south of Ramat Tsofar	**Trip Miles:** 513.00

Shy in his desert 'organic pepper' greenhouse

Day 75: We were blessed to get our laundry cleaned, buy our supplies, and catch up on our journal. We have only 160 kilometers (100 miles) left to go! The section of the Israel Trail ahead should be spectacular, as we will be hiking through Barak and Veradit Canyons. These are some of the largest and deepest in all of Israel. With this in mind, we are resting and preparing ourselves physically and spiritually for our journey ahead. Thank you for your prayers. God has supplied our every need beyond our expectations over the past two months and 800 kilometers (500 miles).

Saturday, November 19, 2005	
Destination: *The Antelope Farm -- Arava Valley*	**Today's Miles:** 5.00
Starting Location: *Moshav Zofar*	**Trip Miles:** 518.00

The Antelope Farm -- Addax and Eland herds

Day 76: With only 100 miles (160 km) left on the Israel Trail until we reach Eilat, we decided to take a second day off and check out the Antelope Farm, which is three and a half kilometers (2 miles) north of Zofar. Therefore, with just a daypack containing food, towels, bathing suits and our camping mats we set out for an Israeli-African adventure on this beautiful Shabbat morning. The weather is ideal with clear skies and temperature in the upper 20's C (70's F).

The Antelope Farm is one hundred and eighty-five acres (750 dunams), lying just off the Arava Hwy. and is an amazing animal sanctuary that took the owners, Yossi and Shlomit Ben, thirteen years to get permission to build. They have created a sanctuary for about sixteen different varieties of antelope and sheep that are now residing together in individual herds in this majestic desert park. The antelope species in the park include: Kudu, Blesbok, Wildebeest, Arabian Oryx, Springbok, Impala, Eland, Sahara Oryx, Addax, and Nubian Ibex. They also have Red Deer, Silka Deer, Barbary Sheep, Cameroon Sheep, Pygmy goats and the African Wild Ass. Inside the park in a structure built to look like 'Noah's Ark' (originally constructed to quarantine the imported antelope), the owners have built a zoo with dozens of different animals and birds, such as the Meercat, Hyrax, Macaws, Cockatoos, etc.

After walking through the park for quite awhile and photographing the different herds, we met an Israeli guide who spoke excellent English, Taliyah, who gave us a personal tour of the 'Ark' and then drove us through the entire sanctuary in the owner's car. What a wonderfully delightful and surprising experience. (We posted twenty-eight pictures of the animals on our complimentary Yahoo website at: 360.yahoo.com/gregandbev2004 in an album called "The Antelope Farm") After touring the park for a couple hours, we ate a picnic lunch on the grassy area nearby the guest bungalows, and then soaked our legs and aching muscles in a beautiful mineral pool that they have built just outside the fenced animal sanctuary for 'human' guests.

The rest of the day we spent soaking up the sun, reading, and relaxing. As the sun set over the Arava we reluctantly left this desert oasis. We hiked back to Zofar just as it was getting dark in order to have dinner and spend the night at our friend's, Shy and Orly's home. Tomorrow we will begin early our hike through the Barak (Lightning) and Veradit (Rose) Canyons. This next week should take us through some of the most spectacular sections of the entire trail. By God's grace, we now feel physically invigorated and spiritually ready to finish our 'walk of faith'.

	Sunday, November 20, 2005	
Destination: Wadi Paran		**Today's Miles:** 15.00
Starting Location: The Antelope Farm -- Arava Valley		**Trip Miles:** 533.00

Climbing down into Varadit Canyon

Day 77: Up at 5:00 AM, and after a quick breakfast, Shy drove us to Wadi Zaeef where we had left off hiking three days earlier. It was a beautiful desert morning that had the appearance of being on a safari in Africa. While driving to the Trail on the 4x4 road that we took from the Arava Hwy, we spotted gazelles (svi in Hebrew) that seemed to be as curious of us as we were of them.

Within ninety minutes of hiking, we reached the ravine entrance to the amazing Barak Canyon. It is a very narrow and deep canyon, which required much skill to climb up by way of cable ladders and brace bars. Without these aids provided by the trail authority, Barak Canyon would be impossible to traverse. Winter floods wear the rocks smooth and it would be very slippery and dangerous if wet.

After exiting from the top of the canyon, we hiked for several hours to reach Varadit Canyon and were very amazed at the awesome beauty and colors of this canyon. We had to climb down this time and it was even narrower with steeper climbs and deeper pools (dry). The rock walls are very colorful with a predominant pink hue (varod in Hebrew) from which the canyon derives its name. We climbed down Varadit Canyon for quite awhile and enjoyed the pleasantly cool temperature, which was a relief in comparison with the desert heat above. After an hour or so, we exited the canyon into one of Israel's largest dry riverbeds, Wadi Paran. In the winter, this area is prone to very dangerous flash floods.

We hiked up Wadi Paran to Kipat Paran where we had arranged for Shy and his family to meet us for a campfire dinner. They brought us water, some good foods, and our backpacks. Shy then surprised us by offering Greg the use of his professional "Jaguar" backpack. What an answer to prayer as now hiking the rest of the Negev Desert to Taba (the Egyptian border) would be less difficult.

It was so nice to have company out here in the middle of the wilderness. The stars were brilliant with billions visible in this vast secluded area far away from any human settlement. After Shy, Orly, and their children drove off that night, the solitude of the desert seemed so remote.

Monday, November 21, 2005	
Destination: Ashram BaMidbar	**Today's Miles:** 10.00
Starting Location: Wadi Paran	**Trip Miles:** 543.00

Hiking along a dusty powdery trail

Day 78: How easy it was to hike today with the new backpack, which Shy had adjusted for Greg's frame. We hiked four kilometers (2.5 miles) through Wadi Tsichor to its entrance off Hwy. 40 in a little over an hour.

For the rest of the day we hiked directly south, parallel to the highway, with Israeli Defense Force firing zones on both sides of the trail. The landscape was beautiful but the trail was extremely dusty, as tanks have ground the limestone to soft dusty ankle deep powder, which penetrated everything.

Around 2:30 PM we arrived at a desert oasis, called Ashram BaMidbar, where fifteen people live in a small peaceful settlement based upon Indian philosophy and community (Ashram). We were warmly received and invited to an Indian style vegetarian lunch. We rented a dormitory room, cleaned up with hot showers, and took a much-needed nap until dinnertime.

The residents of Ashram BaMidbar hold festivals regularly throughout the year and have teaching and meditation workshops. After dinner, we were able to get on-line and check our e-mail. We were thankful to be inside this night for the temperature suddenly dropped dramatically because of a cold front that had come in from the north.

Tuesday, November 22, 2005	
Destination: Kibbutz Naot Smadar	**Today's Miles:** 10.00
Starting Location: Ashram BaMidbar	**Trip Miles:** 553.00

Artist's Center -- Kibbutz Naot Smadar

Day 79: We started hiking at 9:00 AM, southward along Hwy 40, and completed the fifteen kilometers (9.4 miles) to Kibbutz Naot Smadar in only four hours. We had decided to hike on the shoulder of the highway rather than the adjacent Israel Trail because the firing zone on both sides of the road and trail made deviation impossible, and we were clean and did not want to continue walking through the powdery dust as we had the day before.

Instead of camping at the junction where Kibbutz Neot Smadar has a restaurant, gift shop and picnic area, we decided to hike to the kibbutz through their organically cultivated orchards. They grow olives, dates, plum, pears, peaches, apricots, pomellos, figs, kumquats, and numerous other fruits and vegetables.

At the kibbutz office they received us very warmly an organized a tour of the settlement for us and then showed us to a guest house (hot water and a tub) and invited us to dinner and breakfast in the morning in their dining hall with all of the members and volunteer workers.

Eighty families live communally with no private property or allowances. Everyone receives whatever he needs as seen fit by the community.

Surprisingly, in the center of this modest settlement, a very dramatic structure stands that the kibbutz members have been building for twenty years. This artistic cultural center is nearing completion. It is truly an amazing architectural structure (see picture).

The temperature here was now dropping with the wind chill near freezing. We were so blessed to be indoors. We also enjoyed a very quiet organic vegetable dinner in the Kibbutz dining hall with the many Israeli and foreign volunteers that join the kibbutz from a few days to months at a time. No one spoke out-loud, only a few quiet whispers. Weird!

Wednesday, November 23, 2005	
Destination: Shaharoot - Camel-riders Camp	**Today's Miles:** 13.80
Starting Location: Kibbutz Naot Smadar	**Trip Miles:** 566.80

Protecting our eyes in a desert sand-storm

Day 80: The morning was crisp and clear. We got a ride from the kibbutz to the junction where we had turned off from yesterday and began hiking southward on the Israel Trail parallel to Hwy 12. Again, there were firing zones on both sides of the trail for the first four kilometers (2.5 miles). About an hour later, we turned off onto the road that goes to the desert town of Shaharoot, and an east wind began to pick-up. By 10 AM, we were in the middle of a full-blown desert sandstorm. Being blinded by the whipping sand we covered our faces with hats and towels and packed tissue around the edges of

our glasses. It was impossible to stop and rest or even eat lunch. We just kept pressing on.

As we passed the area of Ovda (Israeli Air force Base) the mountains formed a natural barrier and blocked the wind. We could now walk more easily, but visibility remained poor the rest of the day. We arrived at Shaharoot and learned there was no shop there to buy food supplies. We were driven by one of the forty residents of this outback village to the nearby Camel-riders Camp. Here began a very nice evening. We rented a Bedouin tent, had great hot showers in a clean bathhouse to wash off all the sand, and were invited to have an all-you-can-eat barbecue dinner with an army group gathered for a remembrance service being held in another big Bedouin tent that evening. We made friends with Boaz, a bus driver on vacation from Tel Aviv. Boaz was seeking a spiritual retreat from the city hustle and bustle here in this desert place. We were able to encourage him in his search.

After dinner there was a folk concert put on by the local residents. They played many desert instruments creating an altogether unique atmosphere under the decor of this ancient styled tent. The Camel Rider's Camp is located on the very edge of the cliffs dropping off hundreds of meters to the Arava valley below. The lights from all of the kibbutz settlements in the valley twinkled and reminded us of how far down we would have to go down on the trail the next day. Having feasted well, we were now fully recovered from the sandstorm that had battered us throughout the day. We fell fast asleep, warm and cozy in the Bedouin tent, knowing that we would need all of our strength tomorrow for the difficult descent to Timna.

Thursday, November 24, 2005	
Destination: Timna Park	**Today's Miles:** 15.60
Starting Location: Shaharoot - Camel-riders Camp	**Trip Miles:** 582.40

Day 81: Boaz offered to drive our packs to Park Timna for us since he was going there to spend the day anyway. This was only the second Israel National Trail section out of the forty-four sections that was listed as DIFFICULT.

The Trail down to Timna

We were grateful for the help. As a result, we managed the twenty-five kilometer trail in eight and a half hours. Our descent from Timna cliffs took one and a half hours. It was magnificent. We arrived at the Park entrance at 4 PM and were greeted by Boaz who was so happy to see us. He drove us to Timna Lake where we camped for the night.

We had been praying for warmer weather. Tonight was the warmest it had been in six weeks. What a relief and wonderful answer to prayer! For the first time since we had been camped on the beach on Mediterranean Sea, we were able to sleep on top of our sleeping bags without layers of clothing on for warmth.

Many years ago we had camped by this very lake with our children when they were young, and tonight we especially missed them. We stayed up late and spoke by cell phone to all of our family who were gathered for Thanksgiving dinner in Tallahassee, Florida.

Friday, November 25, 2005	
Destination: Timna Lake	**Today's Miles:** 5.60
Starting Location: Timna Park	**Trip Miles:** 588.00

Day 82: With three days left to hike and fifty-four kilometers (33.75 miles) to go to the end of the INT, we decided that we would need to restock our dwindling supplies by going to Eilat. At 9:30 AM, we began hiking on the Israel trail through Timna Park on the "Geological Trail." This is a spectacular trail, which took us to a very high dolomite plateau (Timna Mountain) with a scenic view of the entire region and the Jordanian Mt. Range. The visibility was excellent, as the sand from the previous storm had now settled. We reached the park entrance by noon and got two quick rides hitchhiking to the "Jumbo" supermarket in Eilat.

On top of Timna Mountain on a dolomite plateau

On Friday stores close early for Shabbat and we arrived just in time to do all our shopping for the next four days. With a backpack loaded with food and charcoals for a barbeque of chicken and turkey for dinner that we had planned for the evening in Timna Park, we quickly hitched back to the Timna Mines. From there, we hiked west for a couple of kilometers to the lake. The Timna copper mines, which date back to the time of the Egyptian pharaohs, which were also utilized by King Solomon, have recently been reopened.

We had a very peaceful Erev Shabbat together next to this beautiful lake in one of the nicest Nature Reserves in Israel. For the first time since we started hiking, we had a candlelight barbecue dinner and a bottle of wine. We listened to a group of Israeli hikers playing guitar and singing in the Bedouin tent nearby as we fell asleep under a canopy of a billion stars.

Saturday, November 26, 2005	
Destination: Timna Lake	**Today's Miles:** 0.00
Starting Location: Timna Lake	**Trip Miles:** 588.00

Day 83: Shabbat Rest Yeah! These past six days we have hiked 112 kilometers (70 miles) and so we decided to take a day off in this beautiful area.

After lunch, we went "noodling," which is an Australian term for picking through mounds of rubble for gemstones. We noodled through the Timna mine piles for beautiful blue-green Eilat stone and had a great time treasure hunting.

In the afternoon we wrote out our trail journal by hand for the past week and will update our website after we reach Eilat next Wednesday. It is hard to believe that our 'walk of faith' on the Israel National Trail will soon be over. The past three months have been more amazing than we could ever have imagined. To God be the glory!

Timna Lake

We enjoyed dinner at the Bedouin Hospitality Tent at Timna Lake eating delicious Middle Eastern food, and then retired to our small tent one hundred meters (100 yards) away. We fell asleep with strange gargling sounds emanating from a group of camels living in a nearby enclosure.

Sunday, November 27, 2005	
Destination: *Canyon Shahoret (The Black Canyon)*	***Today's Miles:*** *13.80*
Starting Location: *Timna Lake*	***Trip Miles:*** *601.80*

The Trail to Canyon Shahoret

Day 84: Our friend Boaz called and wanted to see us again. He arranged to pick up our packs from Timna and met us around 3:30 PM at Canyon Shahoret. With only daypacks, again we were able to make good time hiking up Wadi Raham. While walking through the dry canyons, we were surprised to suddenly hear and see three Sefa (Hebrew for Viper) helicopters descend into the canyon just a few hundred meters over our heads. To our amazement they returned after a minute descending even

lower to check us out. The loud echoes rumbled throughout the canyon walls leaving us in a state of shock.

After passing the canyon area, our next climb was up to Amram Overlook. We could see the Red Sea for the first time now, as well as Aqaba (in Jordan) and Timna behind us. Spectacular colorful canyons lie below (dark red, yellow, and black mountains). From there we had an hours descent to Canyon Shahoret where we where happy to find Boaz waiting for us.

We had a great campfire dinner together with Boaz, and then he departed for his return back to Tel Aviv. Boaz commented repeatedly how we had encouraged him with our 'walk of faith', but he really encouraged us with his kindness and friendship.

Monday, November 28, 2005	
Destination: Ein Netafim (The Netafim Spring)	**Today's Miles:** 8.80
Starting Location: Canyon Shahoret (The Black Canyon)	**Trip Miles:** 610.60

Ein Netafim - The Netafim Spring

Day 85: We were sleeping well when at 2:30 AM a semi-trailer and a truck came rumbling down the washer board dirt road leading to our campsite. What a loud commotion broke our deep sleep for about an hour. At daybreak, we met Hanna. She explained that she was in charge of setting up camp for over a thousand students arriving soon that would be hiking through Canyon Shahoret. Her company, Pashut, provides logistical support for hiking and camping groups throughout Israel. We enjoyed coffee with her and her team then quickly set out for our hike through Canyon Shahoret – getting a head start seemed like a good idea.

The black Canyons (shahoret means black) is a very beautiful area to hike into. We saw an Ibex family skillfully climbing the canyon clefts. Within an hour, we reached the summit of the

Shahoret Mts. Overlook to see a magnificent view of the area on this very clear day.

Now we started descending into Lost Valley. A great-secluded place to film a featured movie nestled between several mountain ranges. We now had named the sandstone colored mountains 'black cherry cheesecake and chocolate Halva Mountains'. When we reached Netafim Wadi, we stopped for lunch. We knew we were about to face a strenuous climb for the next two hours to the Netafim Spring.

Many birds and animals survive the intense summer heat from the water collected into a man-made trough from a trickle of water flowing out of the rock at the base of a shady deep canyon wall. On the climb up out of this area, we needed to remove our packs at several spots in order to pass through small openings in the rock as we then managed to climb up to the top of the cliff. Very exhilarating!

We then hiked a kilometer off the trail to an army border-crossing checkpoint to fill up with water. The water in the Netafim spring was unsuitable for drinking. The soldiers were very friendly and gave us icy cold water and a big bag of fruit (kiwis, apples, oranges, pears). We returned to our trail and found a super place to set up camp for our last night on the Israel National Trail. This was probably the most beautiful sunset yet of our entire trip. God's presence was all around us.

Tuesday, November 29, 2005	
Destination: Taba - The Egyptian border - Princess Beach	**Today's Miles:** 8.80
Starting Location: Ein Netafim (The Netafim Spring)	**Trip Miles:** 619.40

Day 86: The weather had really warmed up (an answer to prayer). We were happy to get an early start to beat the heat of the day on the Gishron Valley Descent. This would be the most dramatic and difficult descent of the entire trail. It took us over an hour to make the descent from Mt. Yoash to the Gishon ravine. The trail provides many cables, handle grip bars, and ladders for safe climbing. Geologically, the Eilat Mts. are considered 'new mountains' compared to the Timna range lying to the north. It took us an hour to get down into Wadi Gishon.

Overlooking Eilat, Israel and Aqaba, Jordan – on Mt. Zephahot

It took only twenty minutes to climb out at the Gishon Ascent. Everyone familiar with the Israel Trail agrees that this is the most spectacular trail of the forty-four trails that compose the INT.

We had two more climbs – Har Bolbosim (Boulder Mt.) and Mt. Zefahot, at which point you overlook all of Eilat, Aqaba, and way into the Sinai, including the beautiful Coral Island south of the border. With the smell of the sea air on this hot day we were excited about reaching Taba for that grand finale swim in the Red Sea ahead.

At 3 PM after eighty-five days and four hours, we prayed at the last trail marker then... dashed for a celebration swim in the Gulf of Eilat. We ate delicious swarma (grilled lamb and turkey) dinner at the Princess Beach in Taba and spent our last night sleeping under the stars on the beach.

It seemed strange knowing that we would not have to wake up early in the morning and put on our backpacks to continue hiking on the trail. We would not have to look for the orange-blue-white Israel Trail markers and would not have to live out of our packs. Life would be different but in a way, the same... for this 'walk of faith' has brought us closer to the land and people of Israel and especially to the Lord God of Israel.

By His grace, we are determined to continue "walking by faith"!

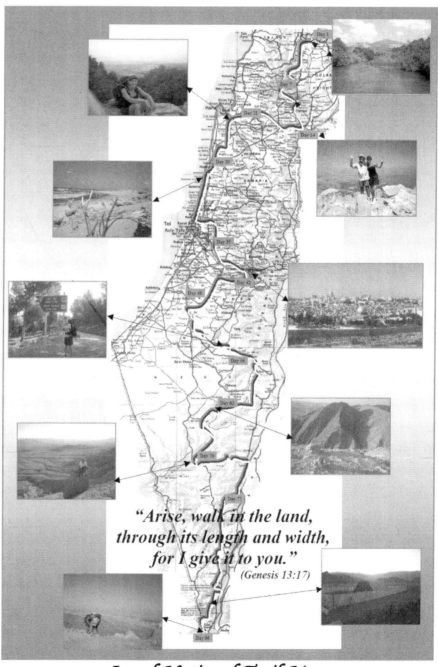

Israel National Trail Map